HOW TO PHOTOGRAPH YOUR CHILD

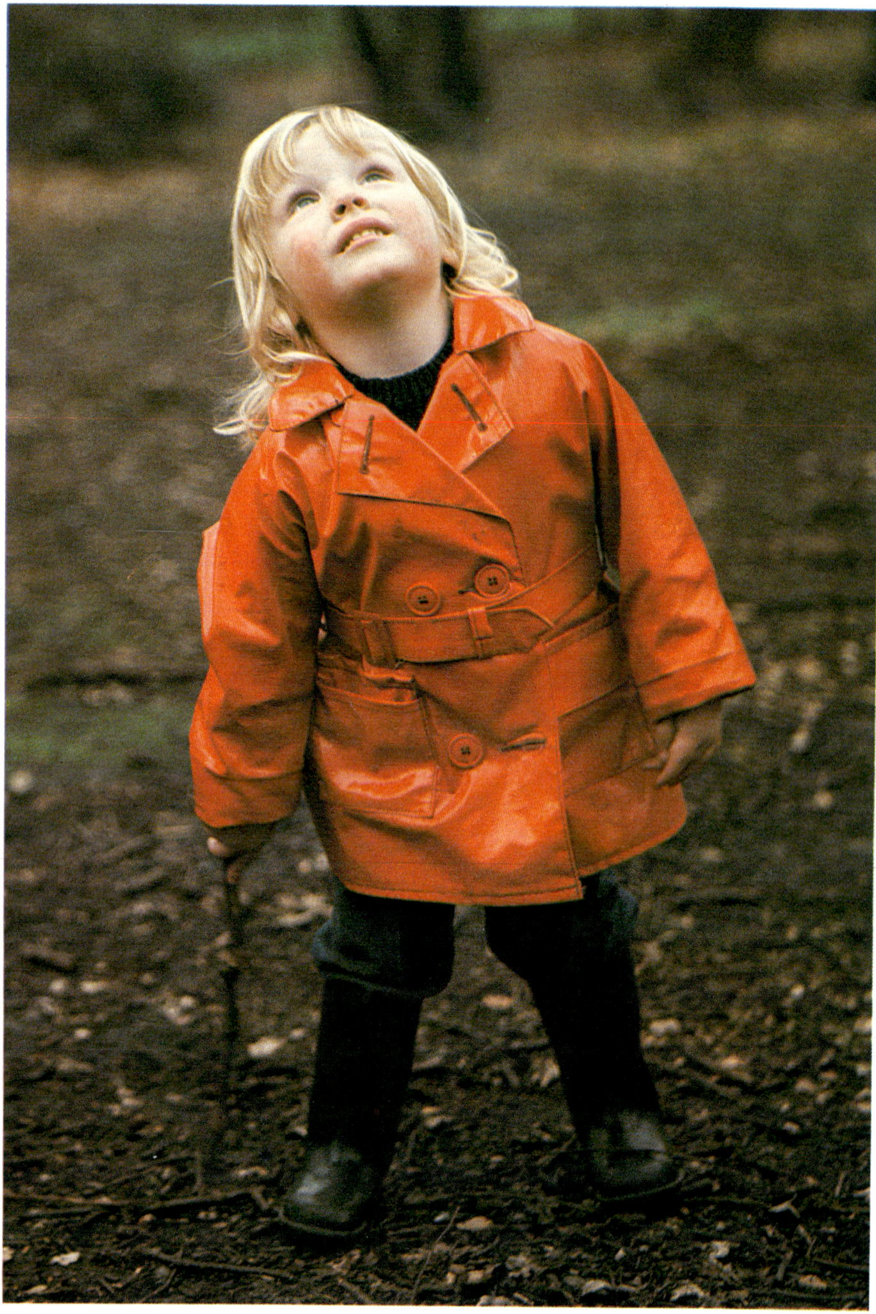

HOW TO PHOTOGRAPH YOUR CHILD

PETER PUGH-COOK

COLLINS

TO LUCY AND JULIAN, PATIENT MODELS FOR MANY OF THE PHOTOGRAPHS IN THIS BOOK

First published 1984 by
William Collins Sons & Co Ltd
London · Glasgow · Sydney
Auckland · Toronto · Johannesburg

ISBN 0 00 411940 1

Designed and produced by
Robert Adkinson Limited, London

Editorial Director
Clare Howell

Editor
Hilary Dickinson

Designer
David Fordham

Phototypeset by Ashwell Print Services Ltd, Ashwellthorpe, Norwich
Illustrations originated by East Anglian Engraving Co Ltd, Norwich
Printed and bound in Italy by **SAGDOS (MI)**

CONTENTS

INTRODUCTION

It is an acknowledged fact that more pictures are taken of children than of any other subject. Since the very beginnings of photography in early Victorian times children have been a favourite subject for the camera. To modern eyes, these first photographs look extremely posed and stilted, a product not only of the technical restraints of the early processes, which often required an exposure time of several minutes, but also a result of rigid nineteenth-century attitudes towards children. However, some of those pioneering photographers, usually amateurs, did introduce an element of romanticism, even fantasy, into their studies of children. Keen amateurs, such as Julia Margaret Cameron and the author Lewis Carroll, overcame numerous problems and produced work of amazing spontaneity and warmth. Some of this work may now be criticized as over-sentimental, but it should be remembered that the photographers of the day were struggling to have their craft recognized as an art form, and in order to gain acceptance many of them attempted to emulate the rose-tinted style of the Victorian portrait painter.

The romantic approach to child photography persisted into the early part of the twentieth century. In America, Edward Steichen was experimenting with new processes to achieve results similar to the Impressionist painters of the period, while Clarence White, a child photographer of considerable reputation, continued to be

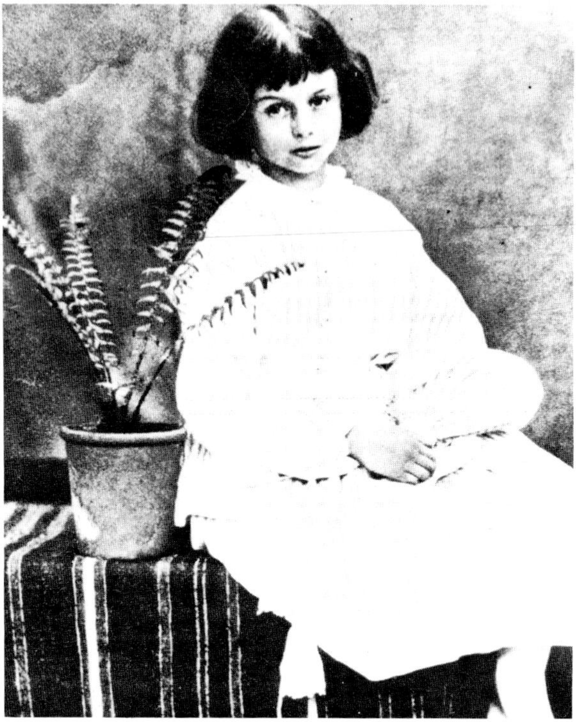

Charles Dodgson, better known as Lewis Carroll, was not only an eminent writer but also one of the earliest amateur child photographers. This early portrait is of Alice Liddell, the inspiration for his well-known 'Alice' stories. Notice how he has been able to capture the sensitivity of the child, even though the exposure time probably ran to several minutes (left).

influenced by the work of the Victorian portraitists. Even in the 1920s, workers such as Imogen Cunningham and Nell Dorr were producing photographs of immense beauty and perfect composition, yet tinged with a sentimentality which completely divorced them from the reality of childhood. It was a case of idealism replacing realism.

Today, attitudes towards child photography have changed beyond recognition. The comparative ease and simplicity of camera operation and the immense improvement in photographic materials now allow a totally different and far more natural approach to the subject. It is no longer necessary to 'set up' a photographic session with a great deal of preparation, and instead the ephemeral moments of childhood can be captured spontaneously and realistically as they occur. It is to this modern, semi-documentary approach to child photography that the major part of this book is devoted. Parents who own a camera have the means of capturing pictorially the entire childhood of their offspring, starting at birth. With the help of this book, every stage of development and every significant occasion can be faithfully and imaginatively recorded. The result will not only be a collection of memorable photographs, each one complete and satisfying in its own right, but also a chronicle, possibly in album form, of the formative years of the children concerned. Many readers will remember with dismay family

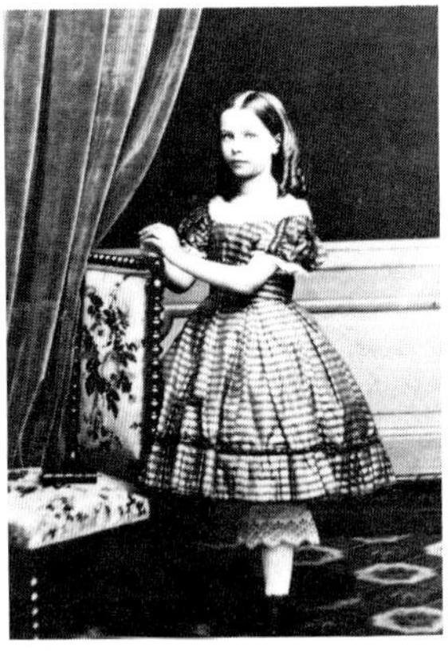

This portrait by an anonymous photographer is far more typical of child photography of the period. The child looks stilted and wooden, and even slightly apprehensive (above).

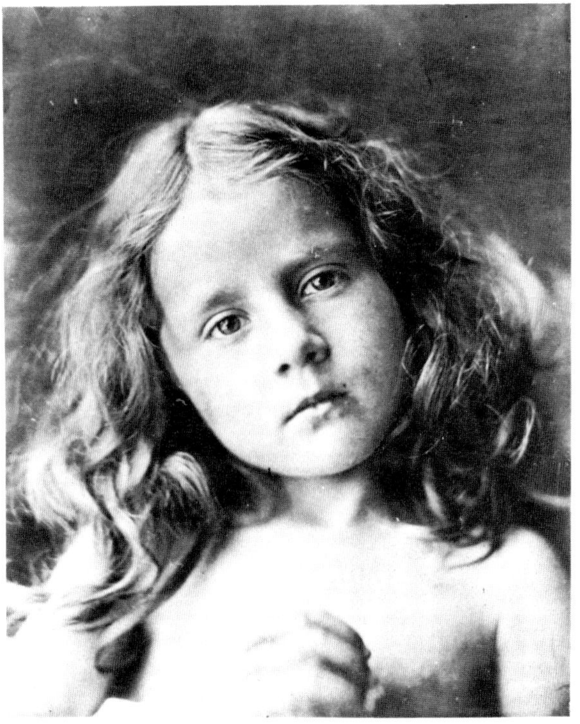

Julia Margaret Cameron, like Carroll, had a great understanding of children, enabling her to photograph in a realistic and sensitive manner (right).

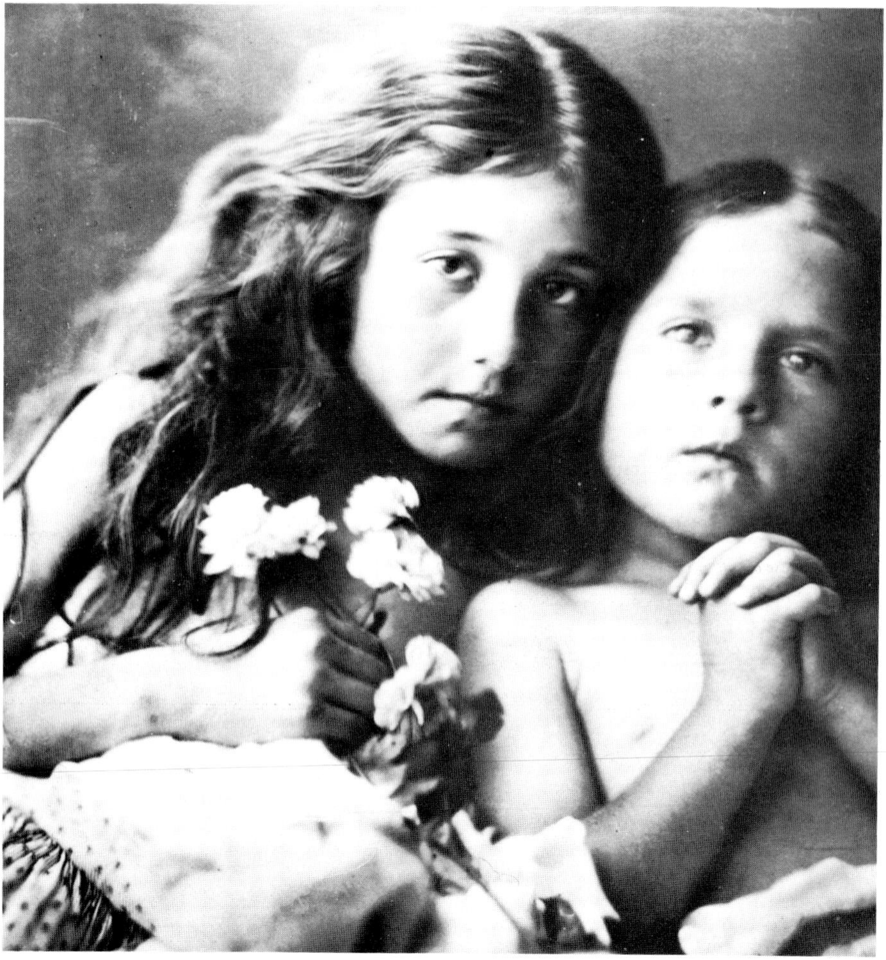

albums of their own childhood, fuzzy snaps badly mounted with no detail of when or where they were taken, with long gaps when the camera had been put away and forgotten. Or holiday scenes so inadequately recorded that the location was unrecognized or forgotten. The well-designed, well-captioned family album will not only be a source of pleasure to the photographer but also, especially in years to come, the subject of great interest and much amusement to the children portrayed inside.

To take successful child photographs it is not necessary to own a lot of expensive equipment. Throughout this book hints and tips are given for users of simple, cheaper cameras: how to utilize them to

Taking into account the technical problems of the period, it seems amazing that in 1865 Julia Cameron was able to convey such a strong feeling of spontaneity and warmth in this picture entitled 'Red and White Roses' (left). Later in the Victorian era, photographers took a backward step, as they attempted to emulate the oil paintings of the time, in order to promote their work as true art.

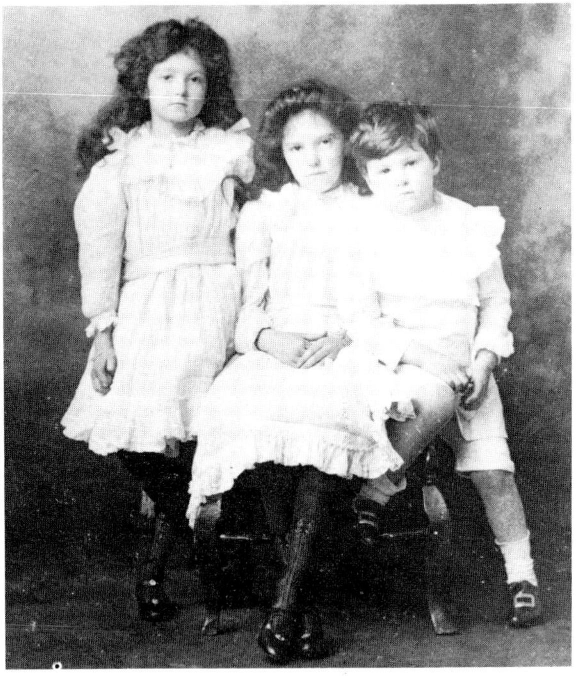

By the turn of the century, photographic techniques had improved dramatically, but photographers were still attempting to copy the work of portrait painters, even down to the use of artificial-looking painted backdrops. Children were made to look like scaled-down adults, and the essence of childhood was lost (right).

the full and minimize their limitations. It is often said – and this is never truer than in child photography – that it is the person who takes the picture and not the quality of the camera that produces a great photograph. Indeed, the finest camera imaginable in inexperienced hands will produce mediocre results. There has never been a camera made that will tell the photographer the precise instant to press the button in order to capture the essential moment, the fleeting expression or the unique opportunity. However, there is no doubt that in certain situations, in very poor light for instance, the flexibility of a more expensive camera will lead to better photographs. The first chapter of the book is aimed at those who are considering renewing their camera or buying one for the first time, with descriptions of the merits of the various camera systems which are available.

Even with a minimum of technical understanding good results can be achieved, as long as the photographer is fully conversant with the functions of the camera. In child photography especially, when actions and movement are unpredictable, it is essential to be able to control all operations of the camera instinctively. Remember, too, that every stage of a child's development is transient. Younger children in particular are constantly changing in appearance and behaviour and any photographic opportunity missed will be lost for ever. The best policy is to keep a camera accessible and loaded all the time, ready for those unexpected situations that will lift your child photographs above the ordinary.

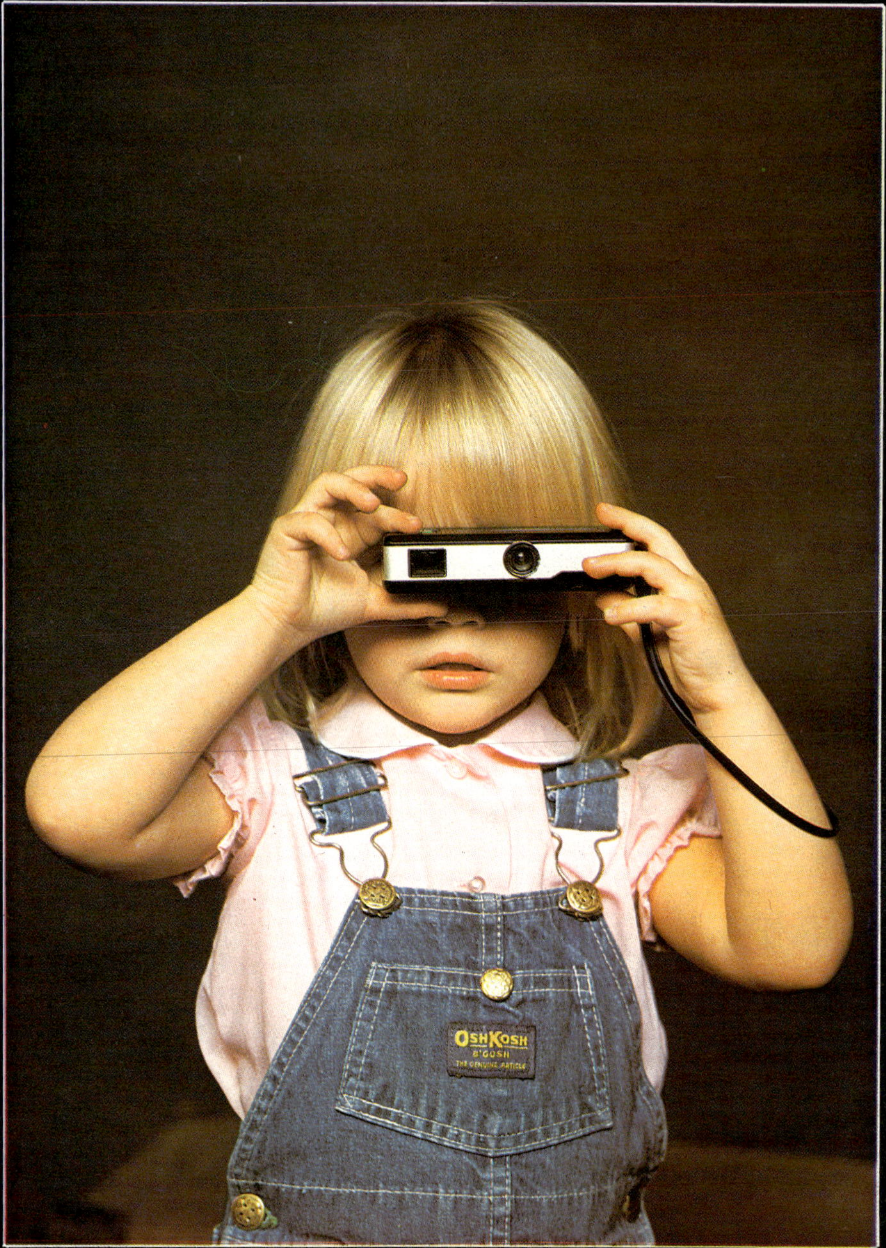
OshKosh
B'GOSH
THE GENUINE ARTICLE

CHOOSING A CAMERA

Many people reading this book will already possess a camera with which they are familiar and have no reason to change. Indeed, there is a lot to be said for not renewing photographic equipment too regularly. Modern cameras do not wear out for a considerable time, and although manufacturers update the specification of their products with great regularity, this is really little more than a marketing ploy. If you already own a camera, you would be well advised to keep it, as long as you are satisfied with both its potential and its results. In return, you will gain the advantage of continuing familiarity with the equipment and will be able to spend any available money on buying accessories to extend the scope of the outfit.

For the occasional or first-time buyer the choice can be bewildering as there has never before been such a diverse range of camera types. Many people ask how much it is necessary to spend on a camera, as after all it can be as little as £10 or as much as £1000. The reason why some cameras are so much more expensive than others depends on two main factors, design specification and manufacturing quality.

Basically, the more a camera has to offer in terms of photographic potential and flexibility, the more it will cost. Advanced technology in the form of light-metering circuitry, optical design and the like is very expensive to develop, and this will naturally be reflected in the price of the product. When considering the cost of a camera the buyer must decide how much of this technical sophistication is actually necessary for his own purposes and whether it will in fact enable him to take better photographs. Many cameras cost a good deal more than others with similar technical specifications because they are built uncompromisingly to very high engineering standards. Better-quality materials are used, and parts manufactured to very much finer tolerances; inspection procedures are far more stringent, and many parts of the mechanism may be built by hand. Cameras in the very high price range such as Leica, Rolleiflex, Hasselblad and the more expensive Nikons are made in this manner. They have a deserved reputation for reliability and durability and are designed to last a lifetime.

Deciding how much to spend on a camera is obviously a matter of personal choice and means. As a general rule, the more you pay, the better the camera will be in terms of versatility. The best approach is to decide which *type* of camera is most suited to your requirements and to fix a price limit. Bear in mind when budgeting that you will probably wish to buy some basic accessories such as a flash-gun and tripod at the same time. Then visit a camera dealer or look through the advertisements in a photographic magazine to find out what is available within your price bracket.

Camera Types

SIMPLE CARTRIDGE-LOADING AND DISC CAMERAS

The cheapest and simplest cameras available are designed to take cartridges or disc film. Cartridge-loading cameras are long and narrow in shape, and almost all use type 110 film. Disc cameras are slim and almost square in shape, and are designed to take the recently developed disc film. Both cameras are light, small and easy to carry about. This type of camera is best suited to the beginner interested in producing small prints on colour negative film. The advantages are low price, portability and simple operation.

Most models feature completely automatic exposure control. On the cheapest models there is no exposure control at all other than a simple slider to select sunny or cloudy light conditions. Most have no focusing control but rely on a fixed-position lens which gives a relatively sharp image at all distances from about 2 metres (6 feet) to infinity. Some models have a supplementary lens which slides over the prime lens to give a close-up or telephoto effect, but this usually lowers the over-all sharpness of the picture. Because of the simple optics, good results are not obtainable in poor light, and for this reason more expensive versions are fitted with a small electronic flash, which gives a rather unnatural effect in daylight, outdoors. Some cartridge and all disc cameras have a built-in motor to transport the film between exposures.

Although these cameras are light and pocketable, their size and weight and awkward shape make them difficult to hold steady in use. The inexperienced photographer is less likely to realize the importance of avoiding camera movement, so the problem is compounded.

The 110 negative is very small and the disc format is even smaller, almost half the size, so that, despite many break-throughs in film technology, large prints of good quality are not possible. Although colour transparency film is available for cartridge cameras, the slides are too small for direct viewing and there are very few suitable slide projectors available.

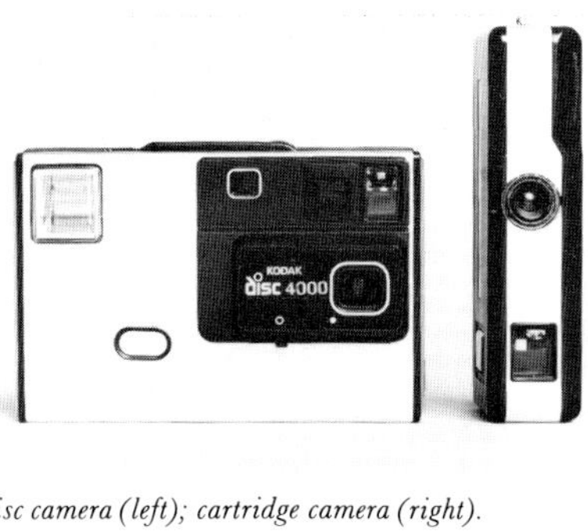

Disc camera (left); cartridge camera (right).

35 MM COMPACT CAMERAS

The 35 mm compact camera is ideal for the person who wants to get excellent results with very little technical knowledge. Not only is there a comprehensive range of film emulsions available, but the larger negative size will give prints and enlargements of much better quality than a very simple camera. Normal-sized colour slides can also be made for viewing in all modern projectors. Despite the film format, most 35 mm compact cameras are almost as small as a cartridge or disc camera, although their more manageable proportions and greater weight make them considerably easier to handle. Some models, such as the Minox and Olympus XA series, are so small that they can easily be carried in a pocket.

These cameras use an optical viewfinder system, which is quite adequate for the fixed non-interchangeable lens. The lens is usually slightly wide-angle, useful in interior situations and in tight surroundings. Focusing is often by a zone

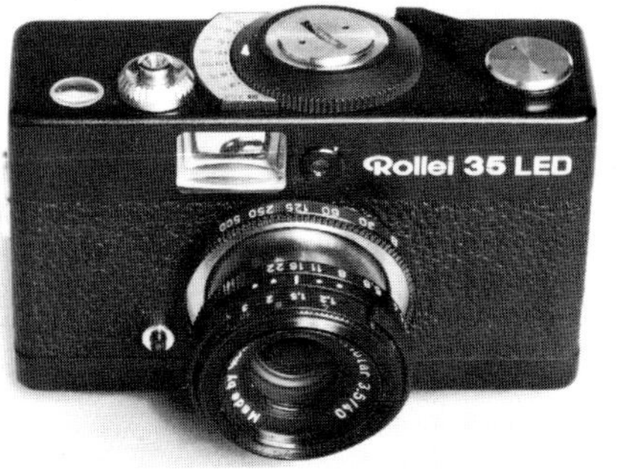

35 mm compact camera.

method, although some compacts have a rangefinding system. More advanced models focus automatically using an infra-red beam. A disadvantage of most compacts is their inability to focus at less than 1 metre (3 feet) so that it is not possible to shoot head portraits without the use of a supplementary lens.

Exposure control is invariably automatic, although on the more expensive models either the speed or aperture can be selected and the exposure computed accordingly. Most make provision for over-riding the exposure read-out under difficult conditions. Most models have a small integral flash unit for indoor use, and some of the advanced compacts have automatic exposure, flash and focusing, even automatic wind-on. Prices vary considerably, the cheapest starting from around £40 to around £100 for the very sophisticated models.

35 MM COUPLED RANGEFINDER CAMERAS

The coupled rangefinder camera is more flexible than the 35 mm compact, although similar in many ways. This breed of camera is losing popularity owing to the rapid development of the single lens reflex system. The rangefinder camera has an optical viewfinder system but it can be fitted with a range of interchangeable lenses. The viewing system is adjusted mechanically to show the field of view of the lens in use. Correct focus is achieved by lining up a double image in the centre of the viewfinder: when the images coincide, the subject is correctly focused. Although there are a few relatively inexpensive models on the market, most rangefinder cameras are expensive and are made mainly for professional use by press photographers and therefore do not have full exposure automation, though most have some form of manual metering. A good-quality rangefinder camera costs in excess of £500, which is very much more than an SLR of similar quality.

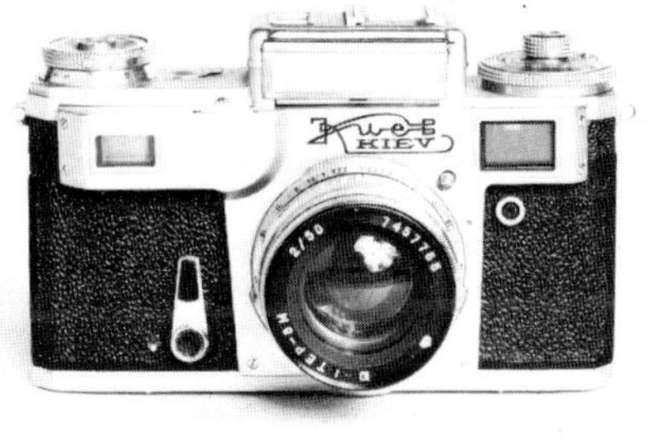

35 mm coupled rangefinder camera.

35 MM SINGLE LENS REFLEX CAMERAS

The most popular and best-known type of camera is probably the 35 mm single lens reflex (SLR). Used by amateurs and professionals alike, these versatile instruments represent the pinnacle of modern camera design, and their names have became household words in countries throughout the world.

The first SLR was a rather unwieldy plate camera, but today's model is an

Camera Types 2

instrument of great sophistication, both mechanically and electronically, and is undoubtedly the most versatile of all camera systems. The reason for its success lies in the focusing and viewing system. The light rays from the lens are diverted via a mirror on to a ground-glass screen within the viewfinder where they form an image which can be focused and composed by the photographer, while precise exposure measurements can be made at the same time. At the moment of taking a picture, the mirror swings away and the film exposure is made. Because the same lens is used for viewing and shooting, the photograph will be an exact representation of what was seen on the screen of the viewfinder. One important point is that all SLRs can be fitted with interchangeable lenses, and no matter what lens is attached to the camera the viewfinder image will always faithfully represent the field of view and focus of that lens. All manufacturers of SLR cameras supply a very wide range of lenses for their products, and several independent companies make lenses to fit the well-known camera marques. A variety of accessories is available, including such items as motor drives which are of great assistance in child photography. The owner of an SLR therefore has a tremendous choice and is able to equip himself with a set of lenses and accessories to suit any photographic situation.

Exposure evaluation is also simplified. The types of exposure read-out and means of measurement vary according to the model of camera. The important common factor is that in each case the metering of light intensity is carried out in the most logical position, within the camera and at the film plane, and the system is precise and easily interpreted. This type of exposure determination is known as through-the-lens (TTL) metering. With the subject composed and focused, the photographer can determine the precise exposure as seen through the viewfinder, irrespective of whatever lens or accessory is in use.

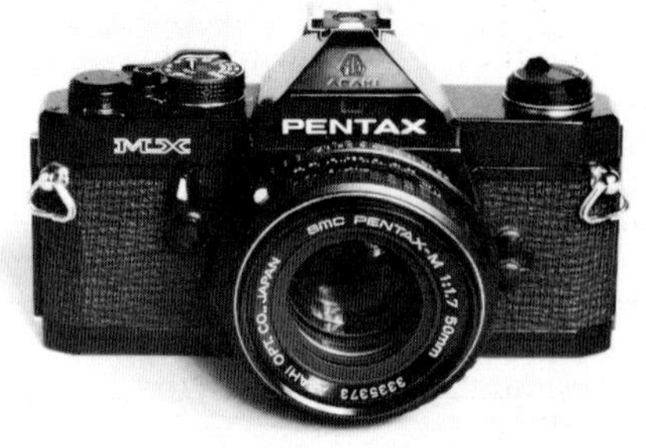

35 mm single lens reflex camera.

Single lens reflex cameras are fairly expensive, with a good-quality instrument costing between £100 and £200, while more advanced models are even more highly priced. It is possible, however, to buy a fairly basic model for about £50; these are usually manufactured in East Germany or Russia and are not very advanced from a mechanical point of view, usually having a very unsophisticated metering system, though often fitted with a lens of surprisingly good optical quality. They certainly offer good value for money and are an ideal introduction to this type of photography.

ROLL-FILM SINGLE LENS REFLEX CAMERAS

There are a number of SLR cameras designed to take 120 roll film. The advantage of these models is their ability to produce larger negatives or transparencies, giving results of higher technical quality. Cameras of this type, such as Hasselblad, Bronica and Pentax 6 × 7, use a film approximately 6 cm in width and produce negatives of 6 × 6 or 6 × 7 cm format. These cameras are usually used by professionals or very advanced amateurs, as although they produce results of very good quality, they are considerably bulkier and heavier than their 35 mm equivalents, and slower in use. For child photography they are best used in controlled studio and posed portrait sessions.

The keen photographer may wish to graduate to this type of camera if he wishes to sell pictures for reproduction, when the highest quality is required. However, the over-all cost must be borne in mind, as these cameras are very expensive and a complete system comprising camera bodies, lenses and accessories would cost several thousand pounds.

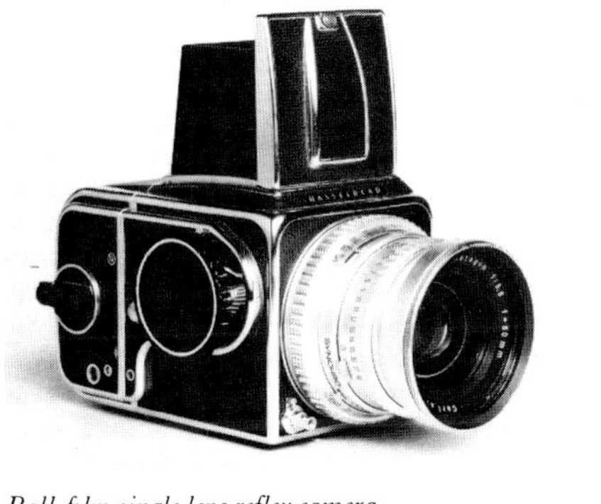

Roll-film single lens reflex camera.

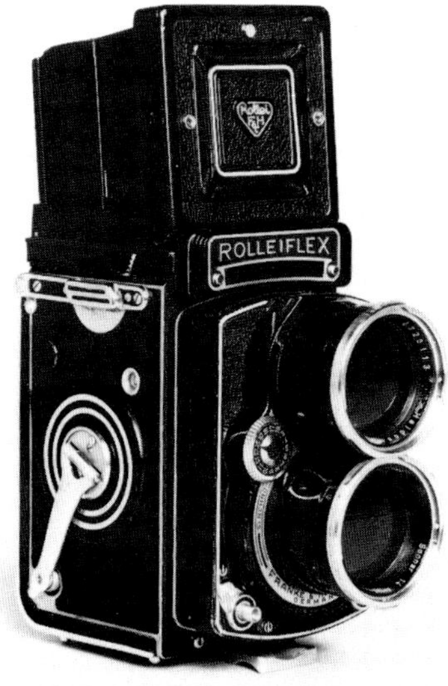

Roll-film twin lens reflex camera.

ROLL-FILM TWIN LENS REFLEX CAMERAS

The twin lens reflex (TLR) is a cheaper type of large-format camera. Taking twelve negatives of 6 × 6 cm on 120 roll film, this camera is like a simplified SLR, but with two lenses, one for taking and one for viewing. The viewing lens is mounted above the taking lens and projects an image on to a ground-glass screen. The two lenses are matched optically and coupled together so that they move together for focusing. The slight difference in the positioning of the two lenses only becomes a problem when working at very close distances. However, special close-up lenses are available which are designed to overcome this.

There are two makes of TLR currently available: the Mamiyaflex, which accepts paired interchangeable lenses, and the Yashica 124, which is a fixed-lens camera. The Mamiyaflex offers greater flexibility and also features a bellows-type focusing mechanism which is useful for extreme close-up work, but it is a bulky camera and not altogether suitable for the quick-reaction shooting required in child photography. The Yashica is lighter and more compact.

The first TLR, the Rolleiflex, built in the 1920s and developed until the last decade, is an extremely fine camera. Although production of the twin lens models ceased a few years ago, late examples on the secondhand market are a

Camera Types 3

very good buy. Although they never featured lens interchangeability, models were built fitted with a fixed pair of wide-angle or telephoto lenses. The Tele-Rolleiflex fitted with paired 135 mm lenses is an ideal camera for the child photographer wishing to use large format.

SPECIAL CAMERAS

There are some special cameras available which warrant consideration for child photography. One is the underwater or all-weather camera. There are several makes now available quite cheaply, for instance the Minolta Weathermatic, taking 110 cartridge film, and at the more expensive end of the range the Nikonos, a 35 mm camera. Both have a plastic body, with sealed components, which allows them to be used safely underwater. Unless your children are accomplished skin-divers, however, the underwater use of these cameras is obviously limited, although they are very useful in situations where a normal camera might get wet, splashed and damaged: for instance, when you are standing in the sea or swimming-pool to take action shots on top of the water, or when children are playing with hoses and buckets of water and you may get drenched. They are also perfect for photography in heavy rain, which can seriously damage a conventional camera. Owing to their sealed construction, they can be safely left on a sandy beach, which would prove fatal to many more sensitive cameras.

Cameras producing three-dimensional effects have existed almost since the birth of photography, but an entirely new type, the Nimslo, has recently been introduced. This camera uses four lenses, mounted in a straight line, exposing simultaneously on a single length of film. The film is specially processed and printed and then split into thousands of segments and mounted on to a special plastic laminate. With the treated print in position, this gives a pseudo-three-dimensional effect, which can be particularly realistic in child photography. The result is certainly interesting, but it is too early to judge whether the system will catch hold. The camera is quite expensive, and both processing and printing considerably more costly.

Instant picture cameras like the Polaroid have been popular for many years, but recently vast improvements have been made in this field in both film materials and cameras. For the child photographer especially, the ability to produce an instant print is invaluable, either as a finished product in itself or as an aid to conventional photography (see also pages 18–19).

Although an instant camera will only produce one print at a time, it is possible to order copies of the photographs from a photographic dealer, but the original must be kept in good condition in order to get a good reprint.

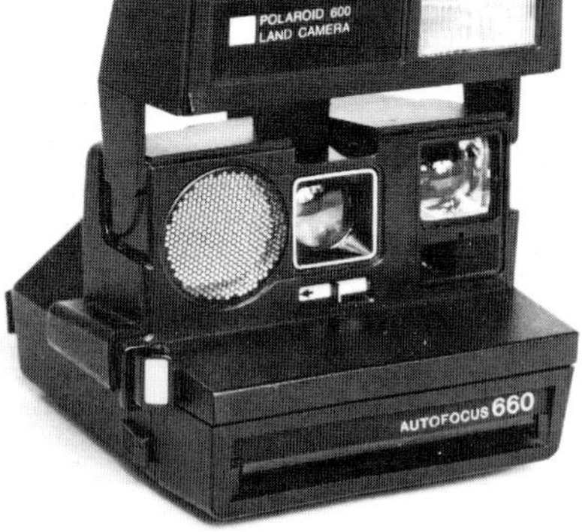

Polaroid camera.

Which Camera?

The chart provides a useful guide to the four main camera types, showing the suitability of each in terms of subject-matter, film materials and general potential. It is immediately obvious that the 35 mm SLR is the ideal choice: quick and accurate focusing, the ability to capture action with fast shutter speeds, lens interchangeability and the possibility of working in poor light and indoors. The outlay is relatively high, but lenses and accessories can be added to the system gradually to build up a very comprehensive outfit.

For those photographers who want to take a less serious approach or who have less money to spend, the 35 mm compact camera is a good compromise. Because it is light and will fit into a pocket, you can carry it with you all day and always be ready to capture the unexpected shot. Ideally, the serious photographer should possess both an SLR outfit and a compact camera, the former for important sessions and excursions, the latter for carrying at all times, like a note-book.

If you only want a camera for occasional use, do not dismiss the cheap and simple models. They demand good light for satisfactory exposure, and are therefore ideal for recording summer holidays and beach scenes. Certain subjects must be treated with caution, but using the advice given in this book it is even possible to portray motion in a pleasing manner. However, there will be many occasions when conditions will be beyond the scope of a simple camera, and the results will be very disappointing; it is at this time that most owners will want to buy a camera with more potential.

ACCEPTABLE ★ GOOD ★★ EXCELLENT ★★★	Simple Cartridge Disc	35 mm Compact	35 mm SLR	Roll-film SLR
SEASIDE PHOTOGRAPHS	★★★	★★★	★★★	★★
HOLIDAY PHOTOGRAPHS	★★★	★★★	★★★	★★
OUTDOOR ACTIVITIES	★★	★★★	★★★	★★
SPORTS AND MOTION	★	★★	★★★	★★
POOR LIGHT	—	★	★★★	★★
PORTRAITS (OUTDOOR)	★	★★	★★★	★★★
PORTRAITS (INDOOR)	—	★	★★★	★★★
FLASH PHOTOGRAPHY	★	★★	★★★	★★★
COLOUR TRANSPARENCIES	—	★★	★★★	★★
COLOUR PRINTS	★★	★★★	★★★	★★★
BLACK-AND-WHITE	—	★★	★★★	★★★
PORTABILITY	★★★	★★★	★★	★
SIMPLICITY	★★★	★★★	★★	★
ACCESSORIES	—	★	★★★	★★★
LENS INTERCHANGE	—	—	★★★	★★★
QUALITY OF RESULT	★	★★	★★★	★★★
AVERAGE PRICE	£25	£60	£150	£500

Instant Cameras

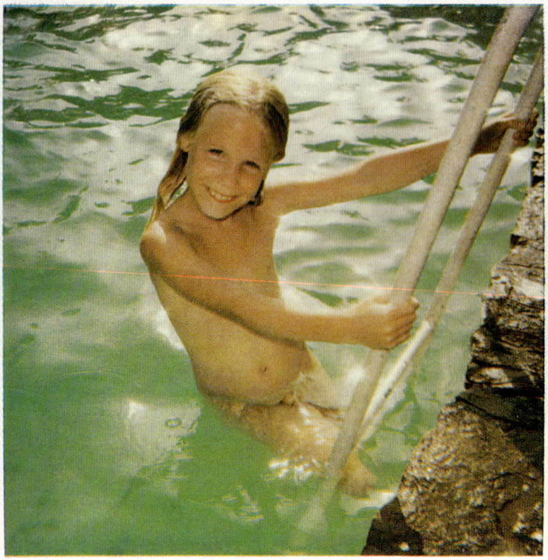

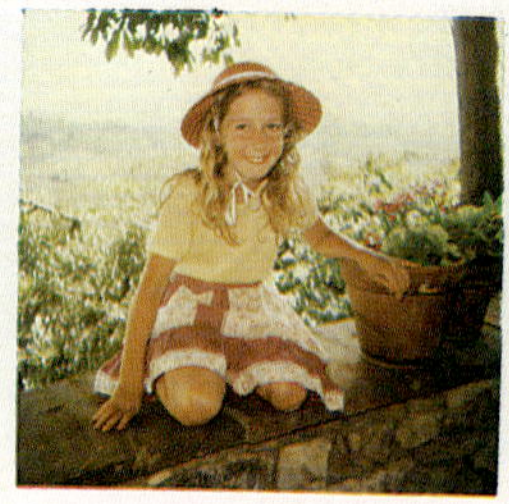

The automatic fill-in flash is ideal for photographing under low light, giving a balanced mix of ambient and flash light (above).

The Polaroid colour process is particularly good for skin tones, giving a warm and natural result (left).

In the late 1940s a new photographic product was launched on the unsuspecting American public: the Land Polaroid camera. This bulky machine, resembling an early bellows camera, was the forerunner of the modern instant camera. It was difficult to load, with two spools of film, and the black-and-white print, once extracted from the works, had to be coated with a layer of liquid stabilizer to become permanent. Nevertheless, the machines worked and gained rapid acceptance.

The instant camera of today is a totally different instrument. It is no longer necessary to peel away the print from a soggy negative sheet, and the modern film packs are compact, easy to load and even contain batteries to power the camera functions. Dry prints are ejected from the mouth of the camera by motor and self-develop to a full-colour image in daylight. Some models feature automatic focusing by sonic beam and self-quenching electronic flash. They have reached such a state of automated perfection that it is difficult to see where further improvements could be made.

It is the magical quality of instant pictures that has made them such a boon to the child photographer. Probably the worst obstacle to be overcome is the boredom of the subject: children tire easily and become restless during a session, but with an instant camera they are able to see results quickly. They are fascinated by the workings of the camera and intrigued to

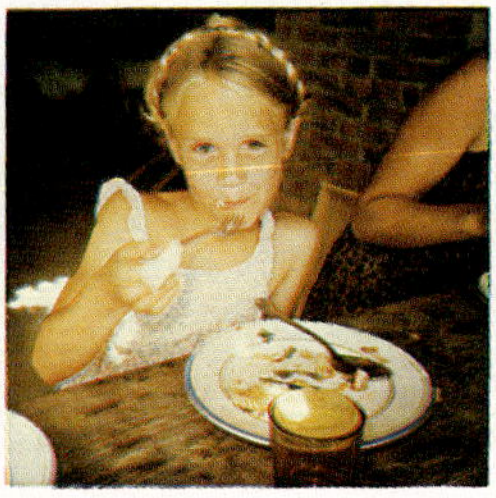

Most instant cameras are completely automatic with no exposure control other than a simple 'lighten or darken' slider, which is rarely needed (above).

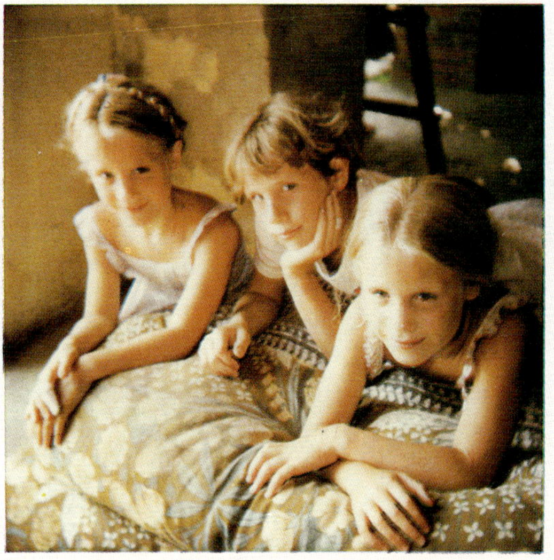

It is often difficult to get three children all looking right at the same time. With an instant camera, you can continue shooting until a perfect result has been achieved and then finish the session (right).

see their own images emerge on film. With the results of the photographer's efforts coming up before their eyes, they rapidly become caught up in the spirit of the occasion.

While an instant camera is obviously not right for every photo session, it is an excellent idea to have one to hand when shooting conventional portraits. The child's interest can be maintained with the occasional 'magic' picture, while the photographer gets what he really wants with a normal camera. The child stays lively and interested and has something to keep at the end of the session.

The instant photograph is also useful for keeping a check on composition and lighting. With a conventional camera you might not notice in the viewfinder that a tree seemed to be growing out of the model's head, but an instant picture taken from the same position would show it up immediately. This is why many professional photographers use a special Polaroid attachment which allows them to produce an instant picture identical to what will be recorded on conventional film.

There is a new development from Polaroid, namely a colour transparency film that can be used in a normal 35 mm camera. The film is supplied in a normal cassette and loaded in the usual way. After exposure it is 'processed' in a few minutes in a special device, which can be carried in the camera case. This new material offers all sorts of interesting possibilities.

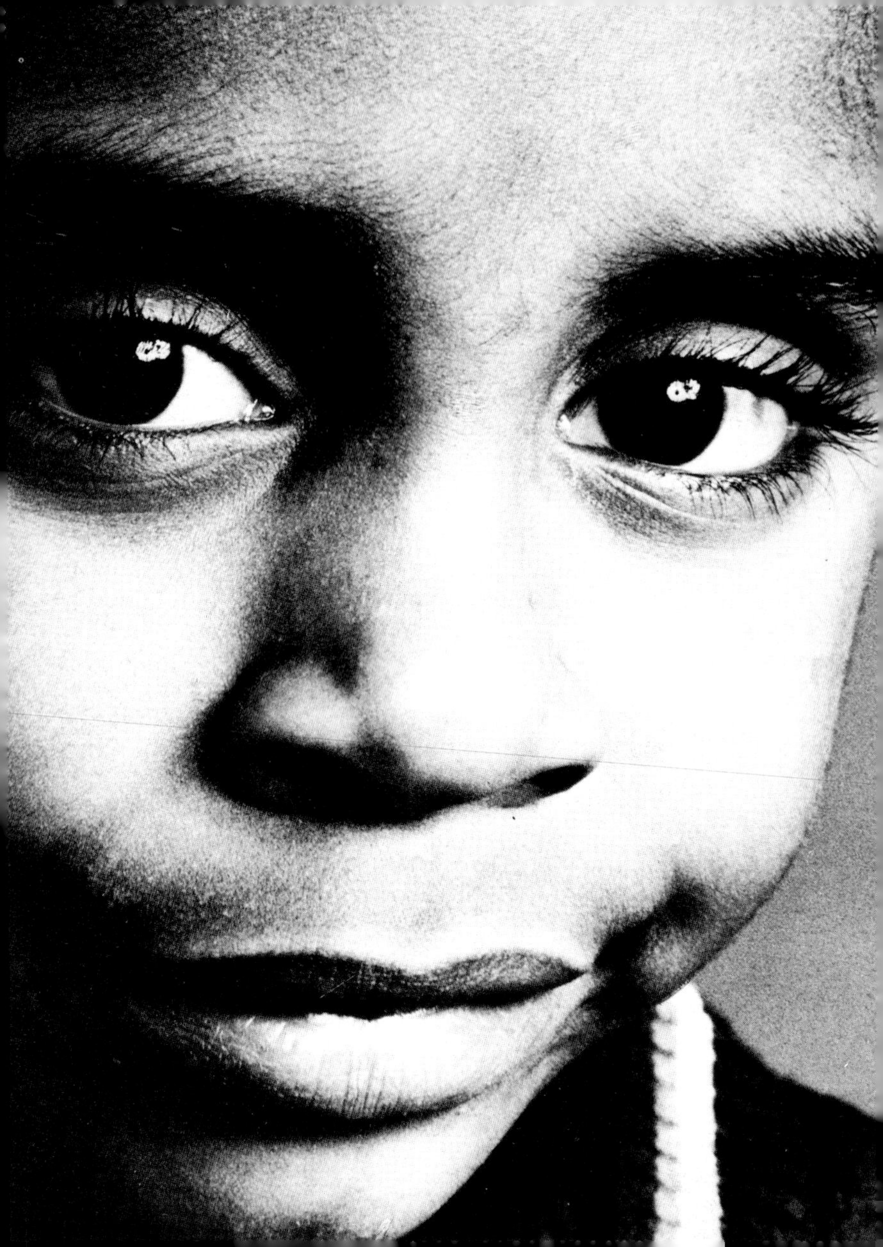

THE CHILD PORTRAIT

The successful child portrait will be more than simply a good likeness – it will capture the character and mood of the sitter and sometimes the spirit of an occasion. Portraiture is one of the most difficult aspects of child photography, demanding not only technical competence and good aesthetic judgement, but also a patient and understanding approach to the subject. An outstanding portrait depends on the establishment of a good rapport, with the photographer giving his undivided attention to the model. It is equally important to capture those fleeting moments, those changing facial expressions that reveal the true character of a child.

Most children, especially the very young, become bored easily when asked to pose for the camera, with the result that the photographs will lack spontaneity. It is therefore vital that, before embarking on a portrait session, the photographer be totally familiar with his equipment and the operation of the camera controls. He must be ready to retain the child's attention completely and lose no valuable time with technical matters.

Careful planning is obviously crucial, and certain questions must be resolved before the session starts. Are the pictures to be of a semi-formal, posed nature, or candid, unposed shots of the child seemingly unaware of the camera? What about the background? Will it be a simple backdrop or a more natural setting? Should the background be purely secondary to the model or play a prominent part in the picture? Once a location has been chosen, the quality and intensity of the light must be considered, whether it is sufficient and not so bright that it causes the child to squint and grimace. If enough time and thought are spent at the planning stage, you will be at least half-way towards achieving a good result.

The Posed Portrait

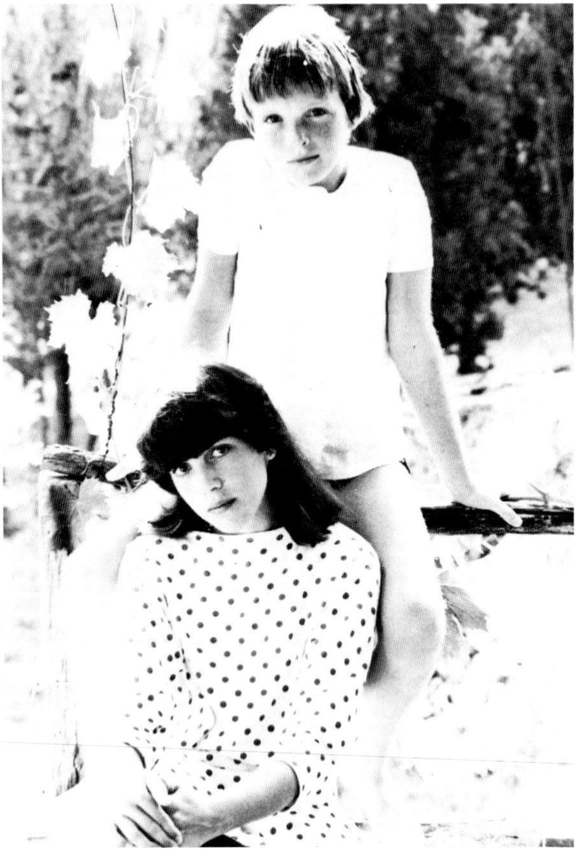

An outdoor setting was used for this portrait shot (left), with the subjects faced away from the evening sunlight, to provide back-lighting. The children were seated in natural positions to ensure a relaxed photograph, with their bodies slightly juxtaposed to give a tighter composition.

Brightly coloured backgrounds are often over-obtrusive, but sometimes a deliberate use of large masses of colour, like these giant balloons, can add a feeling of fun and gaiety to a child portrait (right).

Although most people prefer a natural approach to child photography, there are occasions when a more formal, even stylized approach is required. Since the beginnings of photography in Victorian times, children have been subjected to the ordeal of a visit to the portrait photographer. In those early days this often entailed being clamped to a chair and having to remain still for over a minute – no wonder a visit to the studio was anticipated with dread! Nowadays, of course, the situation is quite different and there is absolutely no reason why a child should not enjoy having his photograph taken, nor for a posed photograph to look stilted or wooden.

The choice of location or background is extremely important in a posed picture and the setting should be unobtrusive and in sympathy with the sitter. The portrait may be taken in a studio set-up, outdoors or in the home. Very fine portraits of children may be made indoors by the light of a large window, with a white reflector used to fill in the shadows. Outdoors, care

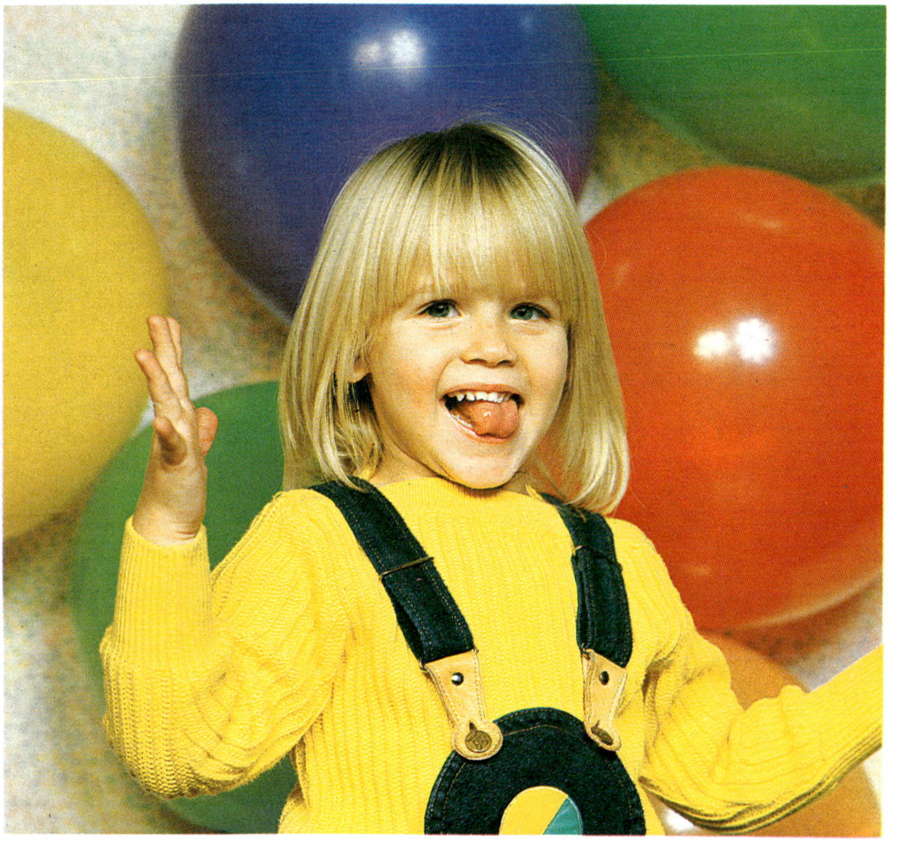

should be taken to choose a background without strong contrast of light and shade as this will prove to be distracting. Similarly, when working in colour, bright splashes should best be avoided and harmonious tones looked for. If the location which you have contains a horizon or other strong horizontal element, make sure that it does not cut through the sitter's head. Trees and foliage can be used to make an ideal background for a child portrait provided that they are photographed suitably out of focus.

When the setting has been selected, all necessary preparations should be made before the child arrives. It can be useful to fit a long-focus or telephoto lens to the camera, as this will ensure a pleasing compression of facial features, with the added bonus of throwing the background well out of focus, eliminating unwanted detail and concentrating attention on the subject. The camera should be loaded with the required type of film, and the correct exposure determined and set. Then, with the camera in the shooting position, the

The Posed Portrait 2

background should be checked through the viewfinder, preferably with the lens stopped down, and any distracting elements eliminated.

When all preparations have been made, the child may be introduced to the shooting area. Great care should be taken to ensure that he is in a comfortable position: he may stand, sit or kneel at the photographer's direction, and if the position *feels* comfortable, it will usually look relaxed in the photograph. It is a good idea to give very young children a favourite toy or book to hold, as having a familiar object will help them to feel comfortable.

When the child is settled, put him at ease by talking to him and perhaps making him laugh. At this point his complete attention is required, and a rapport must be established. After a few exposures it should not be necessary to direct your sitter any longer as he will soon discover what is expected of him, and continuing to give him instructions will only make him self-conscious and awkward. Instead, manipulate the conversation to produce the right range of expressions, bringing in an element of humour or seriousness as required. If you own a Polaroid camera, this is a good time to bring it out and take a couple of shots to show him how good he's looking in your photographs. This will keep the interest going and also give him greater self-assurance.

Although some photographers prefer a hand-held camera, there is a definite advantage in using a tripod in this situation. The presence of a camera between the photographer and the child forms a physical barrier which can break the rapport between them. With a tripod-mounted camera which is correctly framed and focused on the model, the photographer can move away from the apparatus and, by using a cable release, can take his photographs while retaining eye and verbal contact with the child. Obviously, if the child is moving around a great deal, periodic checks must be made in the viewfinder for framing and focus. Using a winder or motor drive has the added advantage that the camera will need no

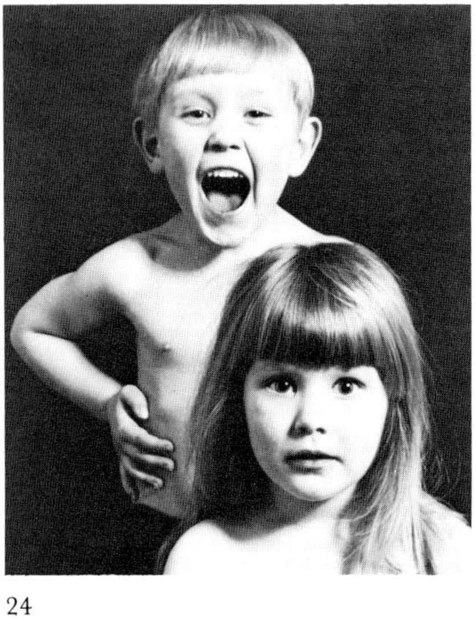

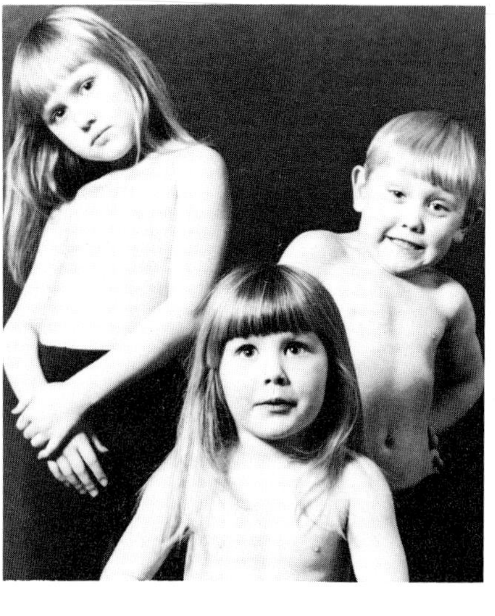

A low camera angle was used in this portrait of a young baby (right). Small children tend to look foreshortened and distorted when photographed from above, although this is natural because of their small size. This photograph was taken with a single flash bounced off a white card.

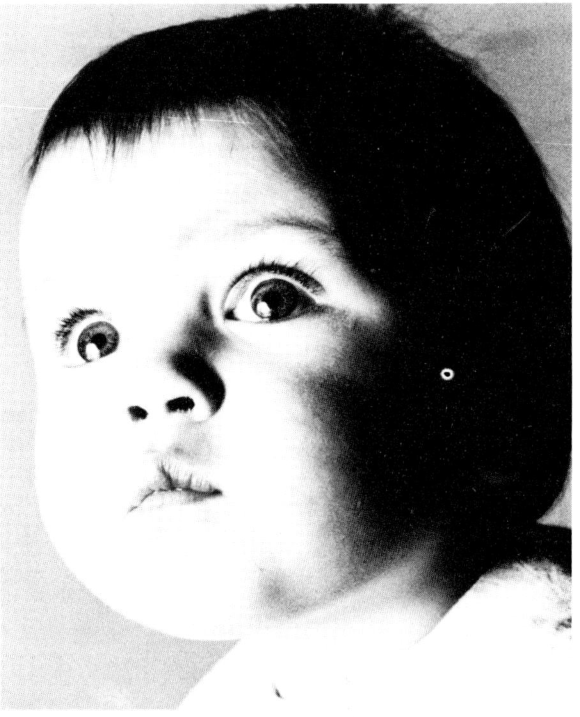

The strength of this portrait (right) relies on the compelling eyes of the model. When shooting a close-up portrait, the eyes should always be focused sharply, even if other facial features are not defined clearly.

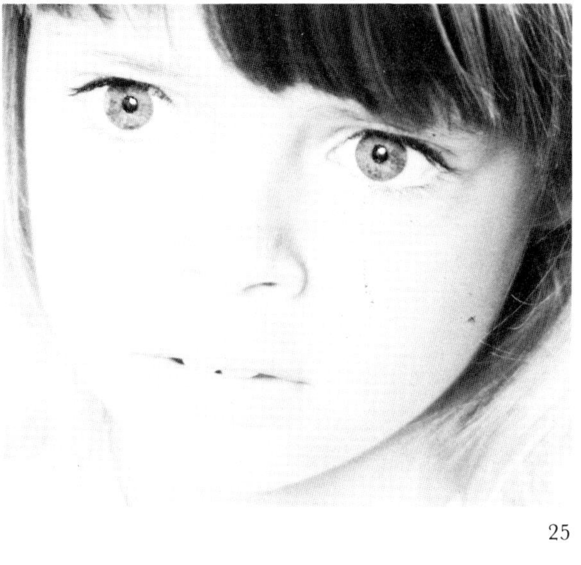

When photographing two or more children together, a more interesting effect will be achieved by arranging the models at different levels and by placing them in varying positions within the picture to form a satisfying composition (left and far left).

The Posed Portrait 3

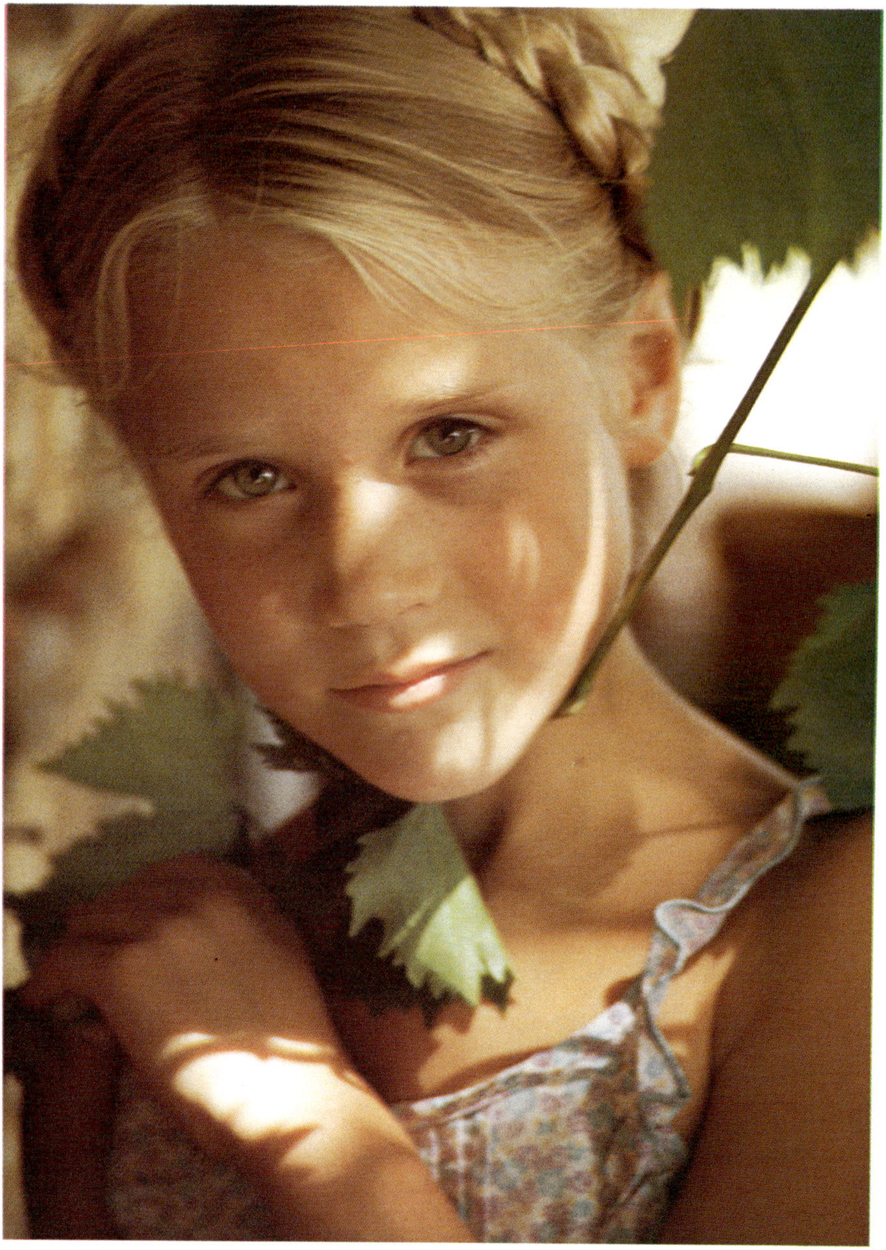

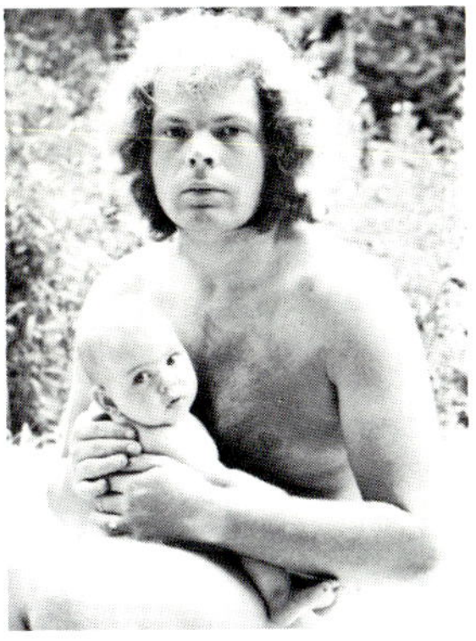

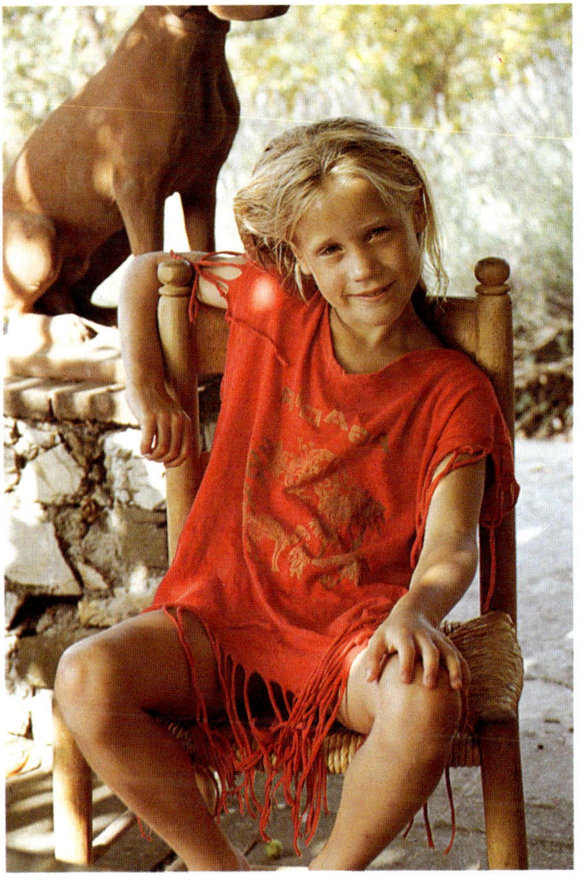

A photograph of the author with his young daughter (above). This is not only a treasured record of a newborn child, but also shows effectively the diminutive size of a small baby.

This close-up portrait (left) was taken by the dappled light of an over-hanging vine. Shots taken under such conditions will only be successful when the patches of light do not obliterate important features, especially the eyes and mouth.

In this typical posed portrait (right), the child is aware of the camera yet is thoroughly relaxed. The choice of colours and the outdoor location are expressive of a general feeling of well-being.

manual operations between exposures. This enables the photographer to work at a fast pace, missing fewer good opportunities, while at the same time allowing maximum concentration on the model.

The use of the zoom lens is also very useful as the variable focal length gives the photographer the ability to re-compose the format of the portrait without moving the camera or disturbing the model. He can expose a range of shots from a close-up head-shot to three-quarters or even full length, without having to move the camera and breaking the continuity of the session.

By using these techniques you will make the best of your time with the child, but do not forget that children, like adults, sometimes have their off-days and that no amount of cajoling and encouragement will make them cooperate. When you feel that the child has had enough, stop; there is no point in carrying on, and to do so may endanger your chance of having a good session next time.

The Unposed Portrait

The posed portrait is sometimes known as 'eye-contact' photography. The child, aware of the photographer's presence, is expected to look into the camera lens, thereby establishing eye-contact with the viewer of the finished photograph. Eyes are probably the most expressive and revealing facial feature of any person, and this is especially true of young children. For this reason 'eye-contact' portraits have a very direct and strong appeal both visually and emotionally.

There are many occasions, however, when it is desirable to portray children in a more natural and less formal manner. Because some children are shy when confronted with a camera, and others will assume uncharacteristic expressions, it is sometimes better to capture them in a situation where they are not expected to respond to the photographer's demands. To achieve this successfully, the child must be involved in some favourite activity of a fairly immobile nature, thus relieving him of the pressure of having to react to the camera. This enables the photographer to observe his subject through the viewfinder and shoot as the opportunities occur.

Setting up a session for an unposed shot requires just as much planning as for a more formal portrait. Bear in mind that a child is often most relaxed in his own territory and so, if suitable, choose the child's own room or a favourite part of the garden as a location. Settle him down with a game, toy, favourite pet or some activity which will keep him absorbed and relatively static for a few minutes. For this type

These portraits of two small children (right and far right) were taken by window light. Very quick reactions are needed when shooting sessions like these, because movements and changes of facial expression will occur with great frequency as the models form a rapport with each other, as well as with the photographer. A motor drive is very useful in situations such as these, as many excellent shots are otherwise likely to be missed. Although winders and motor drives are quite noisy, small children soon get used to the sounds and are not disturbed by them.

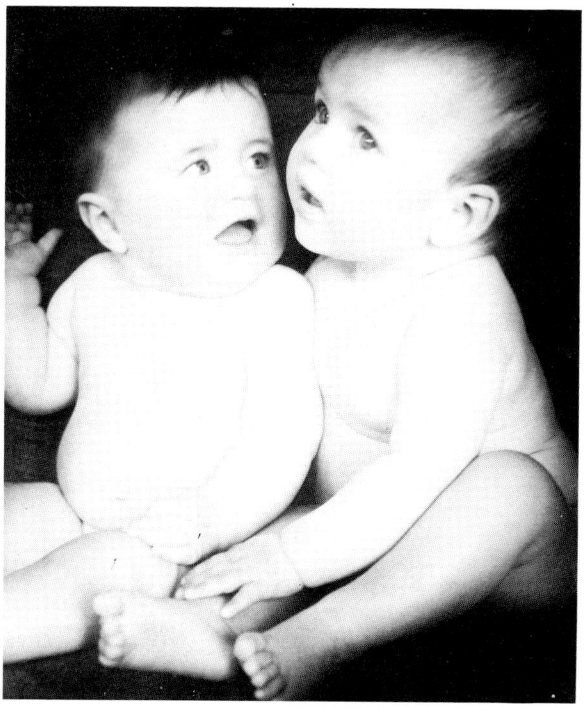

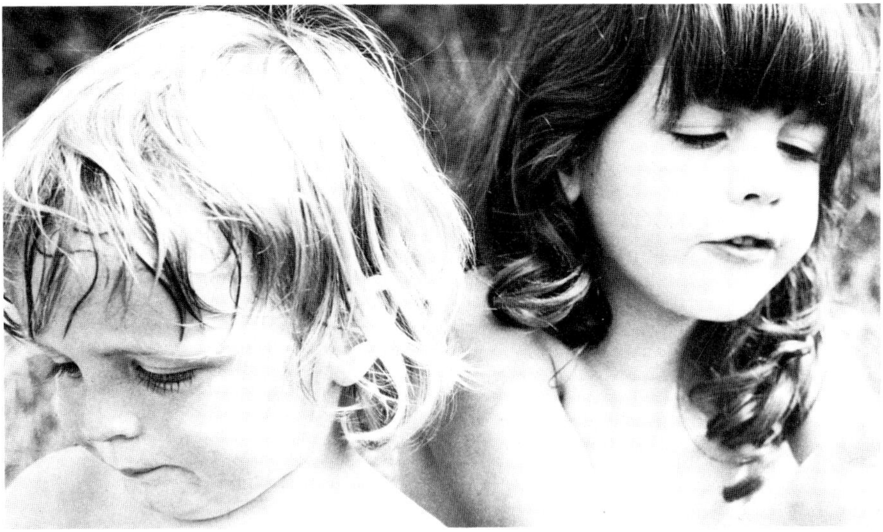

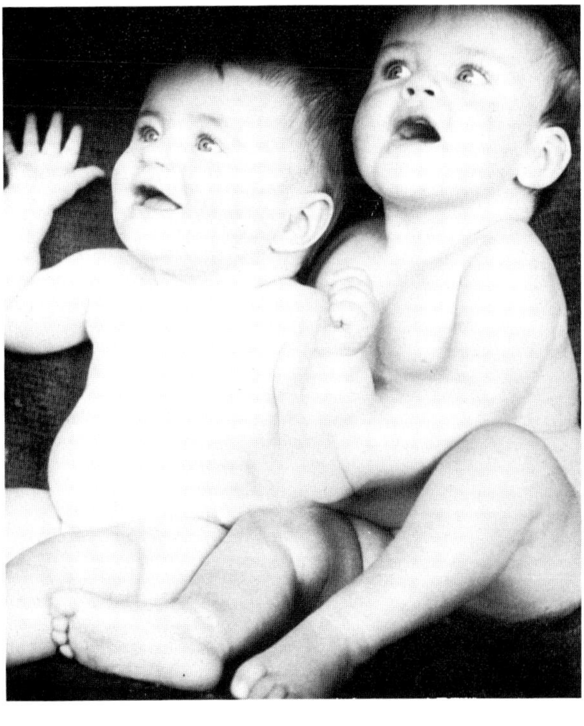

A telephoto lens was used in this shot (above) to bring the images of the children's heads closer together by compressing the effect of perspective. Although the models were sitting some distance apart, their images are of almost equal size in the picture. Another advantage of using a telephoto lens was that the photograph could be taken without the children's knowledge.

The Unposed Portrait 2

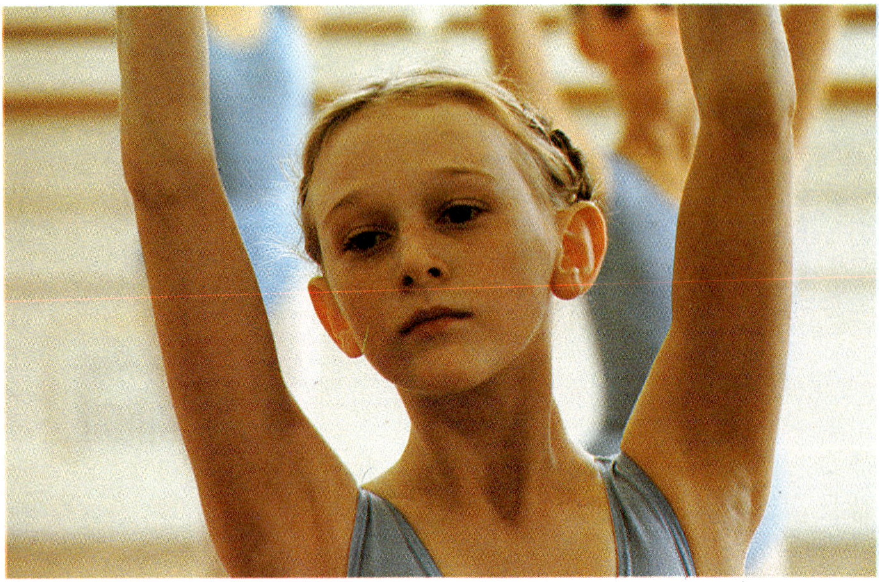

of shot, available light is better than flash, which can be distracting. As children shift quickly and unexpectedly, many expressions will be accompanied by a degree of movement. Check that there is enough light to enable you to use a fairly fast shutter speed and, for the same reasons, use a fast film.

When the child is totally absorbed, introduce the camera quietly. Don't approach too near, as this will divert his attention. Use a telephoto or, better still, a long zoom lens to provide a sufficiently large image of the subject on film. Remember that if the picture is to be a true portrait, the emphasis must be on the child's face. With the model happily preoccupied, and hopefully not too aware of the camera, shoot quickly while the interest lasts. This will not be for very long, so quick reactions are vital, but because the child does not feel obliged to 'perform' for you, the pictures will look natural.

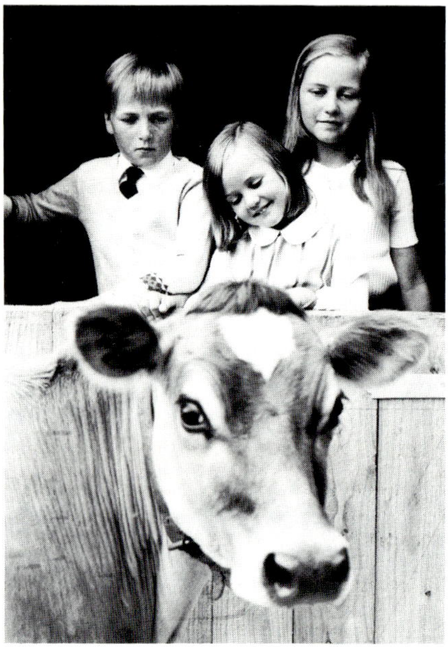

This picture of a young ballet dancer (left) is a typical unposed portrait. Although aware of the camera's presence, the model is totally absorbed in her work routine.

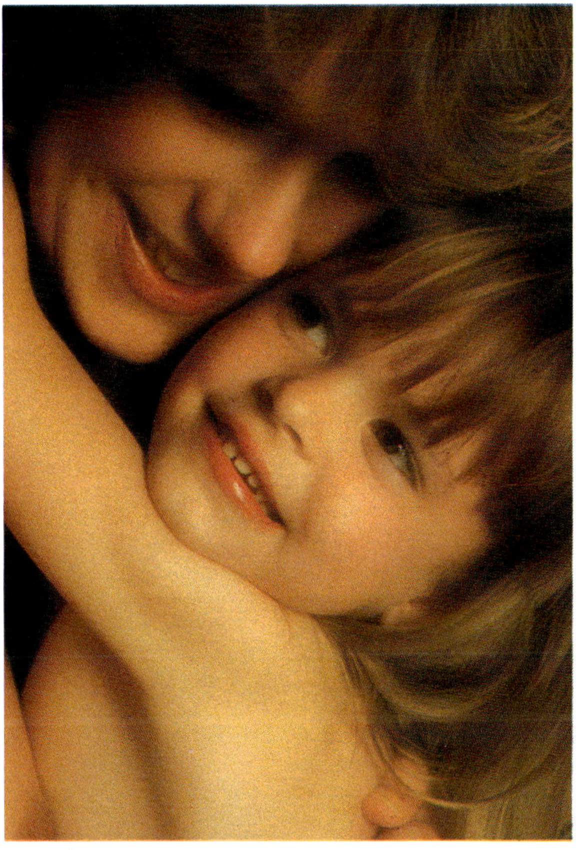

Mother-and-child studies such as this (right) can be most successful as the mother can take on the role of commanding the child's attention, leaving the photographer free to concentrate on recording the ensuing expressions.

Even when taking posed shots, a photographer should be ready to capture the unexpected, as in this picture which originated in a posed session in a farmyard (left). The unheralded and unexpected arrival of a cow resulted in an interestingly varied range of expressions.

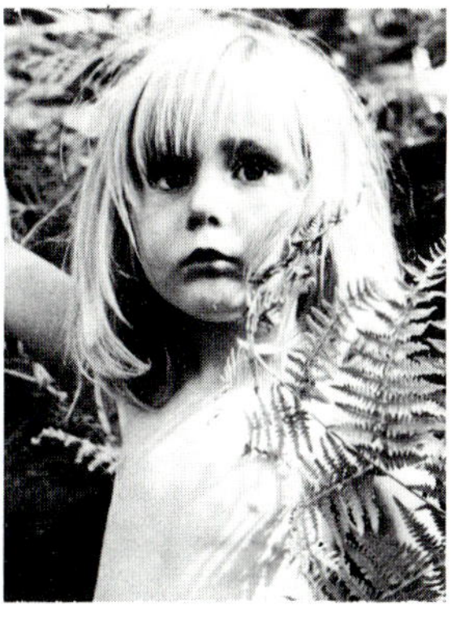

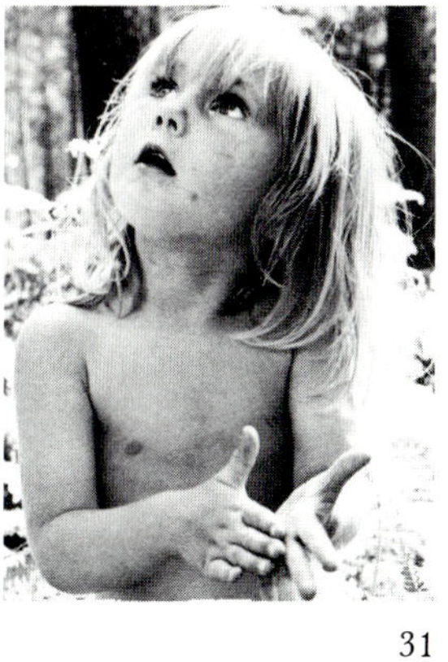

A woodland setting is ideal for unposed portraiture, as the child is unrestrained and free to explore (right and far right). A fast film should be used in such locations as light levels are deceptively low under foliage.

Contact Prints

When you have completed a portrait session and exposed at least one roll of film, it is not necessary to have a full-sized print made of every frame. Some shots will be failures for technical reasons such as subject movement or incorrect focus, and others may be spoilt if the model blinked or assumed an unattractive expression. Rather than waste money, a complete roll of film can be printed by contact on to a single sheet of 8 × 10 printing paper, and the entire set viewed simultaneously with immediate comparison from frame to frame. If you have your own darkroom you can make contact prints using a printing frame, but they can be ordered from the photographic laboratory which is processing your films. Contact prints can be made from both black-and-white and colour negative films, and are reasonably priced.

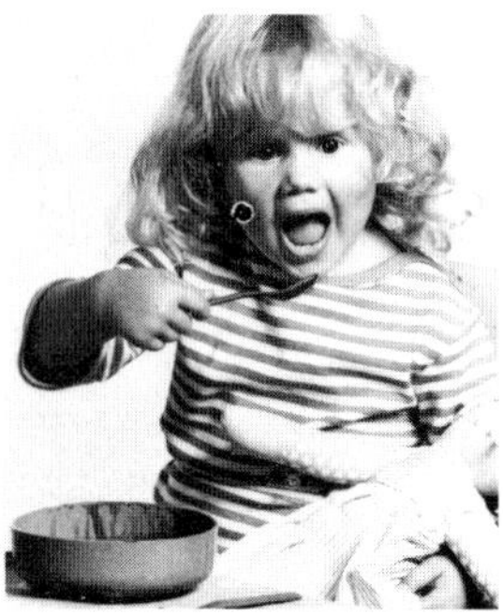

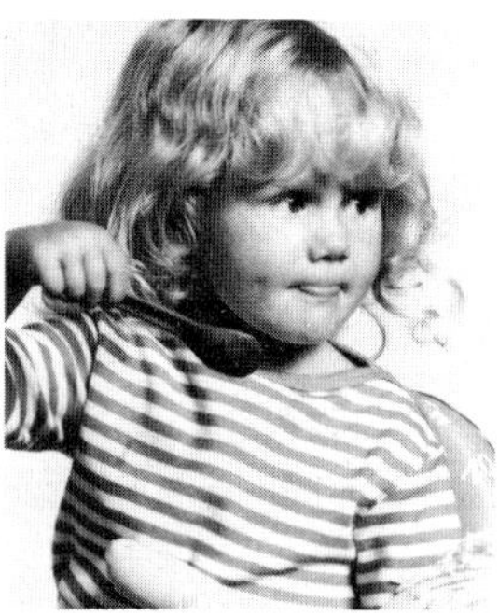

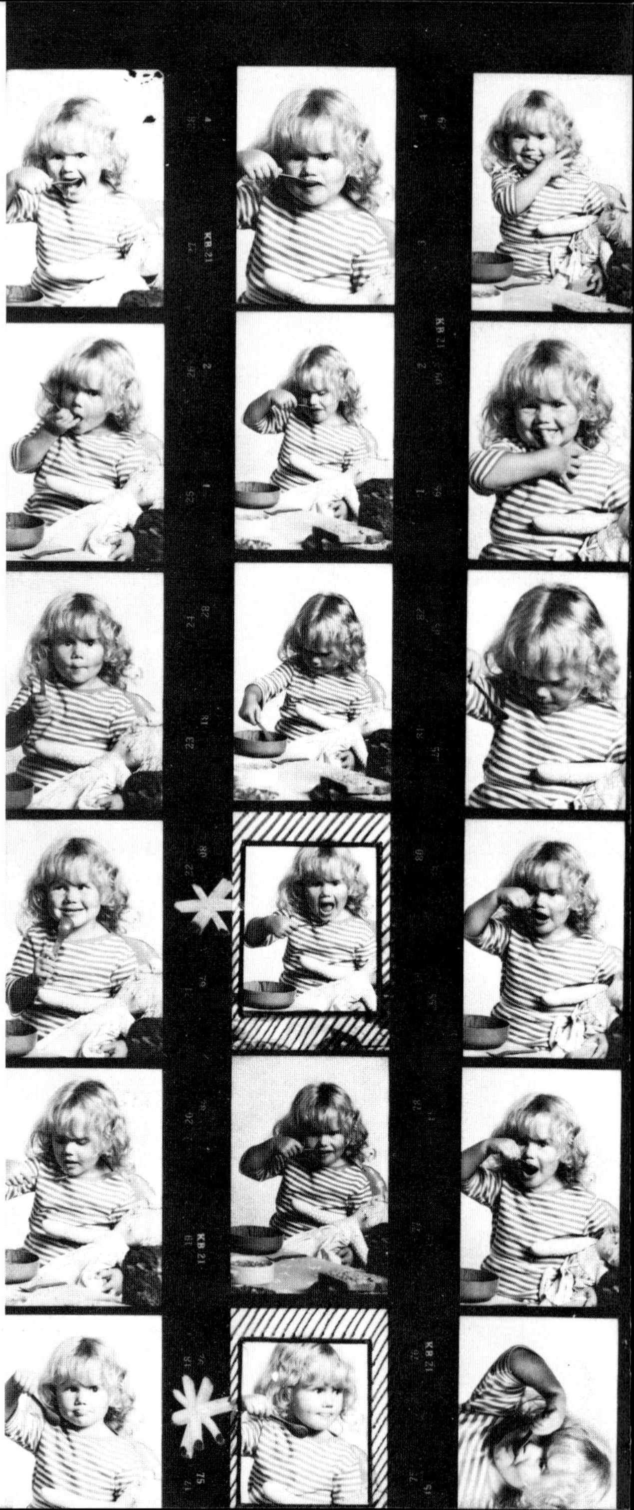

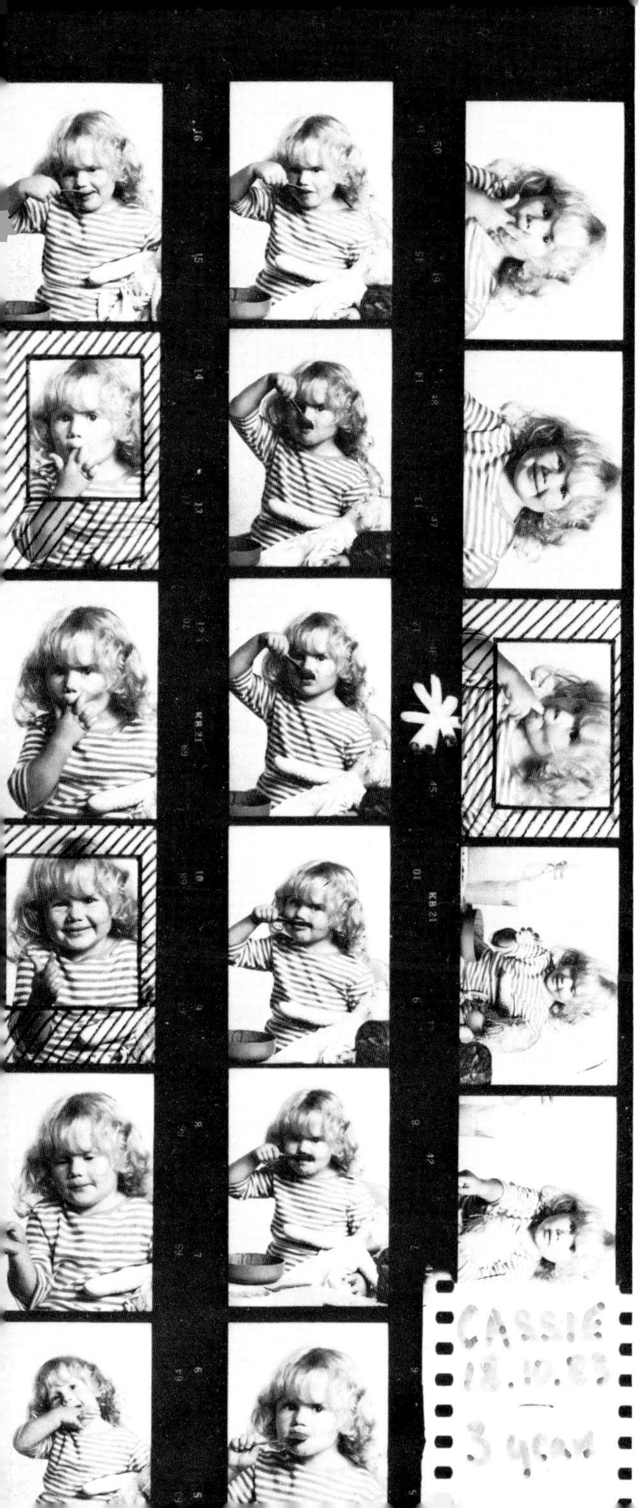

The ideal way to view contact prints is with a high-magnification lens. These are inexpensive and are most useful for assessing both visual and technical quality. In many cases a portion of a negative, rather than the whole, will provide a better composition, and the effects of different cropping can be judged by using two L-shaped cards to mask out the various parts of the image.

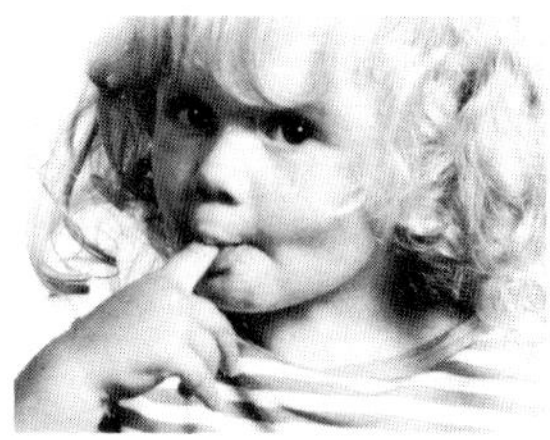

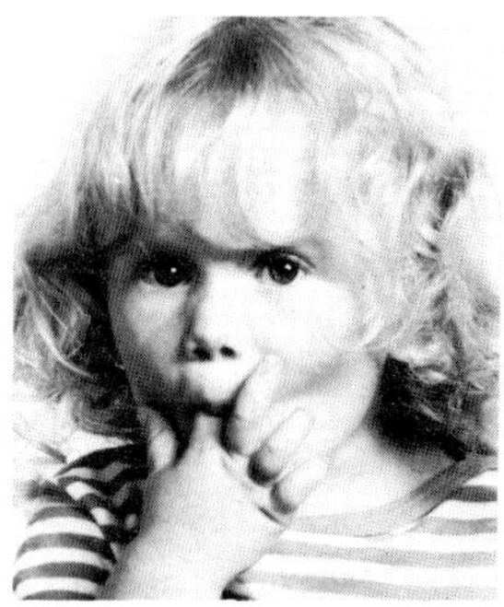

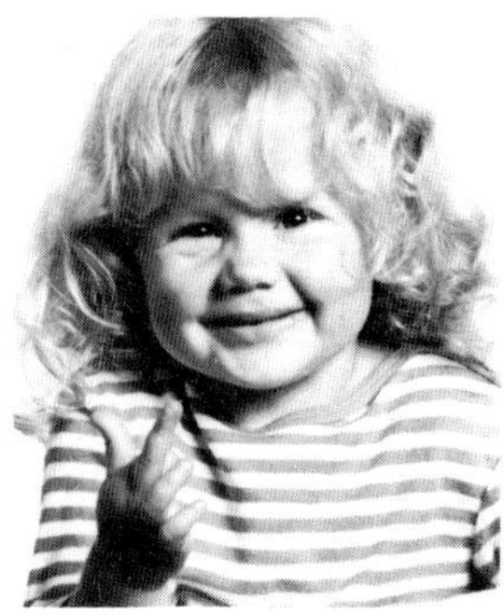

The Candid Portrait

A candid portrait, taken without the knowledge of the subject, captures the essential character and personality of that person. As far as child photography is concerned, candid portraiture is possibly the most rewarding approach, although in actual practical terms it can in fact be very frustrating and difficult for the photographer himself.

Candid photographs are best taken when the child is totally unaware of the camera's presence. For this reason, the ideal camera is an SLR fitted with a long lens. Photographers who use simple cameras and compacts will find candid work more problematical, because the short-focal-length lenses which are fitted to these cameras require a close shooting distance and the subject will be alerted. In the majority of cases, the possibility of taking a candid portrait will occur unexpectedly – you will see a child reacting to a situation with concentration, delight or even momentary trepidation, and you will want to capture the moment. In order to avoid attracting attention to yourself it is

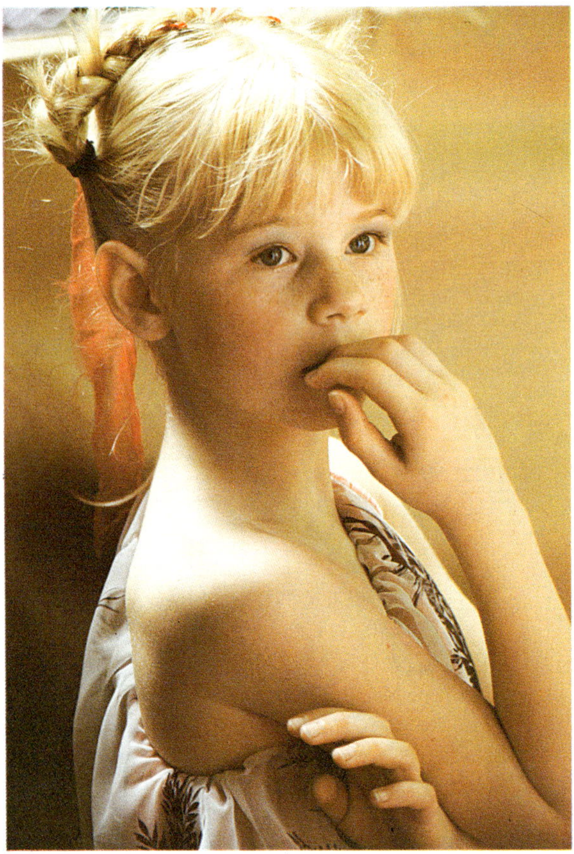

This photograph (left) was taken with the child quite unaware of the camera's presence. By using a long telephoto lens at some distance, the photographer can study the subject's movement and facial expressions and shoot unobtrusively. The use of a telephoto or long-focus lens has the added advantage of throwing the background out of focus and eliminating distracting detail.

In this candid portrait (right), again taken without the model's knowledge, the girl's attention was completely diverted from the camera as she watched the rehearsal for a theatrical event in which she was to feature later. The photograph was taken backstage under low lighting conditions, with the camera mounted on a tripod for steadiness.

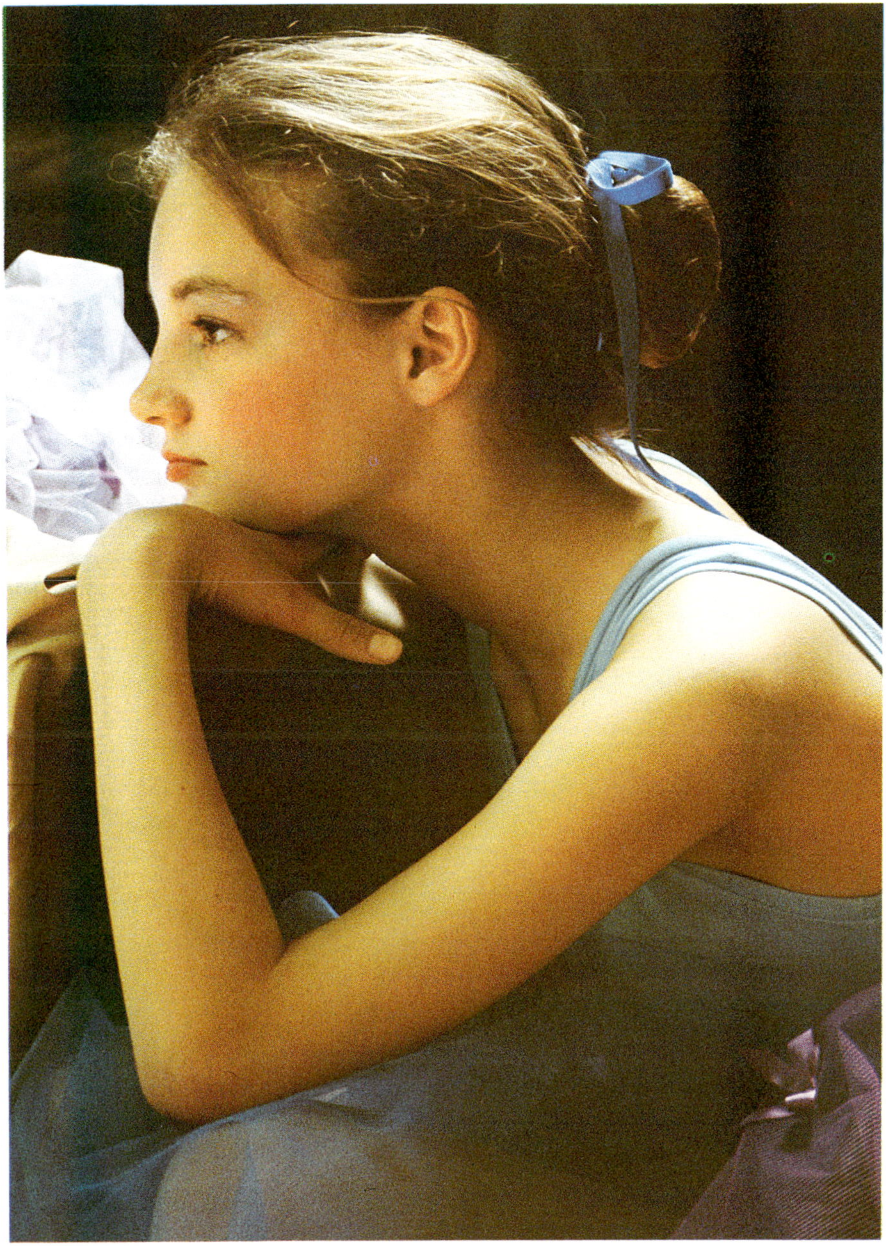

The Candid Portrait 2

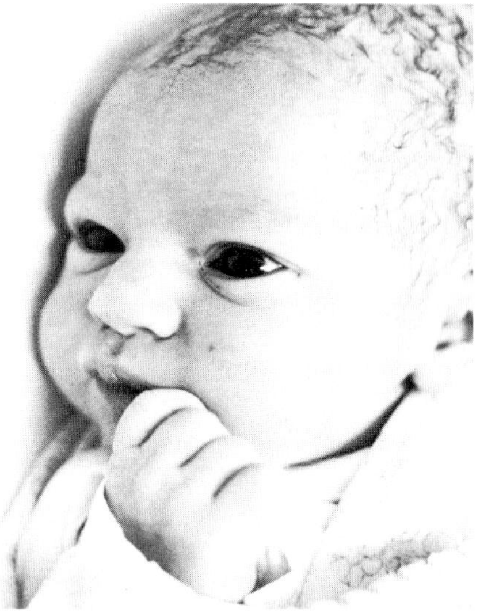

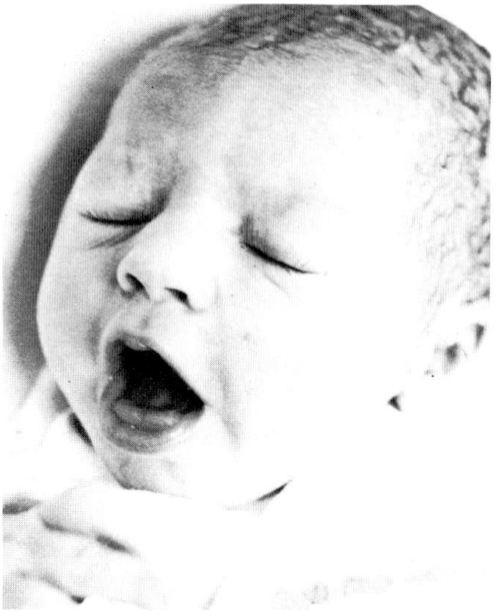

necessary to hold the camera to the eye for as short a time as possible before pressing the button. The way to do this is to have the correct exposure pre-set and the lens focused roughly. Then raise the camera to the shooting position, focus the lens correctly and take the photograph as quickly as you can before the child notices or the moment passes.

Certain situations present particularly good opportunities for candid photography of children, for example when they are watching an entertainment such as Punch and Judy or a puppet show. You will find that the sheer excitement of such occasions will without fail produce an infinite range of reactions and expressions and the children will be so involved in what is going on in front of them that they will be totally oblivious of the camera. Other opportunities for taking this type of shot often occur at the dinner-table, at playtime and in the class-room, in fact in any situation when a child is completely absorbed in what he is doing.

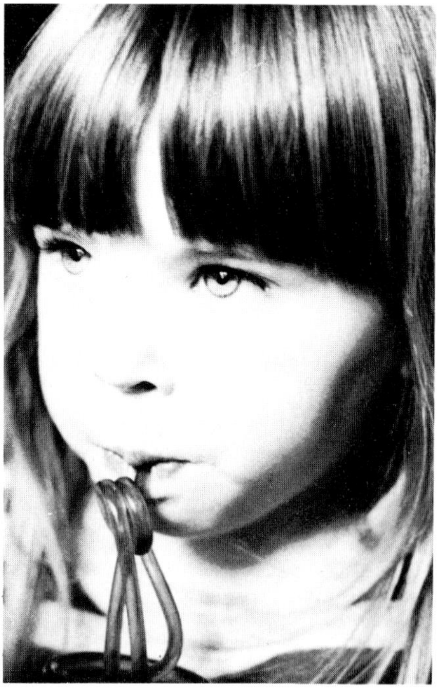

The very first candid portraits of a child will probably be taken of the newborn baby in hospital (left and far left). Most hospitals allow photography in the nursery, and this opportunity should not be missed.

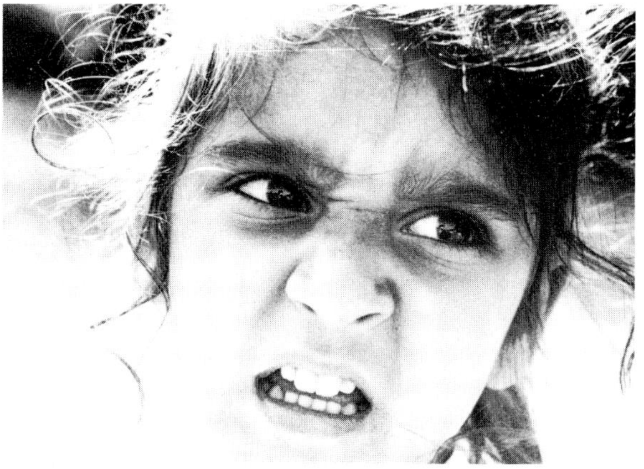

A child's expression is constantly changing, and by keen observation through the viewfinder from a discreet distance these expressions can be captured. The angry child in this picture (right) was photographed with a telephoto lens and a reflex camera from a distance of about 3.5 metres (12 feet).

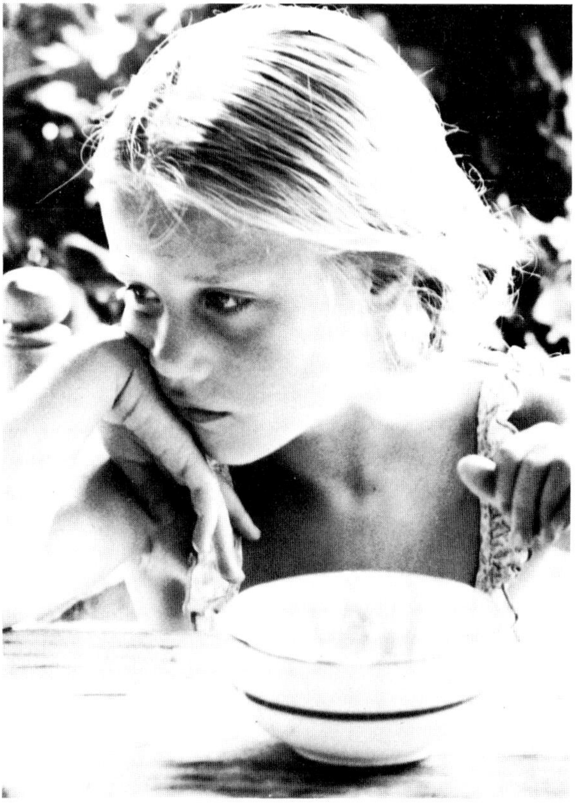

Candid photographs should always be taken when a child is pre-occupied. Eating and drinking are major diversions in a small child's life and, as this shot shows (left), times when a child is least likely to be wary of a camera.

Sometimes an expression will occur on a child's face quite unexpectedly (right). With a pre-set camera it is a simple matter to raise the camera to the eye, focus the lens, take the photograph and lower the camera again, all in a short space of time. In many cases the child will be quite unaware that a picture has been taken.

Taking Portraits with Simple Cameras

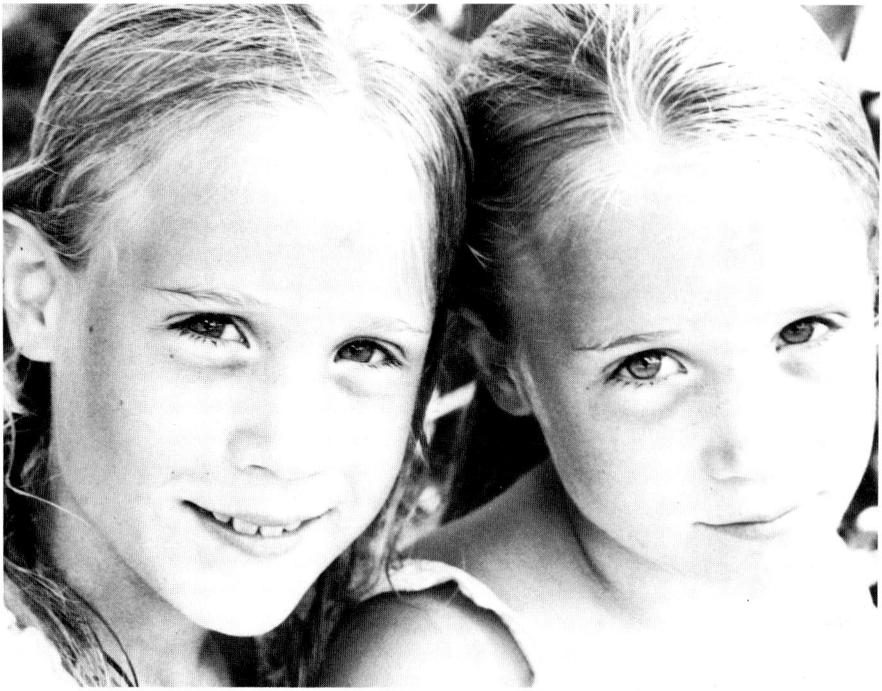

The simple cartridge or disc-loading camera is not the ideal instrument for portrait work but, used resourcefully, they can produce wholly acceptable results. The main problems with cameras of this type are the inability to focus at close distances and the lack of provision for shooting in conditions other than bright light. Some simple cameras are fitted with a telephoto or close-up lens; the telephoto will enable the photographer to get a larger subject image within the camera's normal focusing range, and the close-up attachment will enable him to approach nearer and also gain a larger image. Using either of these supplementary lenses on the camera will make it possible to shoot head-and-shoulders portraits. Simple cameras which do not have this facility will only focus to about 1.5 metres (5 feet) and are restricted to full-length photographs.

If you have one or other of these supplementary lenses, you will be well advised to use it. As a general rule, close-up portraits have more visual impact, especially when they are to be printed relatively small, as is the case with pictures taken with cheaper cameras. Using a supplementary lens will result in a perceptible loss of image quality, which will affect both sharpness and contrast. This is not always a disadvantage for portrait work, however, as there is no fine detail to worry about, unlike landscape photography, for instance. In fact, the softness of the image can sometimes work in the photographer's favour, producing a diffuse, romantic effect. You can take both posed and

This straightforward portrait (left) is quite within the capacity of a simple camera with a close-up or telephoto supplementary lens. When taking a shot of this kind, leave plenty of space around the subjects' heads to allow for lack of accuracy in the viewfinder and for trimming the negative when the picture is printed.

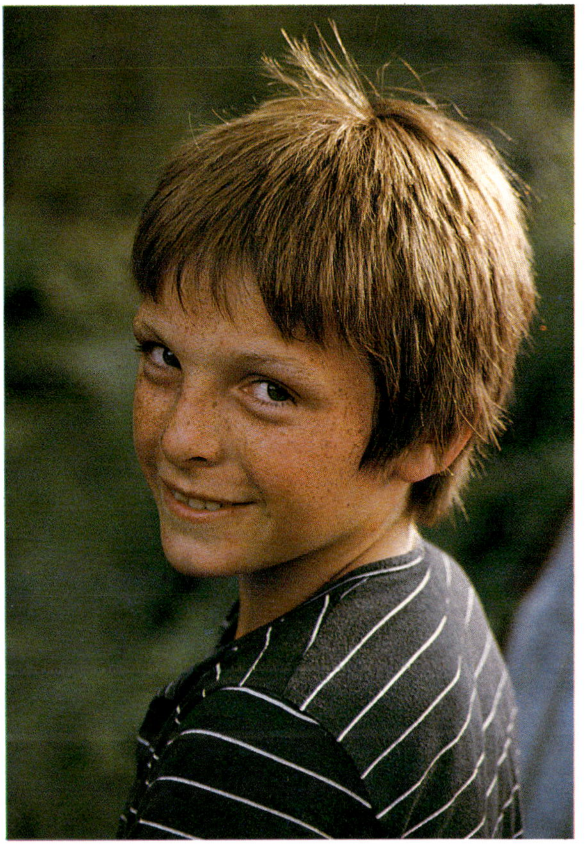

A simple automatic 35 mm compact camera, focused to 1 metre (3 feet), was used for this portrait (right). Shots of this kind should be taken in good light to avoid focusing errors, as the automatic exposure system will select a smaller aperture, giving greater depth of focus. Notice how at close distances the background is thrown pleasantly out of focus.

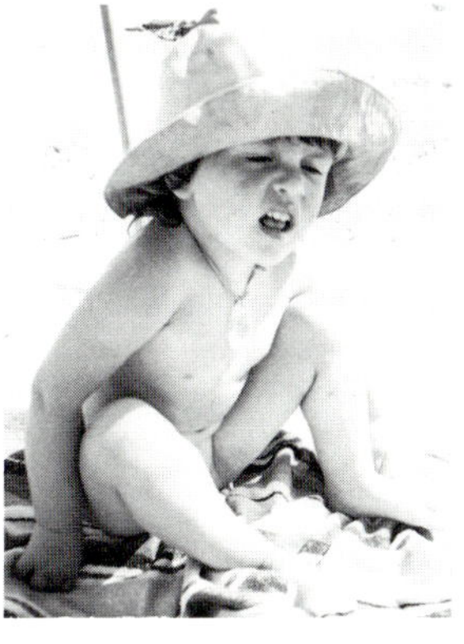

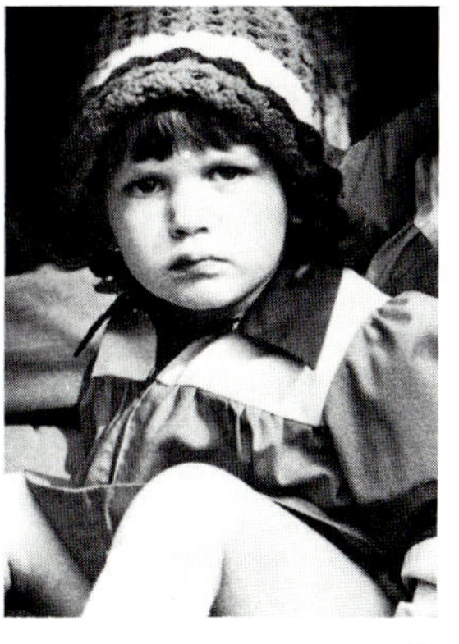

These two very different shots were taken with simple cameras. The beach shot (right) was taken with bright light, in ideal conditions for this type of camera. The study of the little girl (far right), taken under much darker conditions, was still printable because of the wide exposure tolerance of modern film.

Taking Portraits with Simple Cameras 2

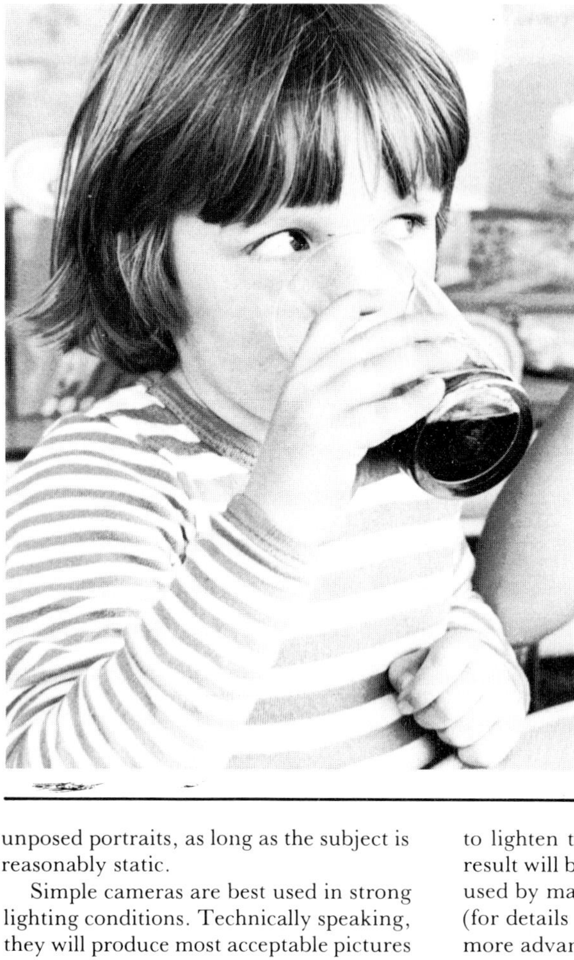

The low light from a restaurant window was combined with the camera flash diffused by a handkerchief to achieve a good lighting balance in this picture (left).

Shot with a cheap, simple 35 mm compact camera, at its closest focusing distance, this picture (right above) is typical of the results obtained easily by daylight.

This outdoor portrait (right below) was taken at a range of about 1 metre (3 feet). When simple cameras have no focusing aid, a tape measure can be used to check the distance.

Most simple cameras can be used away from direct sunlight, and the diffused light of a lightly clouded day will produce the good skin tones and modelling required in a portrait (far right).

unposed portraits, as long as the subject is reasonably static.

Simple cameras are best used in strong lighting conditions. Technically speaking, they will produce most acceptable pictures in sunshine, but the direct light of the sun is not the most conducive to a good portrait as hard shadows are produced under the nose and chin and there is a tendency for the subject's eyes to narrow and squint. Most modern simple cameras have a flash facility, either as an integral unit or as an extra attachment. When the light is too intense, it is a good idea to position the child with the sun behind him, so that the face will be in shade. By using the flash-gun to lighten this dark area, a very pleasing result will be achieved. This is a technique used by many professional photographers (for details of how to use the method with more advanced cameras see pp. 170–1).

When shooting indoors, using a combination of flash and daylight will also produce an attractive effect. Place the child close to a window so that he is illuminated by direct light from outside. This light alone would not be sufficient for a simple camera but, combined with the camera's own flash, a very pleasing lighting balance is achieved. The effect will be far more subtle than with the flash used on its own.

A common problem of flash pictures

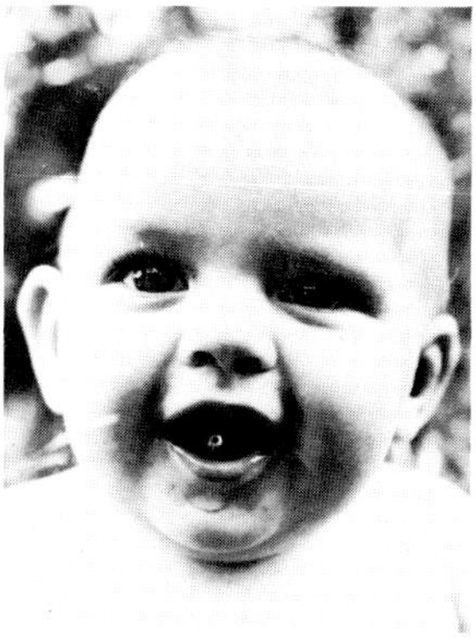

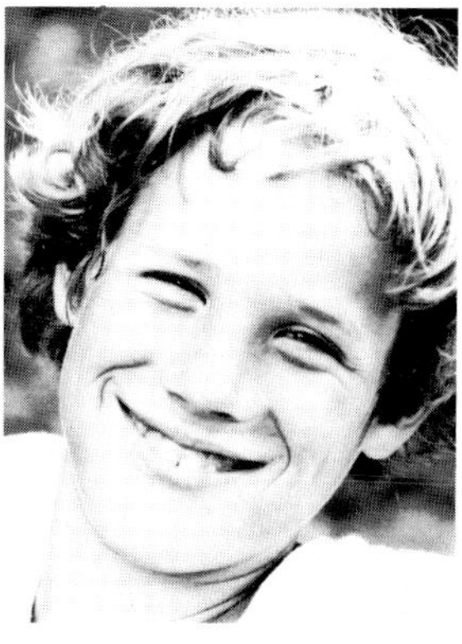

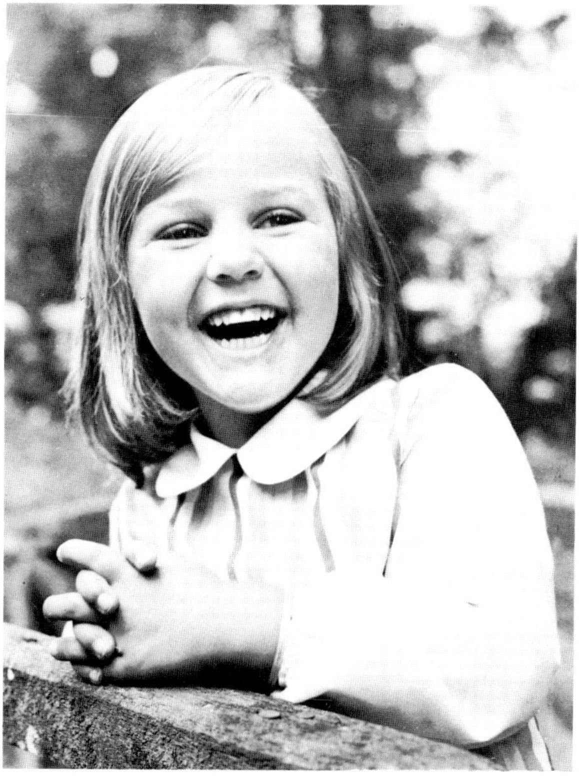

taken with simple cameras is the 'red-eye' effect. This occurs when shooting indoors with a small camera where the flash unit is situated close to the camera lens. Light from the flash is actually reflected from the red-coloured retina of the eye back into the camera where it records as a red spot in the middle of the pupil. To alleviate this, either remove the flash from the camera or, if this is not possible, diffuse the flash. This is done by taping one or two layers of white tissue paper over the flash-head; in an emergency, a single thickness of white handkerchief will do. Diffusing the flash in this way will not only reduce the possibility of 'red eye', but also soften the effect of the light, producing better modelling and less of the 'soot-and-whitewash' effect which is characteristic of so many amateur flash photographs.

A final tip for owners of cartridge and disc cameras is to leave plenty of space above the head of the child when composing a portrait in the camera. There are two reasons for this: the viewfinders of these cameras are very inaccurate at close distances, and the automatic printing machines used in the processing laboratories 'lose' a good part of the image around the edge of the negative. The combined result could mean that your model loses a good part or all of his head.

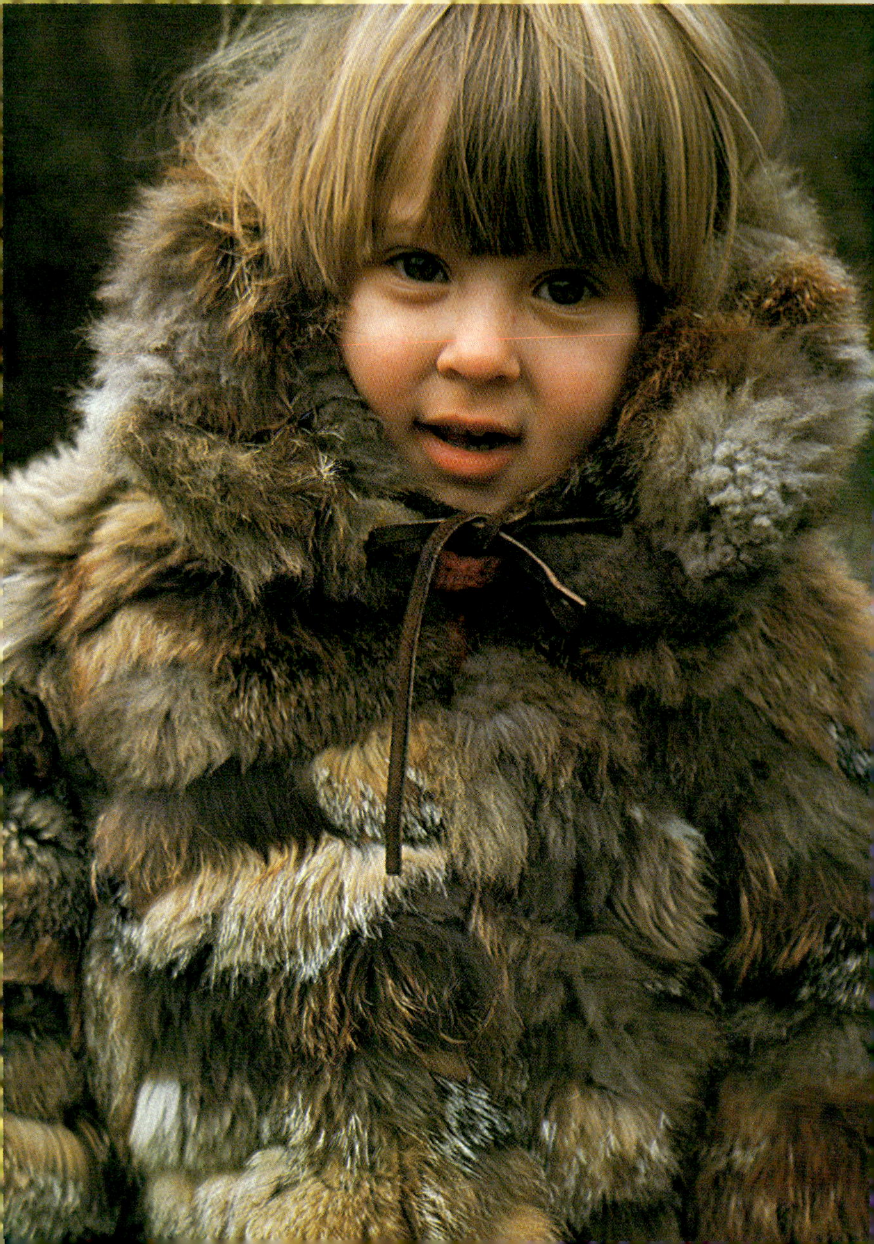

SHOOTING OUTDOORS

Childhood is a time of exploration and discovery, of infinite curiosity and seem-ngly boundless energy. Children need space and the stimulus of new experiences and places, and most children are never happier than when outdoors in the open air. Outside play sets no limits to a young child's imagination; he is in a world of his own, and this makes him an ideal subject for the camera. In later years, as the child's interests develop, hobbies and pastimes will again take him outside, and activities such as fishing, riding and kite-flying all lend themselves extremely well o pictorial treatment.

Given the great variety of possible settings – rivers, lakes, cornfields, sea, sand and snow – it is hardly surprising that most photographs of children are taken ou of doors. The scope is almost endless, and the choice is not limited to the country-side. Towns and cities also offer opportunities for successful child photography

Technically, outdoor photography presents few special problems. There is usually sufficient daylight, although it will vary in character according to the weather and time of day. The knowledgeable photographer will recognize the characteristics of various forms of daylight and use them to maximum effect With modern films and equipment, 'fair-weather' photography is a thing of the past, and it is possible to achieve dramatic results in the most adverse weather conditions. However, the nature of the light must be understood if it is to be used to good creative effect.

Light is not the only consideration, and careful thought must also be given to the background when shooting outdoors. Sometimes it is advantageous to allow the setting to dominate the picture, with the child then becoming part of the over-all scene and the picture telling a complete story. At other times it is mor important to concentrate interest on the child and to isolate the background by judicious focusing or by the choice of camera angle.

Ever since photography became an affordable hobby with the advent of cheap and simple camera outfits, the annual family holiday has been a popular subject and this still provides the ideal opportunity to photograph your child. New places and activities can feed the imagination of the photographer, and the happy relaxed atmosphere is conducive to good pictures. Good light and tanned bodie will provide photographs with sparkle and life, and happy childhood memories will be preserved for the future.

Using Daylight

Many outdoor photographs of children would be improved with a proper appreciation of the use of light and shade. Unless he is shooting off the cuff, the photographer should always assess the direction and quality of the light and use it to its best advantage. The very meaning of the word 'photography' is 'painting with light', and daylight can be manipulated like any other artistic medium.

Daylight varies according to weather conditions, the time of day and the geographical location. On a cloudless day, the sunshine is strong and direct, but, with degrees of cloudiness, the light will be softened or diffused to a greater or lesser extent. As far as photography is concerned, there are four main levels of daylight: direct sunshine, brilliant, with heavily defined shadows; hazy sunshine, still very bright but with lighter, less defined shadows; light cloud, usefully bright, but with soft, pleasantly indistinct shadows; heavy cloud, low-intensity light, with virtually no shadow and low contrast.

The quality and intensity of daylight are not only dependent on the prevailing cloud conditions. From the moment the sun rises, the light builds up in intensity, reaching a peak mid-way between sunrise and sunset. For photographic purposes, however, there is only a measurable change in strength in the two hours after dawn and the two hours before dusk. For the remaining hours of daylight the sunlight remains almost constant.

As regards the photographic quality of direct sunlight, however, this is constantly

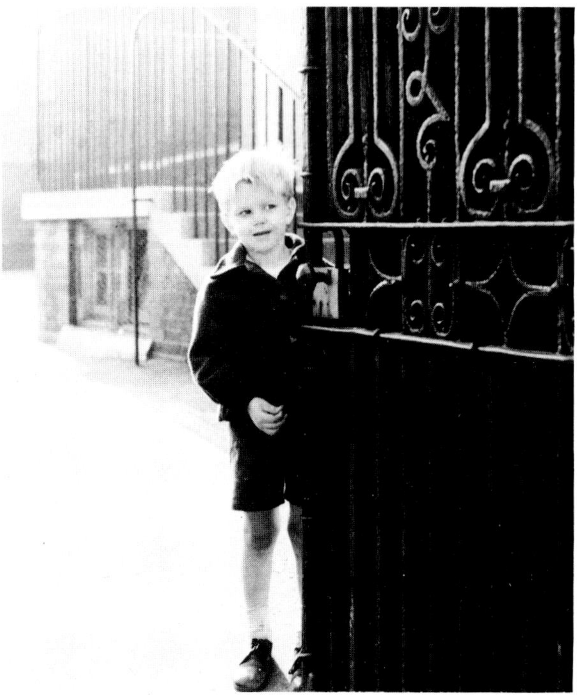

The use of low early-morning sunshine aids the atmosphere in this photograph of a boy attending school for the first time (left). Light can be used in this manner to set a mood and to help tell a story. The back-lighting effect in this picture is typical of that achieved early or late in the day, and especially in the winter months, when the sun lies lower in the sky at all times.

Soft, diffused light is very suitable for child photography. This picture (right), taken beneath trees and foliage, would have been spoiled by hard direct sunshine casting heavy shadows across the scene. Because the sky was still bright, though lightly clouded, a good contrast between the tones is still achieved.

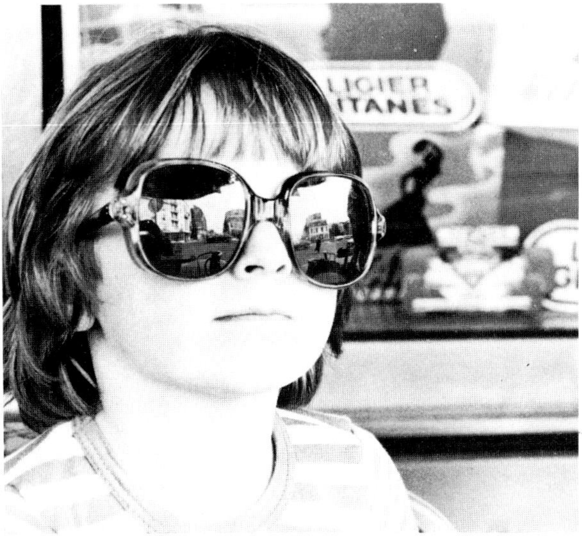

When conditions are too sunny for direct light photography, seek the shade: in this case, the parasol over a café table (left).

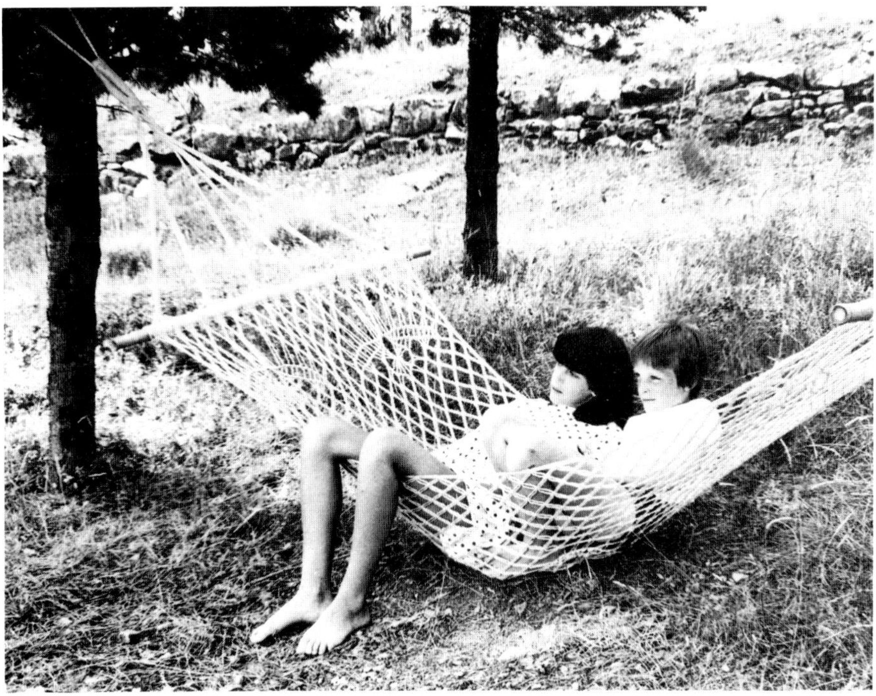

Using Daylight 2

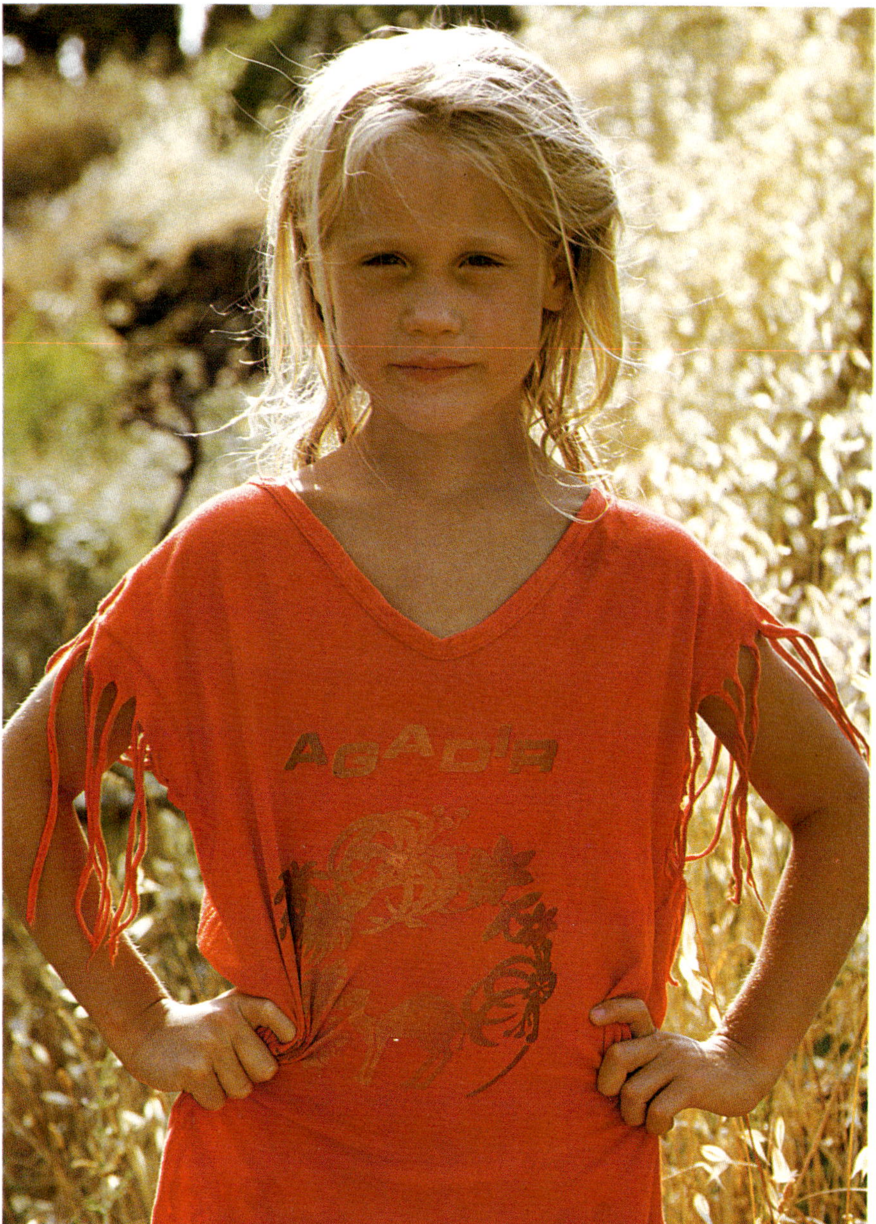

When shooting in the evening, within two hours of sunset, the sun will be low and warm in colour. When shooting into the sun the fringe of light will help the subject stand away from the background (left).

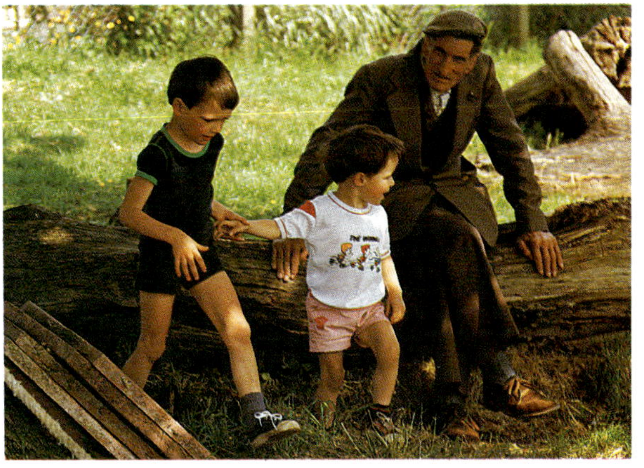

This photograph depicting the contrast of age and youth (right) was photographed in the deep shade of a tree, which required a considerable increase in exposure.

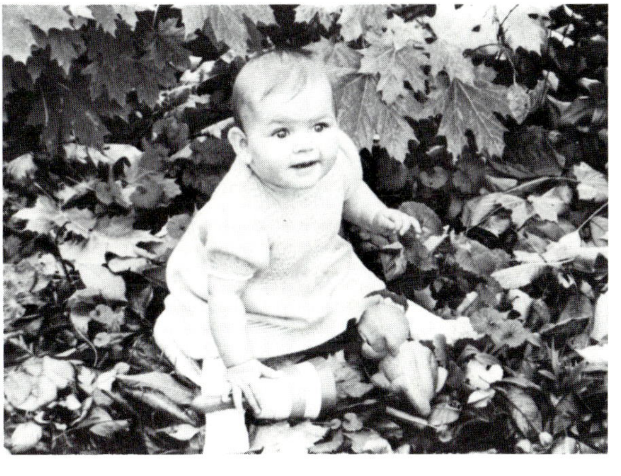

Autumn is an ideal season for child photography, with pretty tinted leaves on the trees and a carpet of fallen foliage below. Although obviously more attractive in colour, it is also an excellent time of year for black-and-white photography of children (right).

changing during daylight hours. In the period after dawn and before dusk the sun is low in the sky and shadows are long and dramatic. As the day progresses, the shadows shorten until the sun is at its highest position at noon, with the angle of the sun to the earth's surface becoming progressively oblique again, with shadows lengthening until dusk. During the periods around sunrise and sunset the light takes on a decidedly golden hue as the sun's rays are diffracted, and only light from the red/yellow end of the spectrum reaches the land surface. Photographically, this produces an illumination of beautifully golden warmth, albeit low in intensity.

Obviously, the photographer will not always be able to choose the time and lighting conditions most suitable for his work. More often it will be a case of making the most of the prevailing weather. When there is a choice, there are some conditions better suited to child photography than others. Hazy, diffused sunshine or light

Using Daylight 3

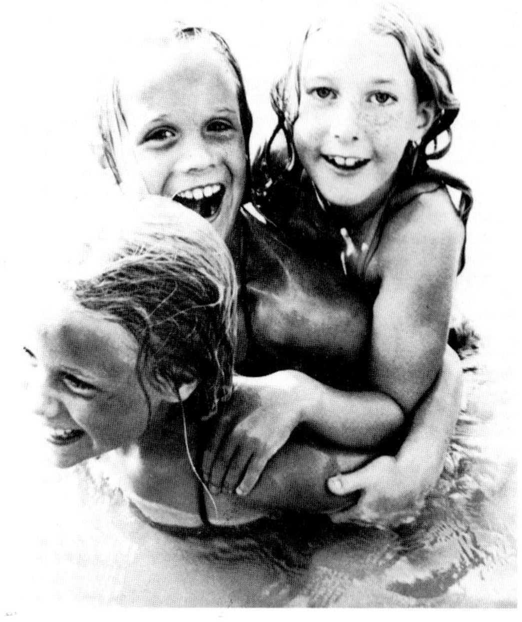

By photographing in sunlight diffused by light cloud, a far softer result is achieved. The faces of at least two of the girls in this shot would have been obscured by heavy shadow if the sunlight had been stronger (left).

The photograph of three children at the edge of a pool was taken by direct evening sunlight (below right). By then moving behind the subjects and shooting into the sun a totally different photograph was created, with more visual interest in the composition of the subject and a more striking use of light and shade (right).

cloud, for instance, is much more suitable than direct sunlight as slightly diffused light gives a much better rendition of skin tones, and the softer shadows are kinder to facial features. Evening sunlight is warm in colour and altogether less harsh than its daylight counterpart.

There are occasions, especially in the summer, when there will be no alternative to photographing in direct sunshine. For distant shots in which the child's figure does not fill the whole frame, this will not matter too much. The same applies to shots in the sea or a swimming-pool, as the brilliance of bright sunshine will add life and sparkle to the water. For close-up shots, however, the harshness of the light and the heavy shadows will spoil the result. Nevertheless, there are ways around this problem. For one thing, avoid photographing in the middle of the day, when the sun is at its highest point and vertical shadows at their worst. Alternatively, seek the shade of a building or tree or use a parasol to provide shadow.

The heavy facial shadows which are caused by photographing in sunshine can also be reduced by using one of two lighting techniques. For distant shots a small flash unit can be used to 'fill in' the dark areas of the subject's face and body. Alternatively, for more close-up work, a piece of white card or even a newspaper can be used as a light reflector, held below the subject's face and out of view of the camera. It must be positioned by trial and error until it effectively reflects light into the shadows.

Shooting towards the light, especially later in the day, will produce a halo-like

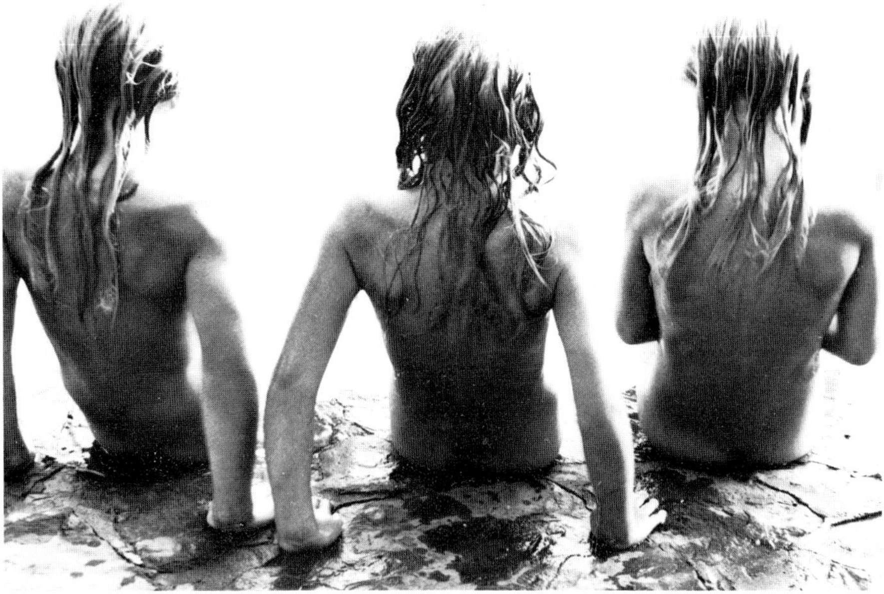

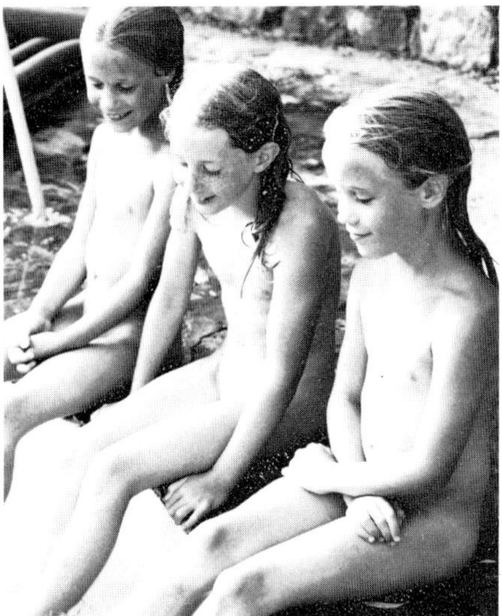

effect of light around the subject's head where the sun shines through the hair. When shooting by this technique, the exposure must be calculated for the subject's face, ignoring the top light shining through the hair. Alternatively, take a general light reading and use a flash to give more illumination to the face.

Whatever the lighting conditions, it is preferable to achieve an even balance of light and shade in a photograph. If you want the child to stand out from his surroundings, it is a good idea to photograph from light to shade or vice versa. When the subject is in the shade and the background lit, the subject will be outlined against a much lighter tone. Conversely, shooting from the light against a shadowed area will set the subject out in relief against a dark background.

Choosing a Location

The best location for a photograph of a child is a place where he will feel happy and relaxed and is interested in the environment. For candid photographs, there should be plenty of things to divert the child's attention away from the photographer. The location should obviously also be attractive to the eye, and there should be sufficient light.

Many outdoor photographs will be taken in conjunction with other activities – fishing requires a river, swimming sessions require a pool or the sea, and swings and roundabouts suggest a playground – and in these situations the choice of location will be self-evident. More often, however, the objective will quite simply be to go out 'somewhere' to photograph the children. For the enterprising photographer, particularly if he has access to the countryside, the range of possibilities is enormous.

Most children love water, and lakes and rivers offer marvellous opportunities for good pictures. Children are at their brightest and liveliest when splashing and paddling, while the presence of water always gives pictures a lift, especially with sunbeams sparkling on the surface. Reflections of the subject and surroundings give photographs an extra dimension. In such locations useful props usually abound, and boats, landing stages and even stepping-stones can be used to add extra interest to the pictures.

Woodland and forests are another perfect location as there are trees to be climbed and branches to swing on. The changing seasons bring great variety to the woodland scene, and autumn in particular is a superb time for child photography. The nuances of coloured foliage and the fallen leaves on the ground are ideal for colour work, especially with the sunlight filtering through the trees. A word of warning, however: light levels are deceptively low throughout the year in wooded locations, so it is best to use a fast film to ensure good results.

In the open countryside, cornfields and long grass make ideal backdrops for child studies. In the evening, the low angle of the

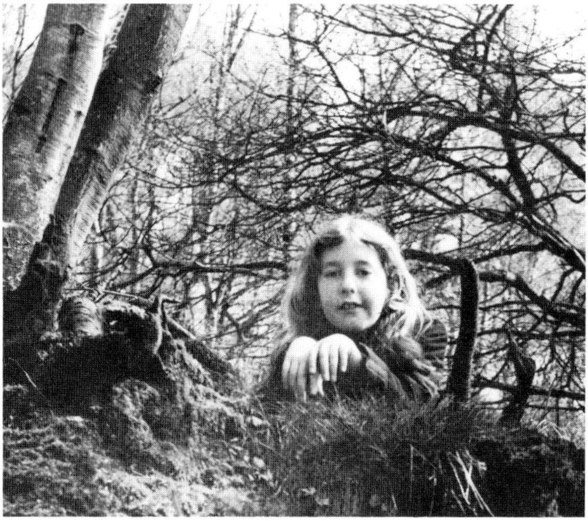

If you want to emphasize a mood or season, the background can be made to dominate a picture, as in this shot photographed in a wood in winter (left).

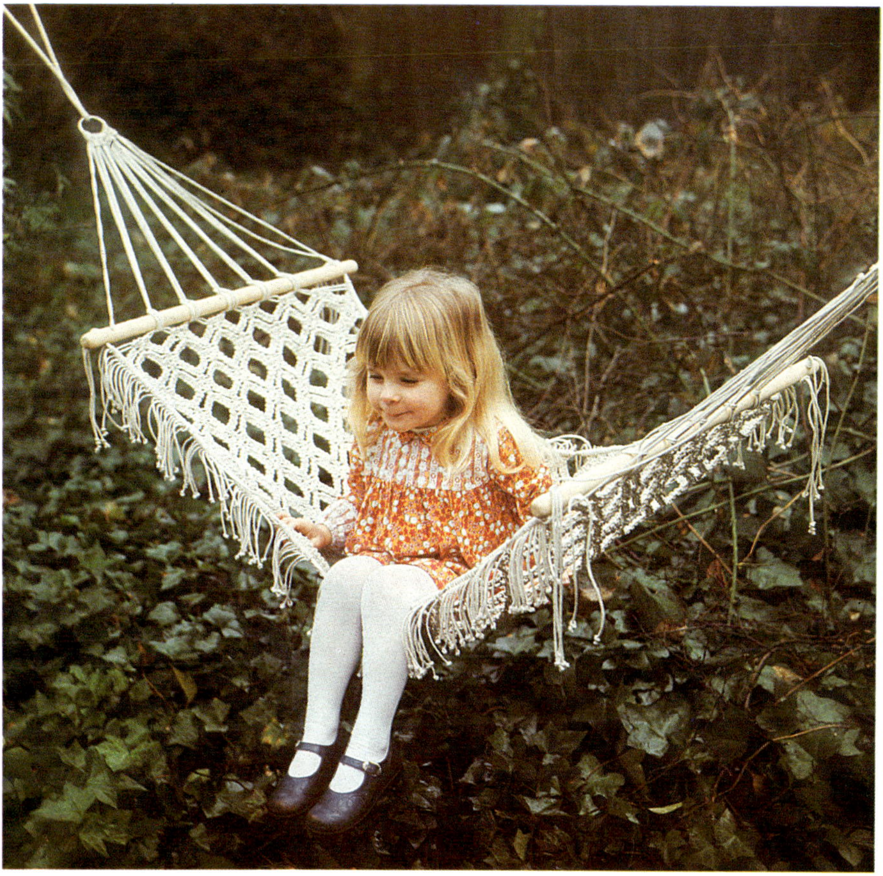

By arranging a hammock in a woodland setting, a more concentrated approach can be made to the subject (above). Natural backgrounds without buildings, fences and the like provide minimum distraction from the subject-matter.

Locations can be used in one of two ways: purely as a background (right) or as an integral and exciting part of the picture as a whole (far right).

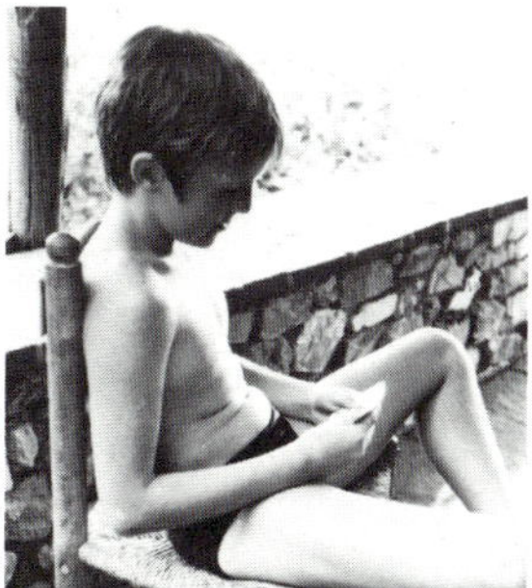

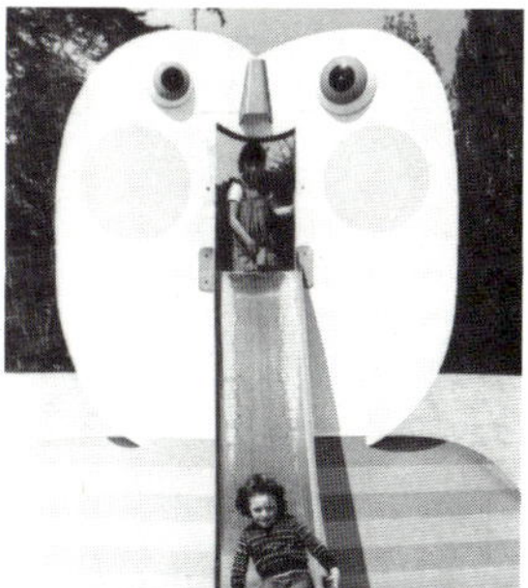

Choosing a Location 2

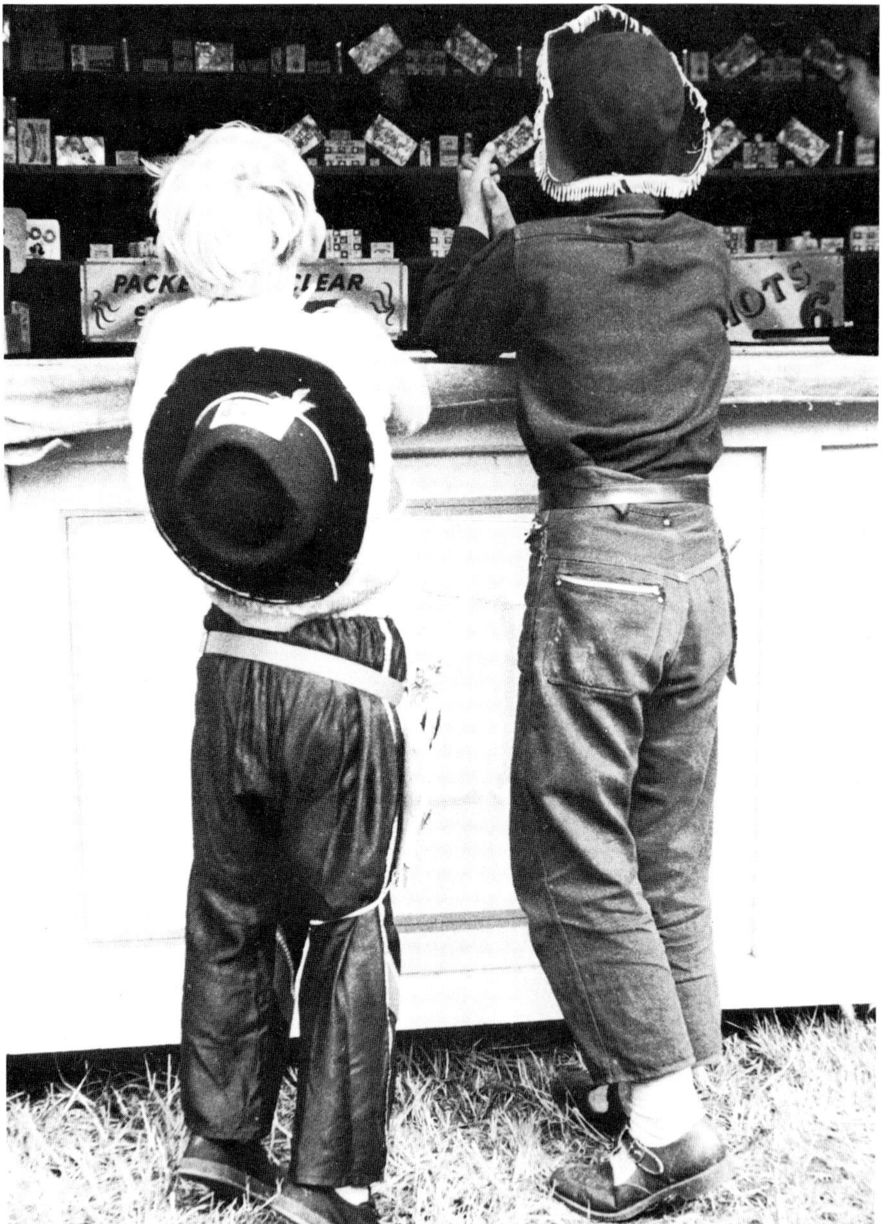

Although the faces of the children are completely hidden in this candid shot, the obvious fairground location and the models' choice of headgear give sufficient information to tell a complete story (left).

City-bound photographers will find a source of inspiration in the local parks and squares. Pigeons will provide interesting subject-matter, especially when a relatively slow shutter speed is used to form an impression of movement (right).

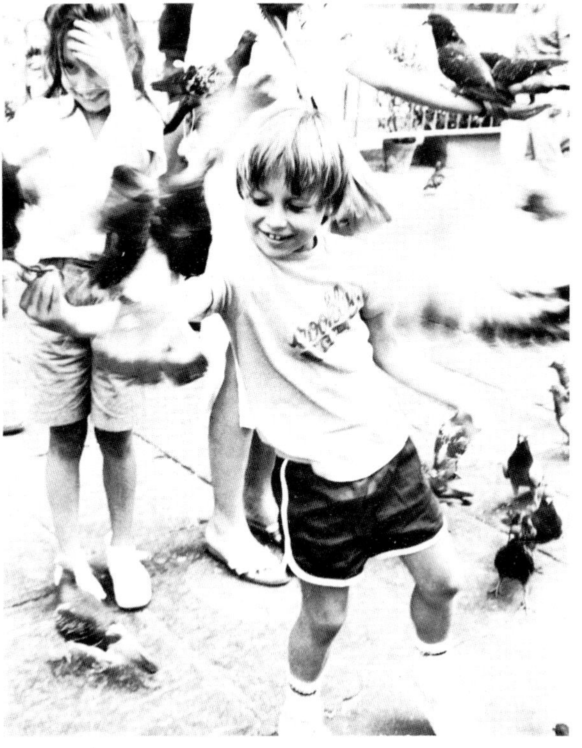

sun will back-light the stems of grass or corn, producing a warm, luminous effect. Do not encourage your children to wade across the cornfield, which will damage growing crops, but instead photograph at the edge of the field. Where there are fields there will usually be a farmhouse near by and most farmers will gladly allow you to take your children into the farmyard to take pictures. The novelty of tractors, cows, chickens and the like will be all-absorbing, and you should be able to take many good candid shots.

The town-based photographer who does not have easy access to the country-side will still find plenty of scope when looking for suitable locations. Most cities contain large parks and playgrounds, as well as zoos and permanent fairgrounds. Some of these locations are discussed in more detail in other places in the book (see pp. 76–7) as well as some of the problems involved in shooting at the seaside (pp. 64–7).

Remember when judging any photographic location that the camera can be selective. Some parts of a place are often nicer than others, and a woodland glade, for example, might well be spoilt by the unpleasant, overflowing litter bin. By careful aiming of the camera, or masking the offending object by judicious positioning of the model, such eye-sores can be eliminated from the photograph.

Backgrounds

The background is the space behind the figure or figures in a photograph. Out of doors, the background can be complementary to the picture as a whole or it can be subdued or almost eliminated by various means. It is important to decide whether the background is to be a true part of the composition or merely ancillary to it.

If you decide that the background should be shown in its entirety, then you should fit a fairly wide-angle lens to the camera. Then, however close you are working to the subject, the wide angle of view of the lens will record a broad sweep of the location with reasonable clarity. Using the same lens but moving away

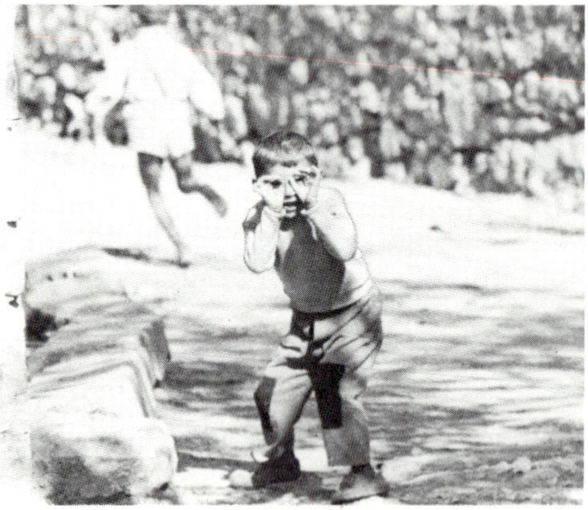

The effects of a confusing background have been reduced by using a large lens aperture and therefore reducing depth of field. The subject stands out more, against an out-of-focus background (left).

By shooting from a low camera position, distracting detail has been eliminated from this photograph by framing the model against a plain sky (right).

Water makes an ideal background as it is visually interesting yet at the same time usually contains no distracting elements or contrasts (below).

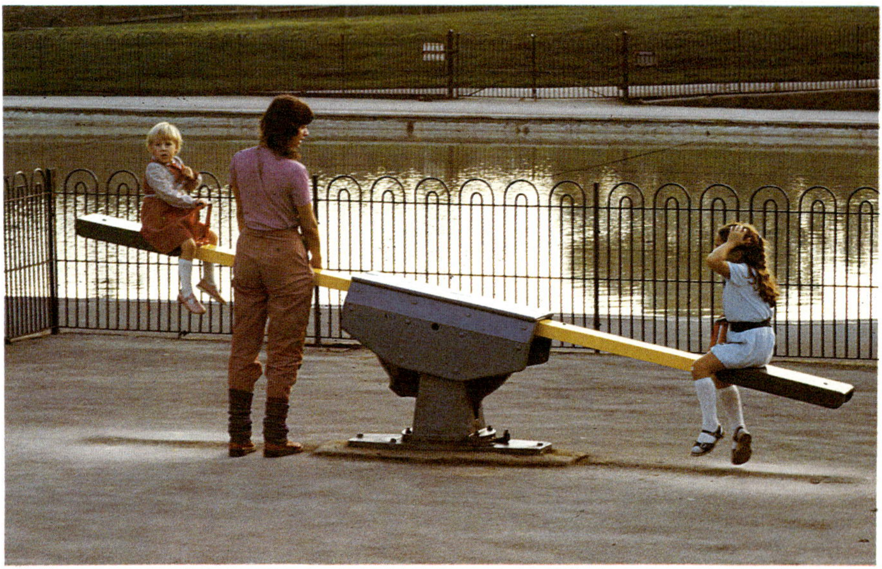

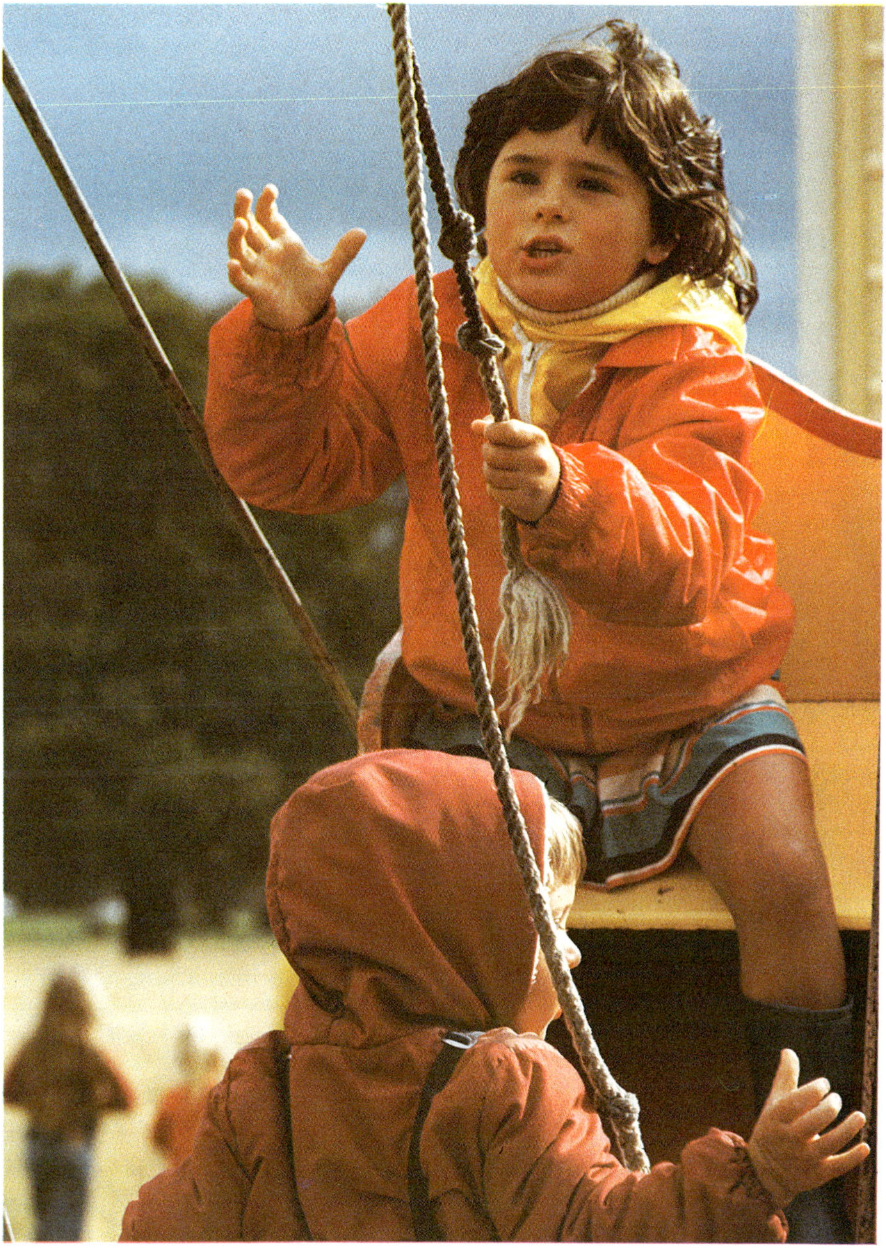

Backgrounds 2

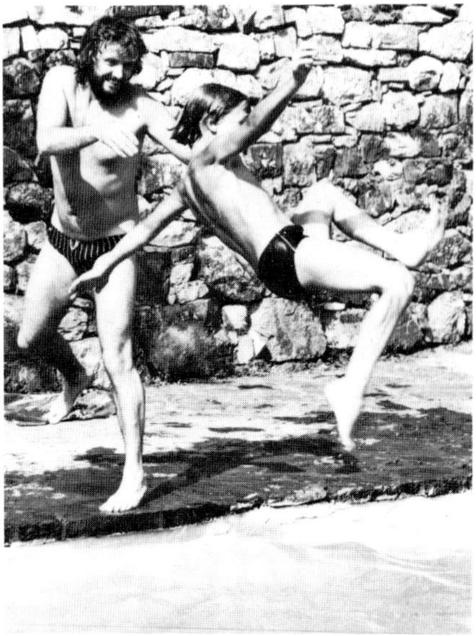

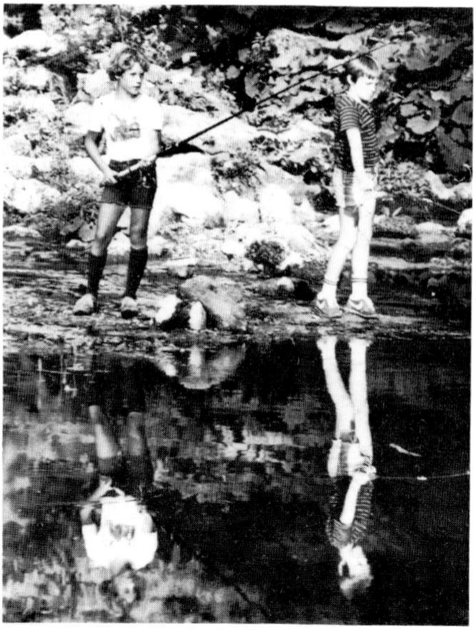

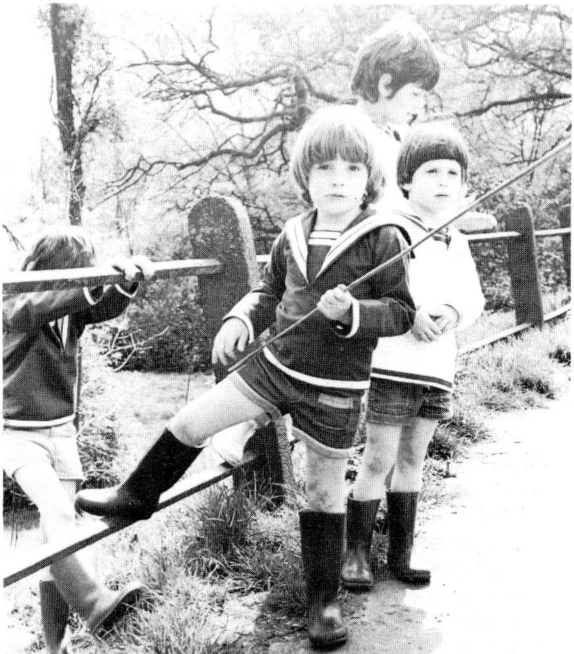

Two potentially good photographs have been spoilt by using over-fussy backgrounds (above). In both cases a better result would have been obtained by looking for a plainer location or, where possible, shooting upwards from a low camera position towards the sky.

By using a semi-wide-angle lens, and shooting close to the subjects, the background has assumed less importance. Note also how the metal railings help to lead the eye into the picture (left).

By photographing the fully lit figures of the children against a background of shadowed foliage, the subjects stand out clearly (right). If the background had received equal illumination to that on the subject, the result would have been far more confusing.

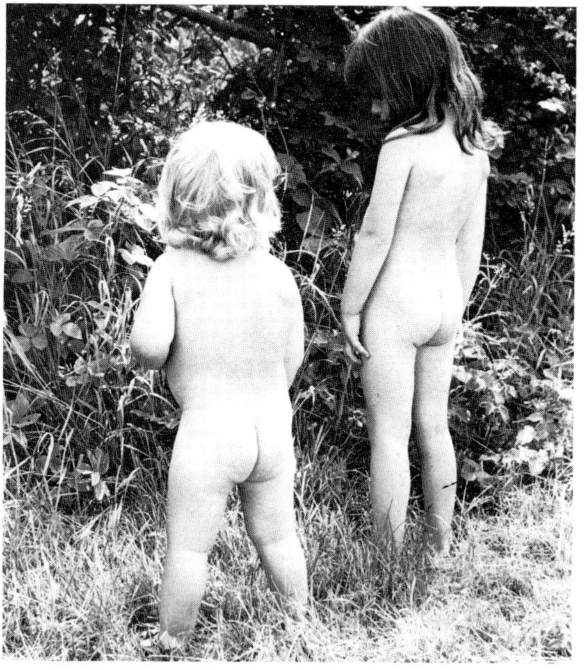

from the subject will result in a smaller figure of the child, in a similar vista.

For close-up studies of children it is more desirable to subdue the background. The easiest method is to use a telephoto or zoom lens, of moderately long focal length. As a lens of this type has a limited depth of field, anything much beyond the focused subject will be recorded out of focus. The effect can be controlled by the lens aperture control: the wider the aperture, the softer the background.

When photographing children, it is important that the background is not fussy or distracting, even when not in focus. Regular patterns such as stone or brick walls should be avoided as these will draw the eye away from the child. Even 'busy' architecture can prove a distraction unless sufficiently out of focus.

In selecting a background it is best to look for areas containing large blocks of continuous tone or colour. When shooting wide-angle backgrounds, more detail can be included as it becomes integral to the scene itself. The background should always be in keeping with the subject and should be relatively inconspicuous. Remember that your child is the main subject in the picture and that the background is serving principally to provide secondary information.

On the rare occasions when a suitable background cannot be found, the child can be photographed from a low angle, against the sky. This is useful in urban areas with a predominance of buildings at eye level, although it is well to remember that the effect might be rather bland unless the sky is particularly dramatic.

Composition

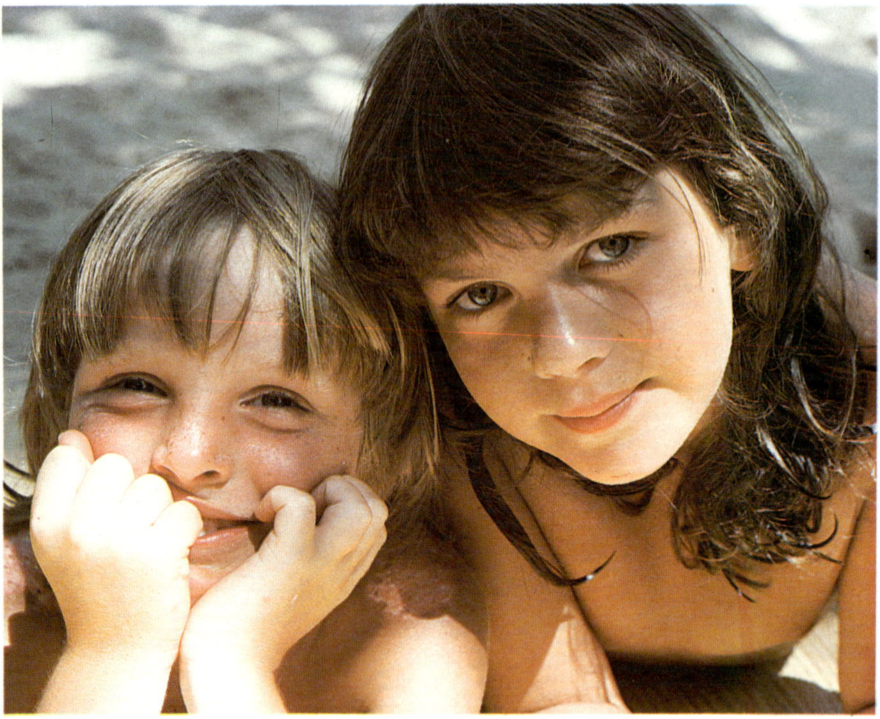

The composition of a photograph is the arrangement of the principal elements within it. The more pleasing or interesting the arrangement, the better composed the picture. In the past, much fuss was made about pictorial composition. Conventions and regulations were created and adhered to, and artists and photographers justified the success of their own work, and that of their peers, by the application of such 'golden rules'. Even in the 1950s, exhibition photographers would produce elaborate thumb-nail sketches to show the compositional lines and thereby justify the creative validity of their offerings. Nowadays there is a good deal more common sense and less pretension attached to the composition of a photographic image.

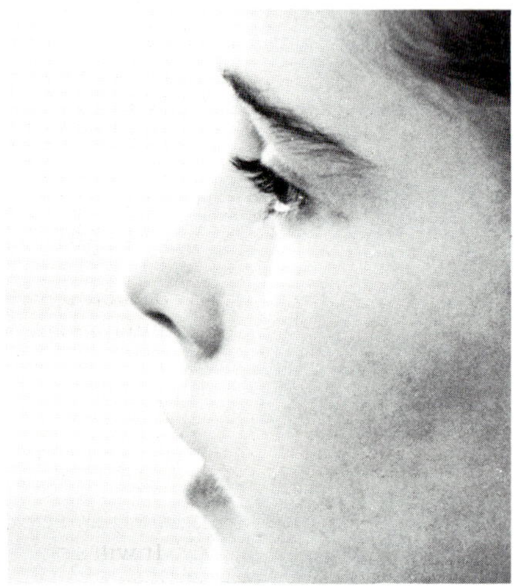

The difference in level of the two children's heads has a balancing effect on the picture as a whole, while the inclination of their faces towards each other gives further cohesion to the photograph (left).

This close-up portrait of a child fulfils naturally the rule of the intersection of thirds (right).

In this shot the composition breaks the rules, the interest being concentrated into a narrow strip running through the middle of the picture (below left).

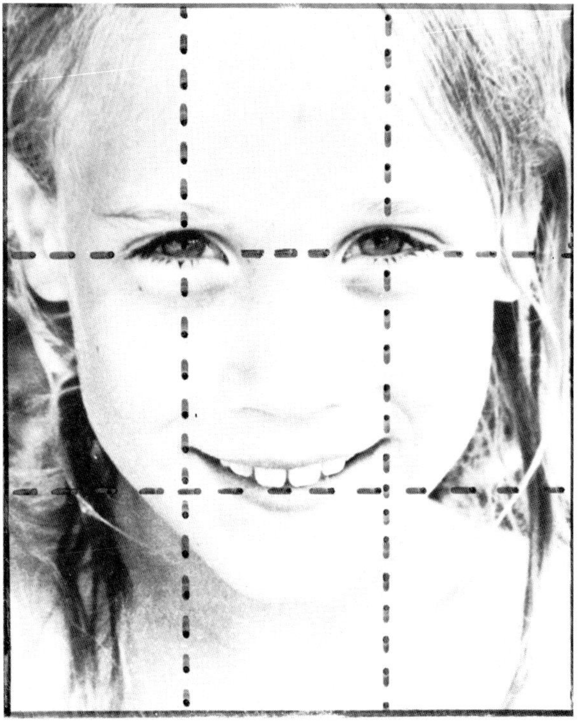

More and more, it is a case of 'if it looks right, shoot it'. Especially when working with children, time spent in worrying over 'correct' composition can mean that a picture is lost completely.

There are none the less certain aids to composition that can be usefully employed by the modern photographer. Such guidelines, however, should be broken at any time to produce a more interesting or unusual result.

One of the oldest conventions of composition is the rule of the intersection of thirds which states that the important element(s) of a picture should emanate from any area at the intersection of the third divisions of each side. It will be seen that the head-on, close-up portrait fulfils this rule admirably (see picture, above). There are many applications of this ruling that will produce well-composed photographs, of a safe nature, showing a pleasing balance of form.

Balance is in fact probably the most important ingredient when approaching conventional composition: balance of light and shade, balance of tones, and balance of line and direction. For instance, to achieve a balanced effect, motion should appear to move into a photograph rather than towards an edge, but like many other 'rules', this can sometimes be ignored for useful effect. Background and foreground, too, should be taken into account, with these elements sometimes being used to create a frame for the subject. One

Composition 2

example is the use of foliage, either in front or behind, to produce an ornamental surround.

Another important aspect of successful composition is emphasis, deciding what is to be the main subject and which other elements you want to include in the picture. A mistake which is commonly made by inexperienced photographers is trying to cram too much in. However tempting it may be to capture the whole of a particular scene, in visual terms the result may be cluttered and unsatisfactory. Remember, only include those things which contribute to the over-all effect of the photograph.

Exciting compositions can be created by the use of strong lines, in any plane or direction, to produce a graphic effect.

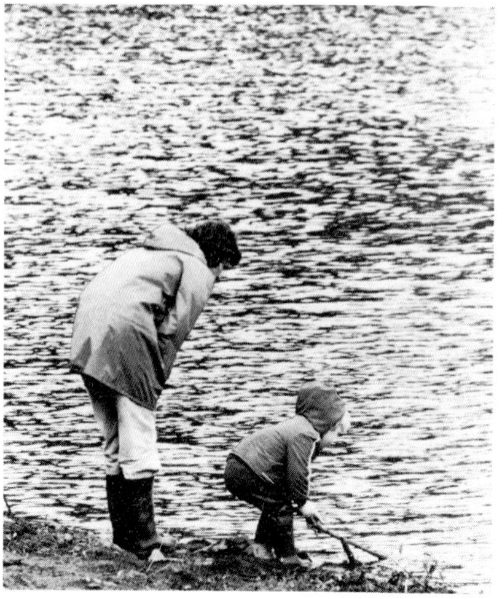

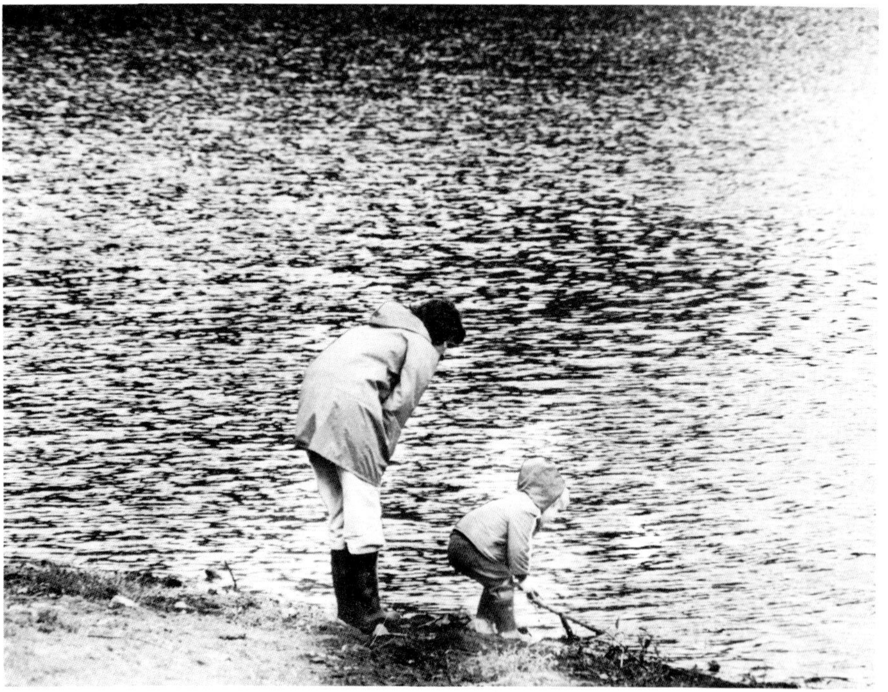

A picture on negative film can be composed again after exposure, at the printing stage. A better crop will often become evident when an exposure is printed full-frame, and sometimes two equally attractive compositions can be made from the same negative (left and below left).

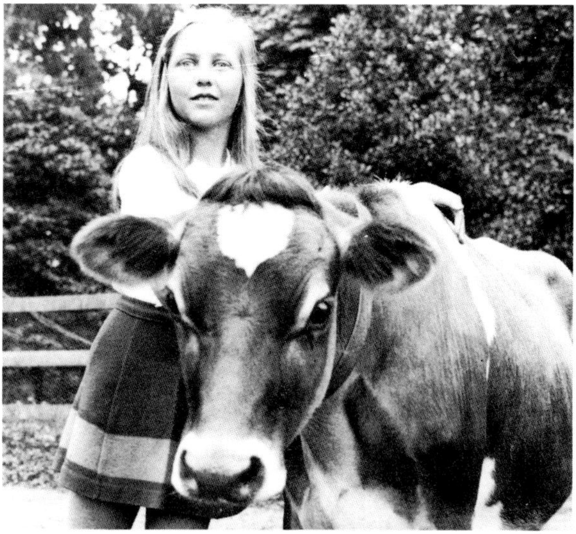

Sometimes you can let one element dominate a photograph; in this case the cow takes on more importance than the child, though the picture remains an effective portrait of them both (right).

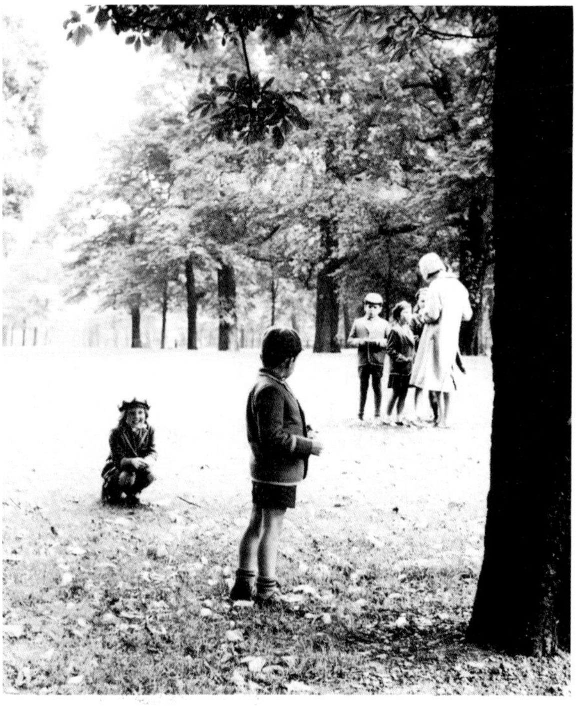

This photograph (right) is composed in the traditional way with strong foreground interest leading the eye through the picture to a middle area and a background.

Composition 3

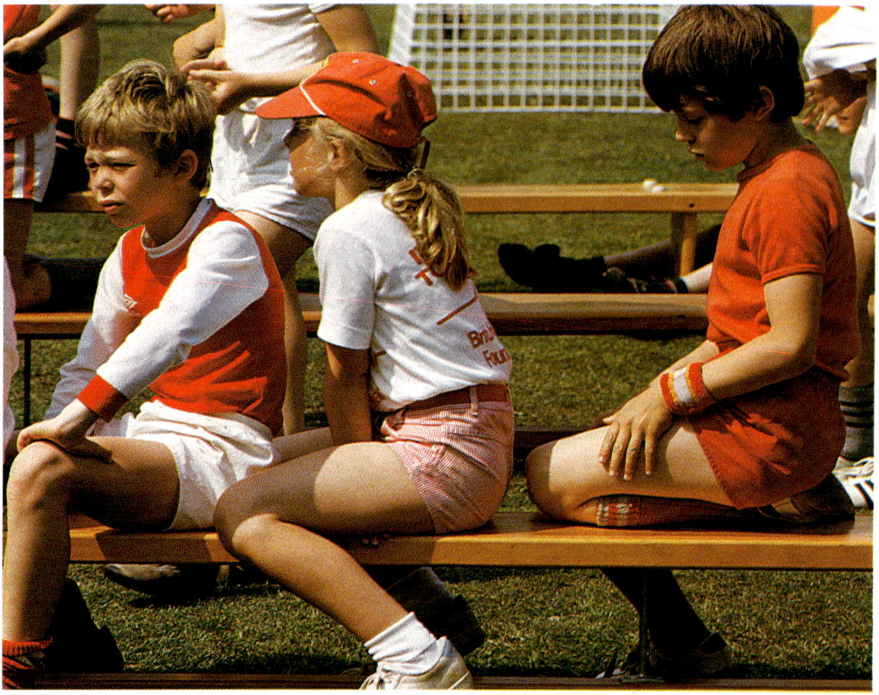

However, this approach is not always suited to child photography, especially for younger subjects, and should be used with care, though it is useful when a definite dramatic effect is required.

These few guide-lines on the subject of composition can be usefully applied in certain circumstances, but the employment of too many rules and regulations will restrict the individuality and creativity of the photographer's work. Many of the most outstanding child photographs owe their interest and impact to the breaking of all conventional ideas about composition. As in all forms of creative work, the photograph is the personal interpretation of an idea. Most photographers develop an eye for a well-composed shot and find that, in time, they acquire an individual style.

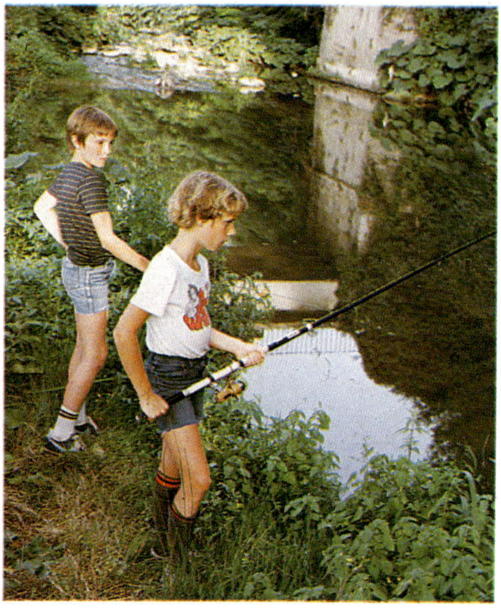

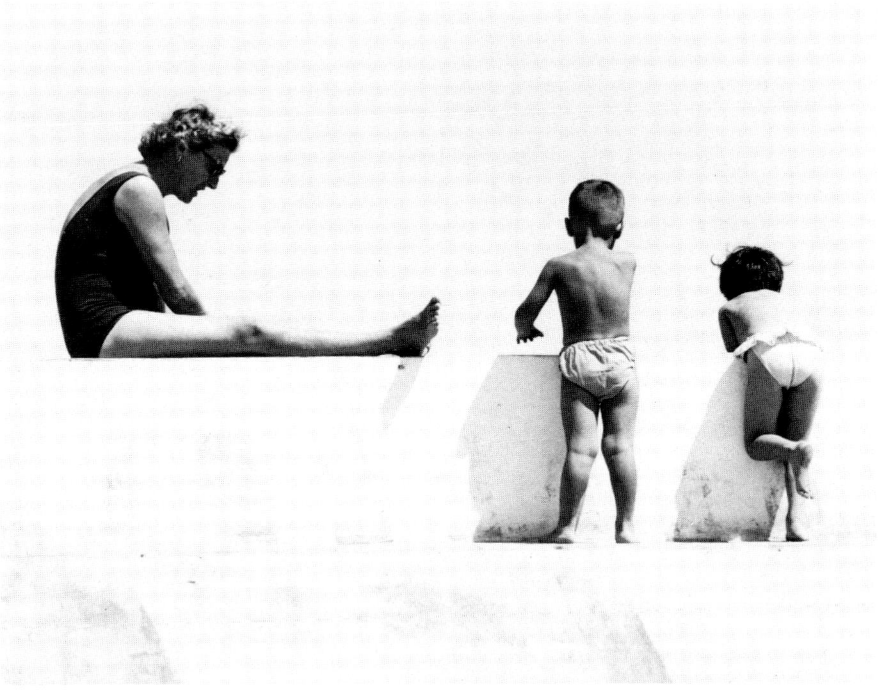

This shot is a more graphic approach to composition, with the main elements arranged along horizontal lines (above left).

In candid shots, look for a pleasing arrangement of bodies and especially limbs, and, when shooting more than one child, a pleasing juxtaposition of positions (above).

This well-balanced composition shows a foreground, subject and background, with an even distribution of light and shade (left).

By using natural props, groups can be photographed in a well-composed arrangement (right).

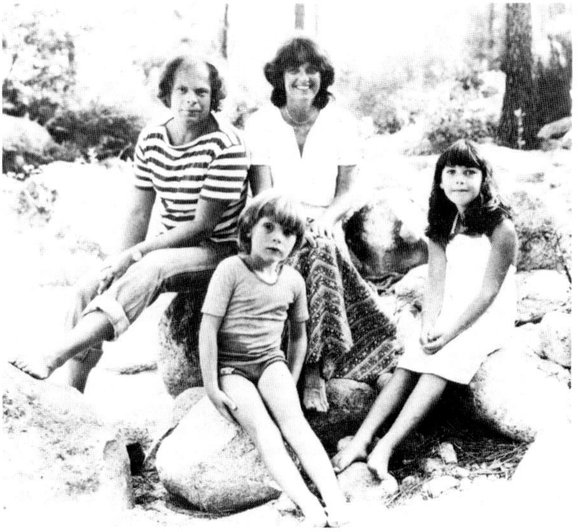

The Seaside Camera

The seaside is probably the most popular location for child photography as it offers great scope for successful pictures. At the same time, there are certain problems specific to seaside photography which warrant detailed discussion. As a general rule, no special equipment is required for photographing on the beach. However, all photographic apparatus has delicate mechanisms and is very much at risk under seashore conditions from sand, water and salt-spray.

Photographing children on the beach is great fun for everyone involved. The children feel happy and uninhibited, both in the water and out. Blue skies, sparkling water and tanned skin are perfect ingredients for successful photographs full of life, so it is an over-prudent photographer who does not take his camera to the beach for fear of damaging it.

The first step towards protecting a camera is to keep it in a case, preferably a zippered type, at all times when it is not in use. As an added precaution the camera case can be put inside a strong polythene bag. This is not only to protect the apparatus from moisture, but also to prevent sand particles getting inside. One grain of sand, penetrating the mechanical workings of a modern camera, is enough to jam it up, necessitating a complete strip-down for repairs. Special care must be taken under windy conditions, when equipment is particularly susceptible to the intrusion of sand. Blown sand can not only damage the mechanics of a camera, but it can also have an abrasive effect on the lens element, literally blasting off a thin layer of glass and coating. It goes without saying that non-sealed cameras must never be left lying on the beach at the mercy of the

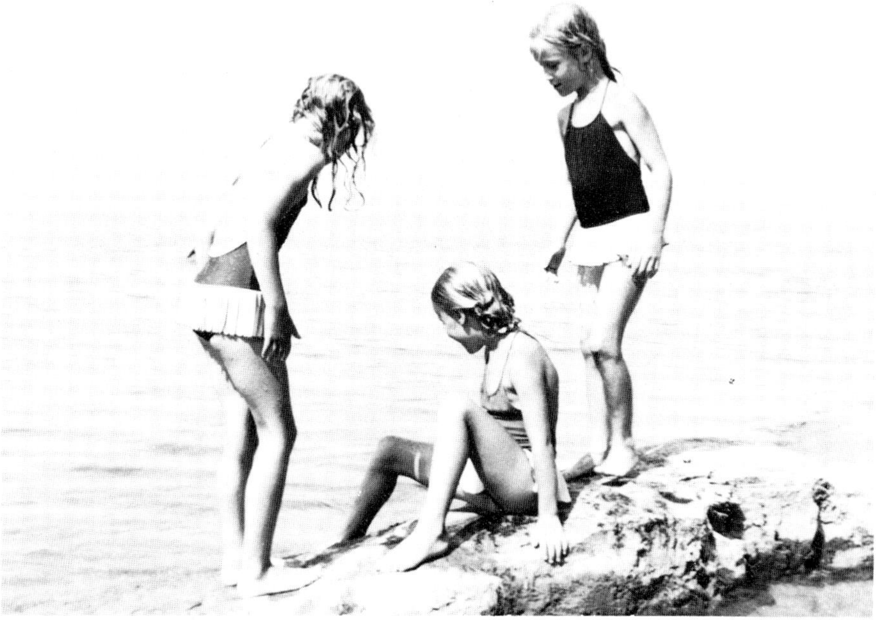

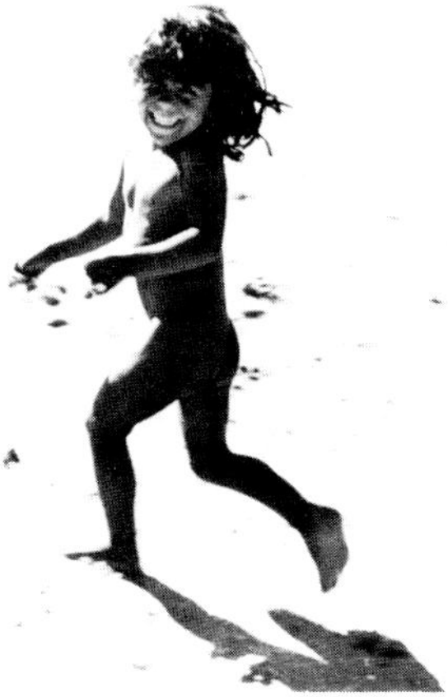

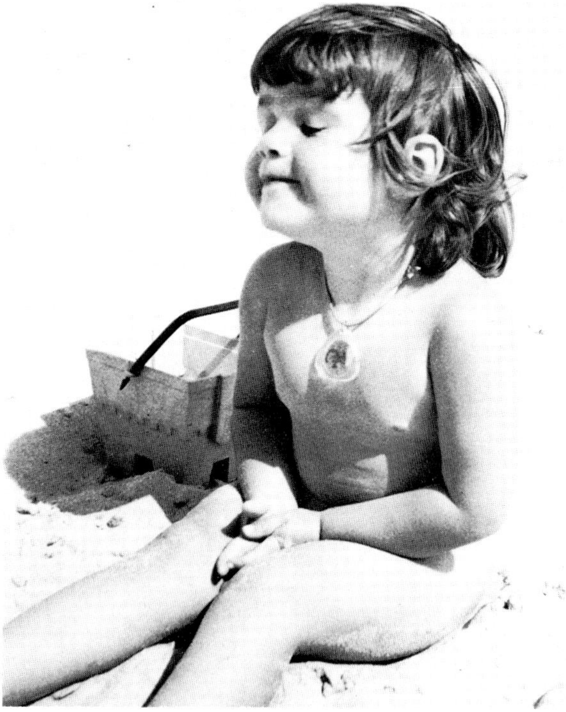

Sunshine and reflections from sand can produce a strong glow of light confusing to some automatic cameras, under-exposing the subject, almost forming a silhouette (above).

Although shot in strong sunlight, the sand has acted as a reflector, bouncing light back into the face of the subject (right).

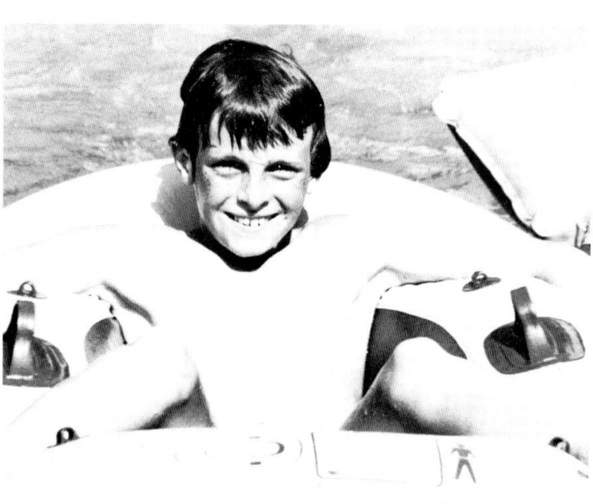

The brightness and reflection of seaside sunlight can often cause the model to squint (right). Use of a fill-in flash will help counteract heavy shadows, but these can be avoided if the model faces away from the sun.

Children at the seaside will be especially preoccupied and uninhibited, allowing the photographer ample opportunity to shoot without attracting their attention. On occasions it is better to leave space around the main action in order to locate the photograph (left).

The Seaside Camera 2

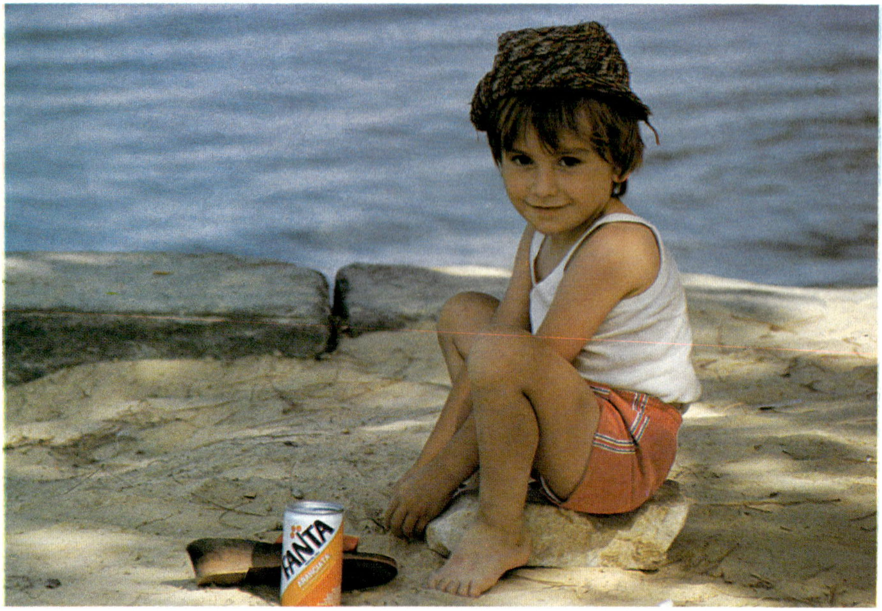

elements without the protection of a case.

When you are shooting standing in the sea, you should take great care to avoid the camera being splashed. The salt in sea-water will not only corrode any metal parts with which it comes into contact, but will also damage the lens coating if it is not carefully wiped away immediately. The best way to protect a lens under such conditions is to fit an ultra-violet filter on to the front element of the lens and leave it on permanently.

If you have the misfortune that your camera becomes completely water-logged, there is probably little that can be done, and it will only be worth salvaging a very expensive camera. However, there are certain things you can and should do if repair is to be at all possible. Immerse the camera immediately in fresh water (preferably distilled) and wash it gently; then seal it in a plastic bag or box filled with fresh water and take it to a reputable repairer as soon as possible.

The sky is very clear near the sea, especially in Mediterranean and tropical countries, and the light will be very cool in colour. This will not be discernible to the human eye, but it will affect colour film. In the simplest terms, the light is high in blue and ultra-violet content, and photographic results, especially in transparencies, will have a slightly blue cast. In order to prevent this, an ultra-violet or skylight filter should be used on the camera lens. If you envisage doing a lot of photography at the seaside it may be worth considering buying a waterproof, all-weather camera such as the Nikonos or Minolta Weathermatic; these cameras are fully protected against all seaside hazards, and can actually be used underwater as well.

The choice of film is important for seaside photography as very high light levels

Because of the glare of seaside light it is a good idea to place the model out of the sun whenever possible. Here, for instance, a tree provided sufficient shade to soften the sunlight (left).

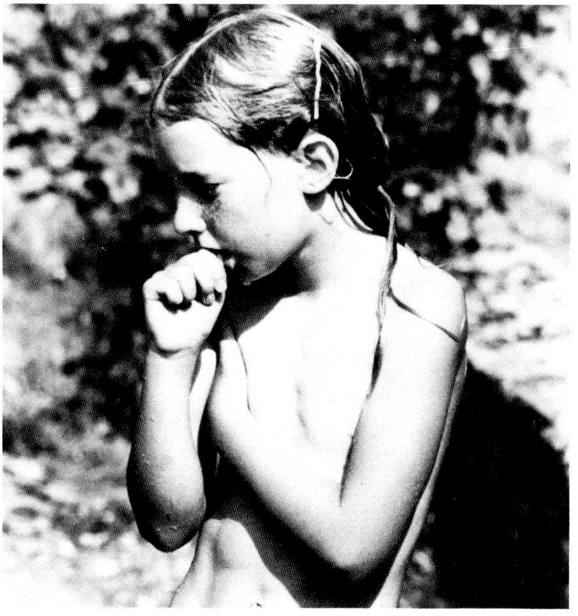

Rock-faces provide interesting but unobtrusive backgrounds at the seaside, as long as they are not in sharp focus (right). For this reason a long-focus lens and the largest possible aperture should be used to concentrate interest on the model.

are often encountered. With a high degree of reflection from near-white sand, exposure levels may be beyond the capabilities of an automatic camera loaded with fast film. It is better to choose a film of lower speed, not more than 100 ASA. This will still enable fast shutter speeds to be used to freeze action, while at the same time giving photographs of better quality.

Care must be taken in calculating exposures. The reflection of light from pale sand can mislead many light-metering systems, causing under-exposure, so whenever possible take a selective light reading from the subject or use the over-ride on the camera. Pictures taken into the light against the sun-lit sand are especially liable to under-exposure, often giving an almost silhouette effect. Heat haze can be another problem, and even if your camera is fitted with an ultra-violet filter it is best not to use a telephoto lens of any length under such conditions, as the image will be degraded.

It is best to avoid shooting in the middle of the day when the sun is high. Waiting until late afternoon will produce better results and the lowering sun will glance off the surface of the water, producing little pools of light, which can be used to very good effect. Later still, in the evening, if you are lucky enough to be in a location where the sun sets over the water, you can achieve attractive, even dramatic results by photographing your children silhouetted against the rosy sky.

When shooting directly into a fiery sunset, automatic cameras will expose for the sky, under-exposing foreground subjects. This will usually be the desired effect. If more detail is required in the subject, the lens aperture must be opened by 2 stops, or by using the + 2 position on cameras with over-ride.

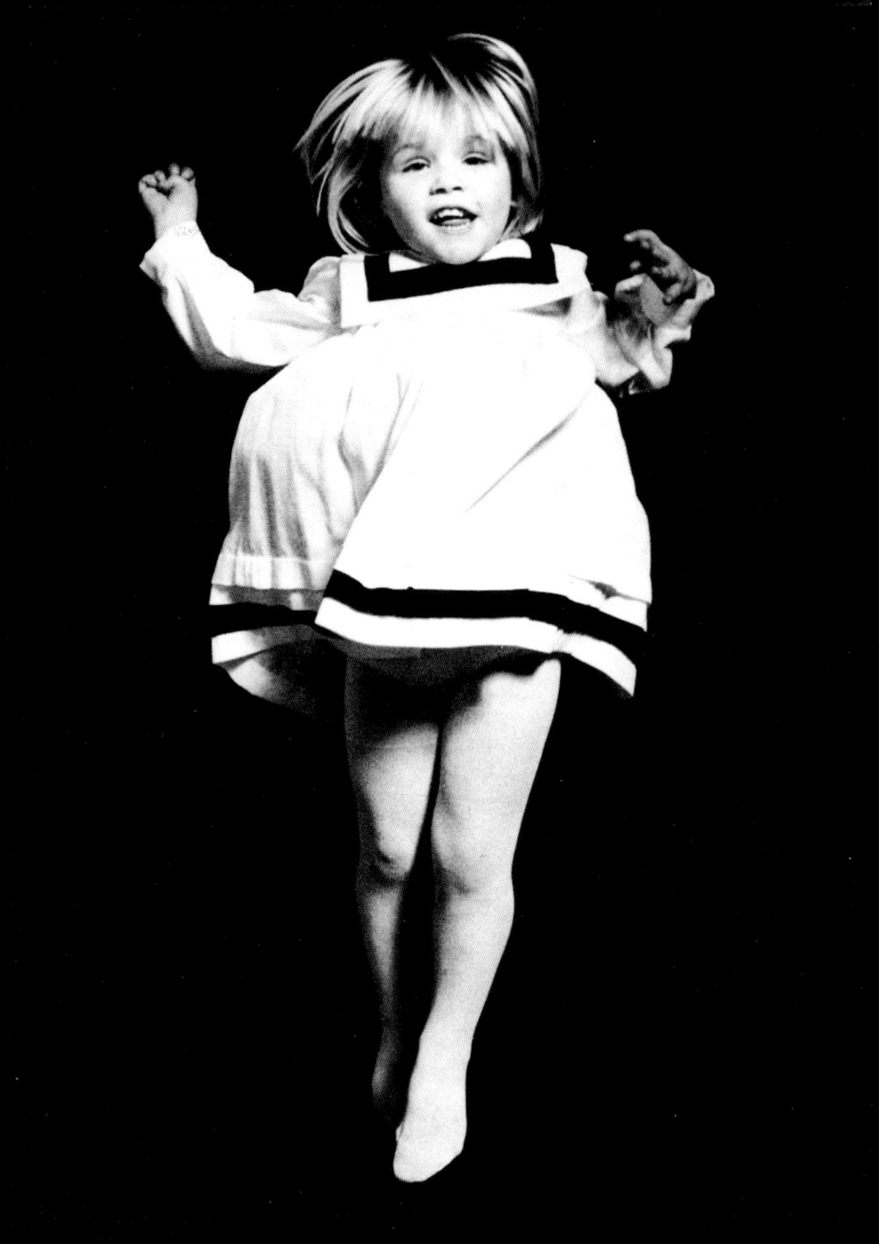

CATCHING THE ACTION

Children are very rarely stationary and seem to have endless vitality and energy. The opportunities for the photographer are almost unlimited as children in motion offer a wealth of interesting, and challenging, subjects. For many years, camera-owners, especially those with simple models, were warned to avoid any form of motion in their photographs in case they be disappointed by the inevitable fuzziness of the result. However, even the most modest camera, if used knowledgeably, can produce pictures interpreting movement in an interesting and exciting manner.

As still photography is a static medium, unlike the ciné and video, it can only attempt to represent true motion by a system of clues, and when these clues are arranged skilfully, a powerful feeling of movement can be created.

There are three basic techniques for interpreting motion photographically. *Freezing* the movement completely by using a fast shutter speed will produce a photograph of over-all sharpness. With no blur, the sense of action will be conveyed by the arrangement of the body and even the facial expression of the subject. The second technique is *panning*, in which the camera is moved in a controlled manner with the moving subject centred in the viewfinder. Using a relatively slow shutter speed, the result is a sharply defined image of the subject, with a deliberately blurred or streaked background giving the impression of movement. The third technique, which is really a development of the panning method, is known as *deliberate* or *controlled blur*. Using a slow shutter speed, the subject is allowed to blur to such an extent that it forms an impression of movement rather than a clearly defined image. Depending on the length of the exposure time various effects can be achieved, with extreme cases representing movement in an almost abstract manner. With child photography, however, such graphic treatment is not recommended, and a slight over-all blurring is enough to convey motion. Under perfect conditions, any one of these techniques can be used to good effect.

All sporting events produce excellent action photographs, especially of older children and teenagers who have developed a high level of style and accomplishment. Action photography also includes cycling, football and roller-skating, and a visit to a playground or fairground will provide good subject-matter.

Children are rarely self-conscious when doing something active, so this is an ideal way of photographing a shy subject, with the least upset for both photographer and child. After a while the child will virtually forget the camera.

Action photography is not difficult, though the photographer must possess quick reactions and be able to anticipate the course of events. Familiarity with his equipment and speed of operation are important, and at sporting events knowing about the particular sport can be a help in choosing camera angles and positions.

Interpreting Motion

FREEZING MOVEMENT

Timing is absolutely vital when attempting to freeze movement in a picture, and in many cases it is necessary to prejudge the moment of exposure. There is a time lapse between the moment when the camera is triggered and the time when the shutter actually fires. This lapse can be as long as a tenth of a second, and during this period a fast-moving subject can travel a considerable distance. Take, for example, the photograph of a young boy diving into a swimming-pool (below). His hands can be seen just entering the water, with the rest of his body seemingly suspended in mid-air. To capture this moment, the camera had to be triggered fractionally before contact with the water had been made to allow for the time lapse of the camera mechanism. When photographing subjects of this kind, the action has to be studied and an appropriate time allowance made.

When taking frozen-action photographs, the sense of movement can often be lost if the camera is not triggered at the right moment. In sports work, for instance, it is advisable to photograph the participant with one foot, if not both, raised clear of the ground, for a true impression of movement to be conveyed. Motion is best captured and frozen when the position of the subject's body emphasizes effort or speed.

There are many occasions when the technique is not suitable, however. One example is a child sitting on a roundabout at a playground where with the use of a fast shutter speed the motion of the roundabout would be lost and the child might just as well be sitting on a stationary object; the panning technique would be far more suitable in this case.

In certain forms of continual motion there is an instant when the motion becomes stationary. For example, a child on a swing will become temporarily motionless at the highest point of the swing's travel, and in the same way a child jumping straight upwards into the air will actually stop moving for a fraction of a second before dropping down to the ground again. Such moments are known as the 'peak of action'

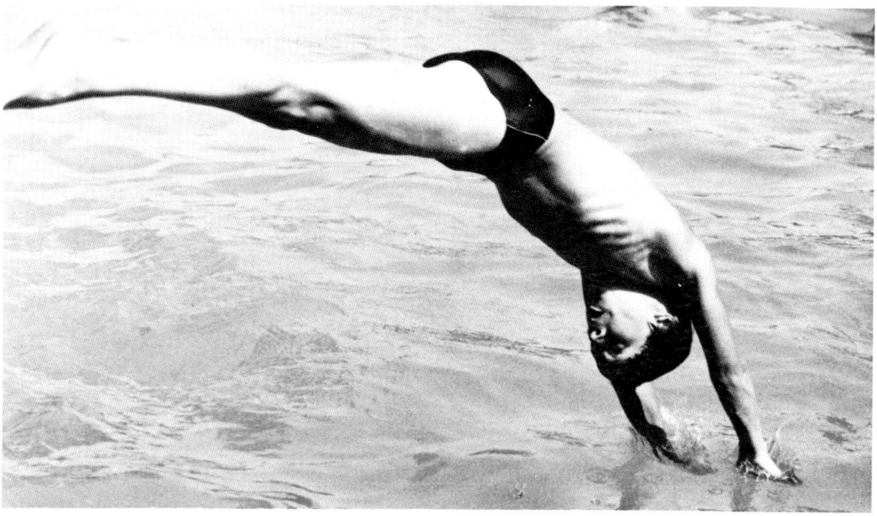

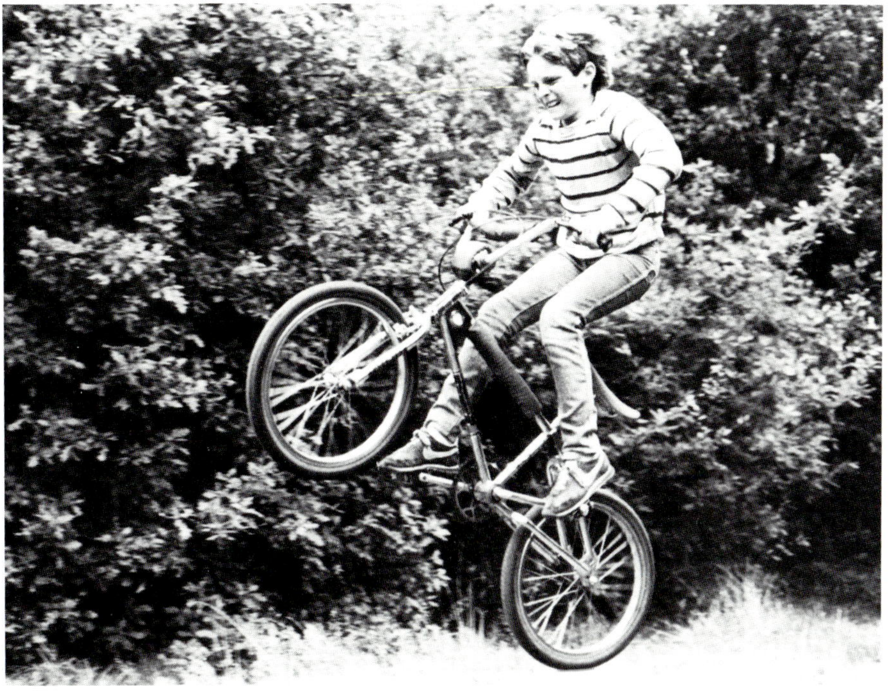

For the freezing technique, use of a fast shutter speed gives an over-all sharp image. Motion is suggested by the position of the bike and the expression of the rider (above).

For horse-riding shots either the panning or frozen-action technique must be used. The example shown here was frozen by using a shutter speed of 1/500 sec (right).

Action must be studied in order to trigger the camera in advance of the motion. In this case, to catch the diver's hands at the moment of entering the water, the exposure was initiated when the subject was still clear of the surface (left).

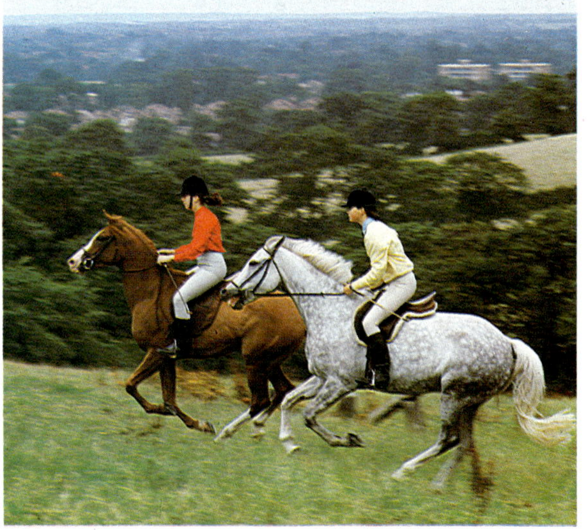

Interpreting Motion 2

and are an ideal time to take a photograph, especially with a simple camera with no high shutter speed. Again, timing is crucial.

Frozen-action photography normally requires the use of a camera capable of working at a high shutter speed. In order to freeze children in motion successfully, a speed of at least 1/250 sec is required, and preferably 1/500 or even 1/1000 sec, depending on the activity. Most cameras have the ability to shoot at such speeds, either by direct selection on the camera or, on aperture-priority models, by choosing the appropriate aperture to compute the required shutter speed. Shooting with a fast speed necessitates using a fairly wide lens aperture, which makes focusing more critical, so for action work a faster film than normal should be loaded in order to use a reasonably small aperture.

Except when motion is contained in a limited area, focusing is a major problem in child action photography, and especially so when working relatively close, as with small children. With an SLR camera it is possible to 'follow-focus' a moving subject in the viewfinder, if the motion is not too rapid. However, the technique is difficult, and is best practised with an empty camera until a certain amount of skill has been achieved. With non-reflex cameras, and when the path of action is reasonably predictable, it is often better to 'zone-focus'. This means focusing in advance on a particular area and waiting until the moving subject reaches that point, the exposure being made within the focused zone. With both of these techniques there is more margin for error if the smallest aperture allowable can be used.

Many modern cameras, especially certain compact models, have quick-reacting automatic focusing systems that can 'lock on' to a moving subject. Such systems make action photography a great deal easier, and any photographer who envisages doing a lot of this type of work might do well to consider buying one of these cameras.

For action photography indoors, an electronic flash is ideal. The duration of the flash is less than 1/800 sec which is

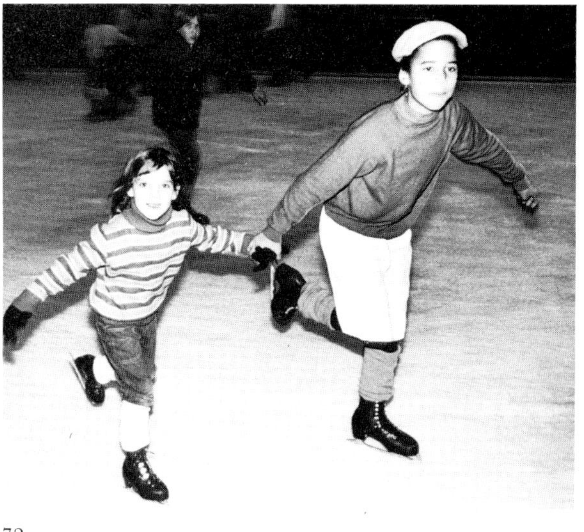

In the panning technique, the use of a slow shutter speed, and the camera moving with the subject, blurs the background to give an impression of speed and motion, while keeping the main image relatively sharp (right).

Electronic flash was used to freeze the motion of these two skaters, photographed in the subdued light of an indoor rink (left).

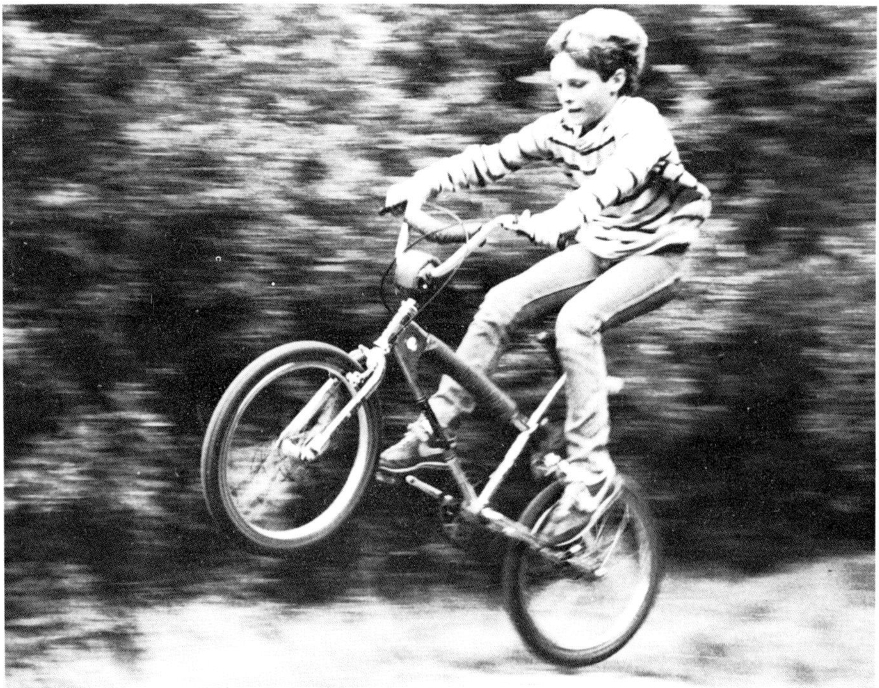

perfect for freezing the most rapid action likely to be encountered inside the home. Flash can also be used effectively outdoors, at night, to photograph all manner of situations, from bonfire parties and barbecues to full-scale dances and galas.

PANNING

The panning technique is best employed when there is a fast and continuous action moving across the horizontal axis of a picture. It is ideally suited to subjects such as cycling, running and roller-skating, where the emphasis is on the participant and the background is of secondary importance or needs to be subdued.

The technique requires the use of a slow shutter speed, usually 1/30 or 1/60 sec, depending on the degree of blur required in the background. The subject must be followed accurately in the viewfinder and the exposure made with the camera *moving* with the subject. A little practice will be needed to learn to keep the subject stationary in the viewfinder, with the camera on the move, and it is advisable to leave excess space around the subject to allow for slight errors in framing. Focusing will be simplified by the fact that a relatively small lens aperture will be in use to compensate for the slow shutter speed and there will therefore be good depth of field.

Once learned, the technique is easy to use and the results will be arresting and interesting. The effect is to give a relatively sharp image of the subject, with a totally blurred background. However, the subject will only be sharp on the planes moving in

Interpreting Motion 3

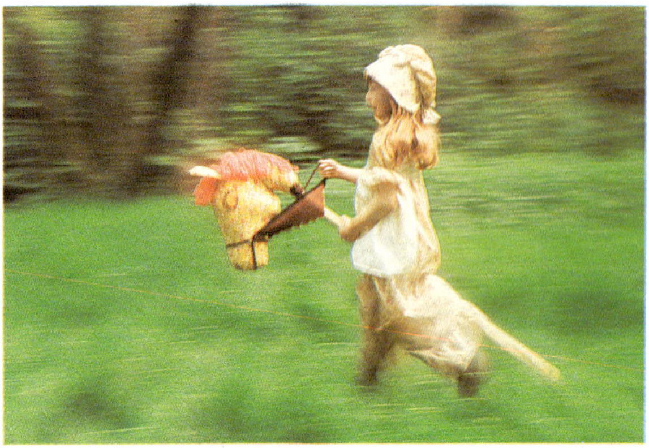

By using a very slow shutter speed (1/8 sec) and panning the camera, the background has blurred considerably, with a lesser degree of movement still evident in the subject (left). This is a combination of the panning and controlled blur techniques.

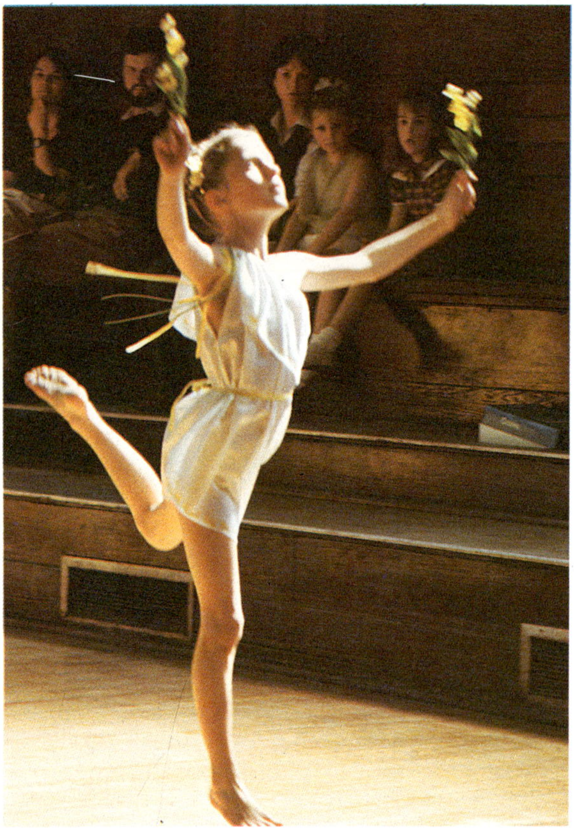

For the deliberate blur technique, by using a very slow speed of 1/4 sec no part of the picture is well defined; the image blurs with an almost abstract pattern, giving a strong feeling of motion (right).

By using a faster shutter speed and freezing the action completely, any feeling of motion would have been lost in this study of a young dancer (left). Instead, by using a speed of 1/125 sec, a degree of blur has been retained, giving a more fluid effect to the picture.

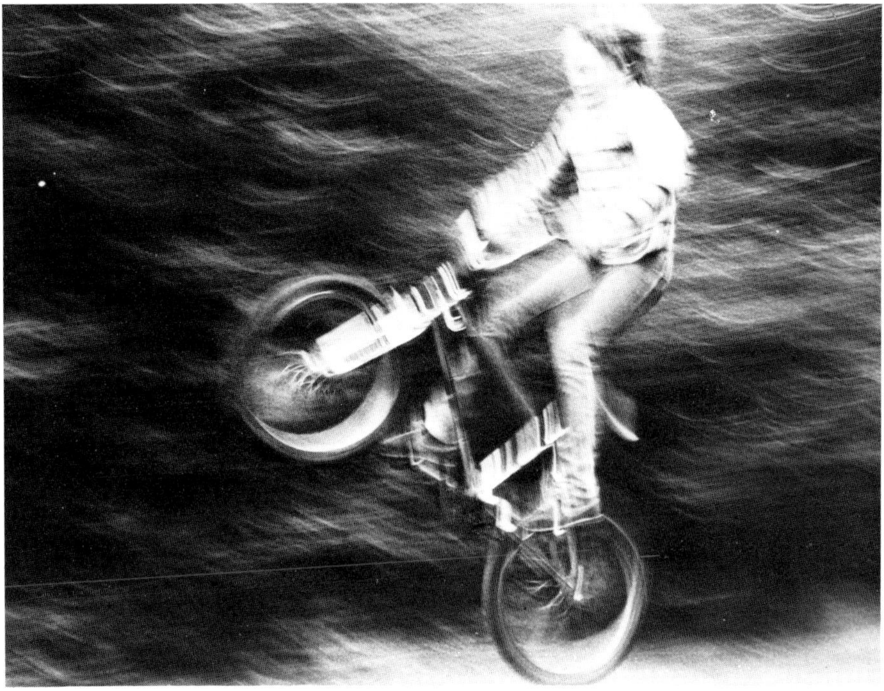

the same direction as the over-all motion. Arms and legs, for instance, may be blurred, as they will be moving in different directions, upwards and downwards, from the main direction of motion.

The slower the shutter speed used, the more pronounced the effect of movement in the subject, and at speeds of 1/15 sec and longer this will be a degree of blur over the entire image. This brings the photograph into another classification, that of controlled or deliberate blur.

CONTROLLED AND DELIBERATE BLUR

Very often, a moving subject frozen by a fast shutter speed will appear too static in a photograph because the effect of movement has been lost. In this case, it is necessary to use a slower shutter speed to produce a slight element of blur in the subject and recreate an impression of motion. For instance, a photograph of a young girl performing a ballet routine might appear too static and statuesque when frozen at a speed of 1/250 sec. By selecting a slower speed of 1/125 sec a slight blur would be restored to the image, giving more life and movement to the shot. This technique can be used to extremes with exposure times of considerably longer duration. At a speed of ¼ sec, for example, an abstract impression of speed can be made to interesting effect, but showing very little detail of the subject. At such long shutter speeds, the technique is very hit and miss, so several exposures must be made to be sure of getting a satisfactory result.

The Fairground

Fairgrounds combine human excitement with mechanical movement, and are a challenge to any photographer wishing to photograph children in unusual circumstances. Most activities will occur with varying degrees of motion and speed, and in order to freeze them the light must be good or a very fast film used. Several rides, such as swings and seesaws, have peaks of movement and are momentarily almost stationary, and then slow shutter speeds or simple cameras can be used. Rides with a circular motion can also be photographed using a panning technique.

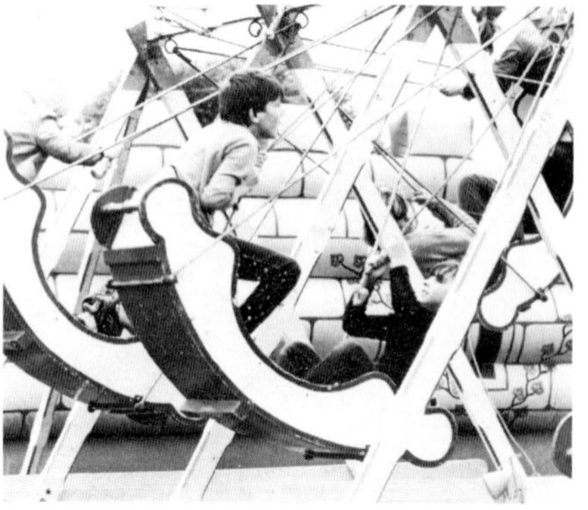

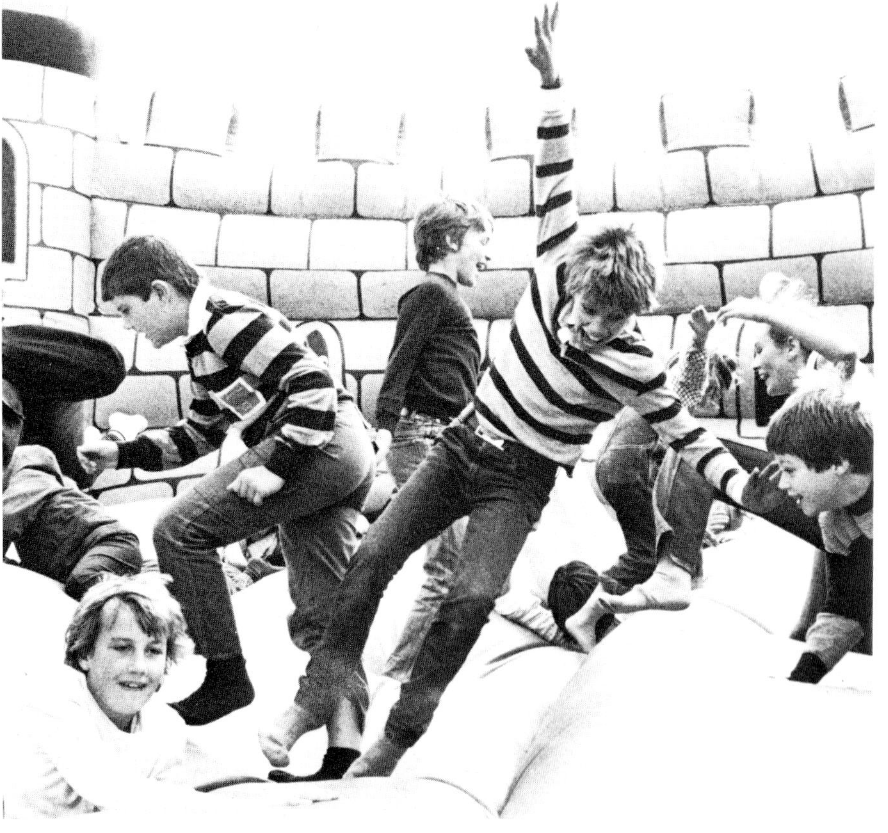

Swing chairs reach a peak of motion, so that if they are photographed at the end of a swing a fast shutter speed will not be necessary (left).

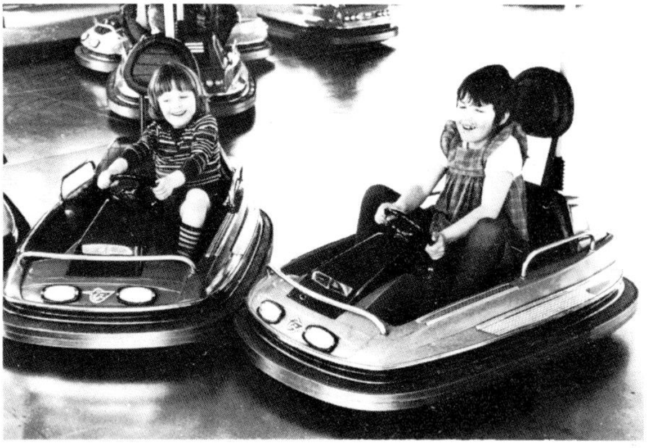

Bumper cars move rapidly and are often difficult to focus (right). Use the smallest aperture possible, while retaining a fairly fast shutter speed.

In this situation (left), there is motion occurring in several different directions, all at the same time. It is therefore necessary to freeze the action completely, and a fast shutter speed must be used.

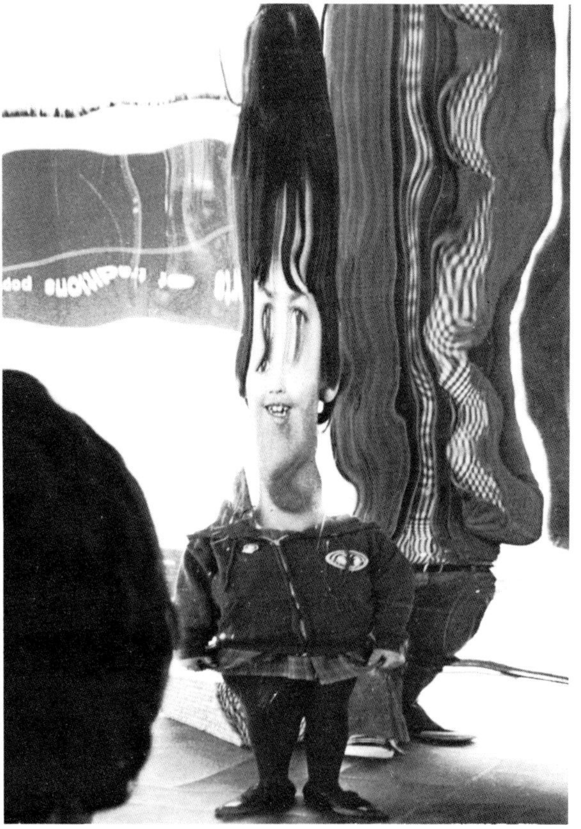

Distorting mirrors are a constant source of amusement to children (right). It will often be impossible to photograph without including the camera operator's image as well. Always focus on the reflected image itself, not on the surface of the mirror.

The Playground

The playground is an ideal place for action photography and a location where children will enjoy playing without being over-aware of the camera. Swings, roundabouts, slides and see-saws offer interesting photographic possibilities, and all the techniques described can be usefully employed in the playground for the production of a variety of effects. Once they have overcome their initial excitement at realizing they are being photographed, you will be free to shoot quietly and at will.

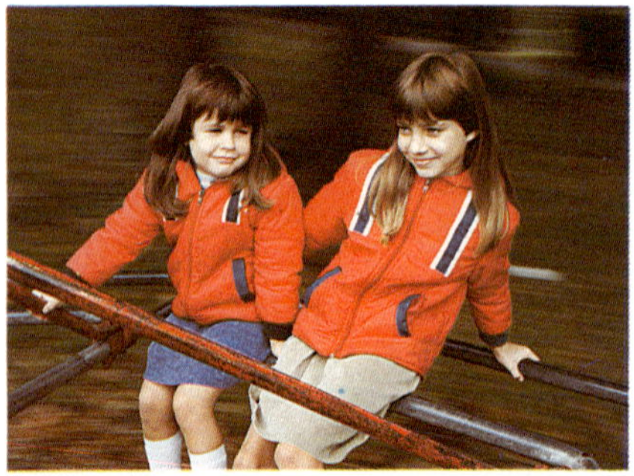

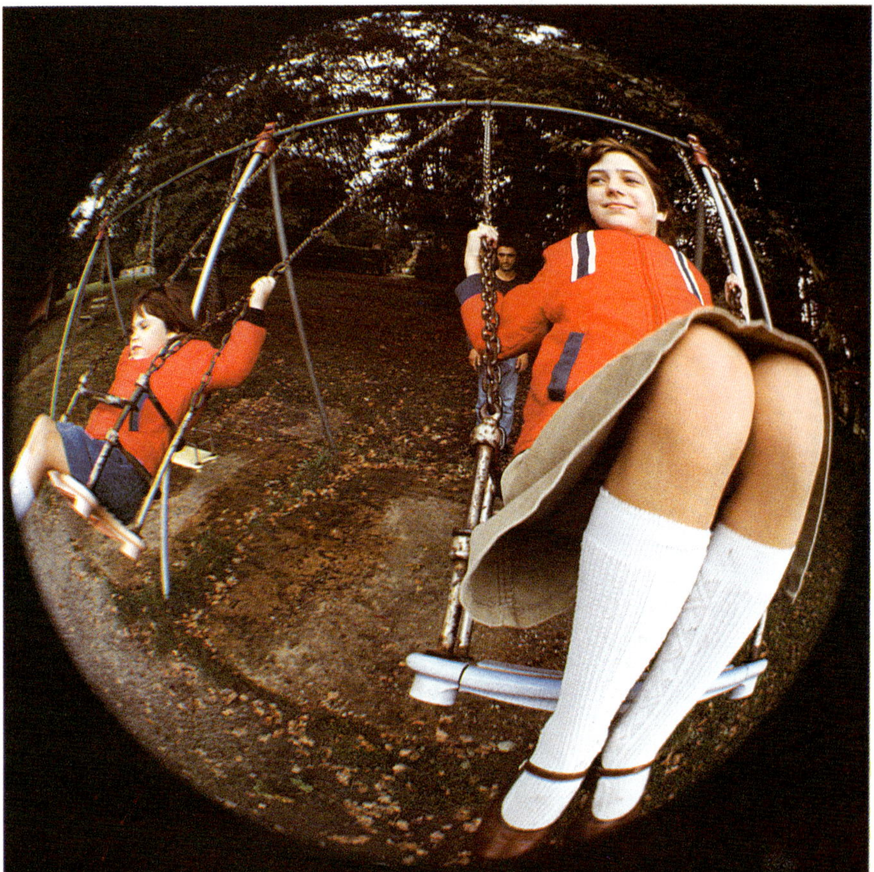

With a shutter speed of 1/15 sec the image of the models has been kept sharp, and the motion of the fast-rotating roundabout suggested by the blurred background (left).

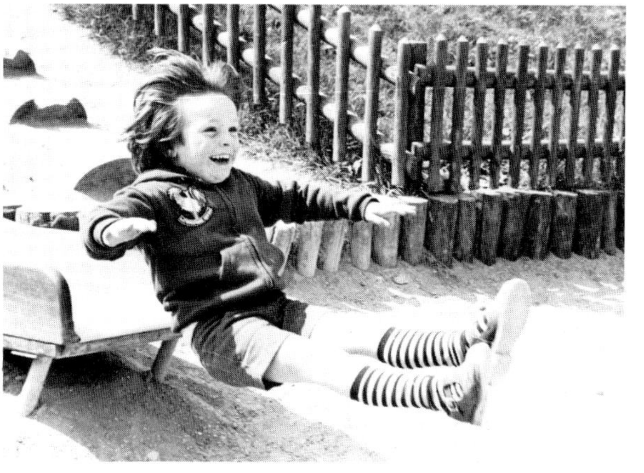

The shutter speed required to freeze action depends upon the direction of motion. Movement travelling towards the camera can be frozen with a slower speed than motion across the field of view. The child on a slide was photographed simultaneously from the side and the front. The frontal motion was captured with an exposure of 1/250 sec, while the side-on movement required a 1/1000 sec exposure to freeze the action (right, above and below).

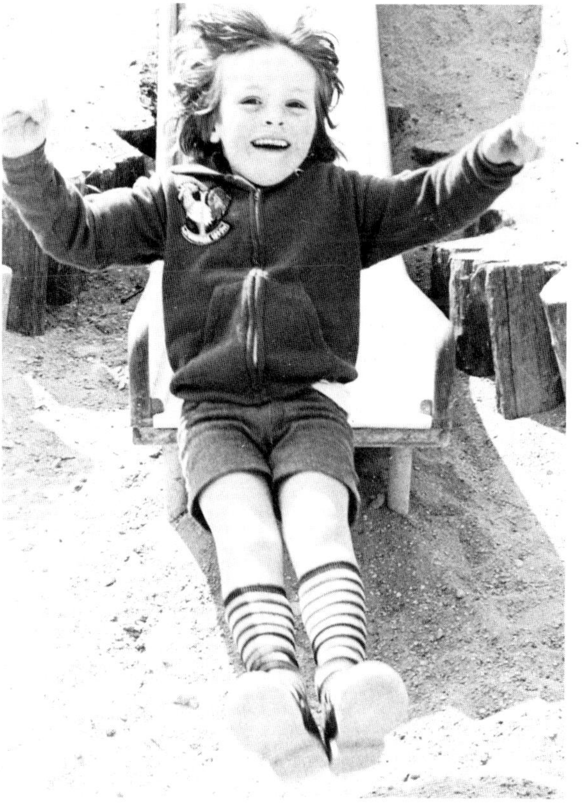

Photographed with a fish-eye lens, the child on a swing has been captured at the moment of peak action where, for a split second, she remains motionless (left). Such shots allow the use of a slow shutter speed, but the timing of the exposure is crucial.

Picture Sequences

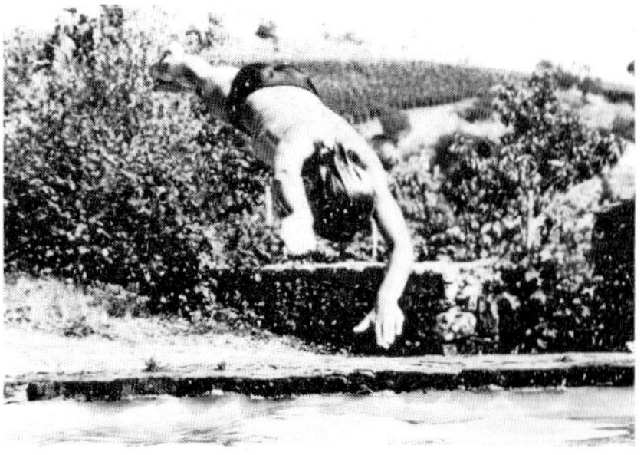

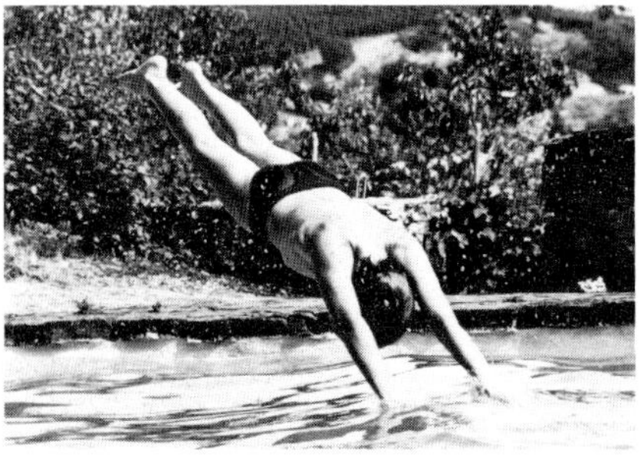

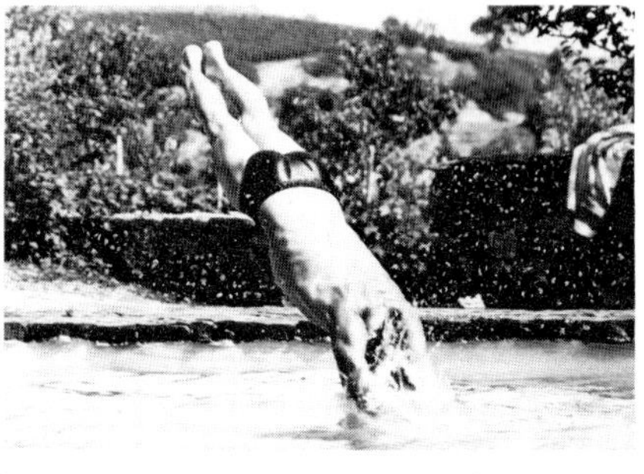

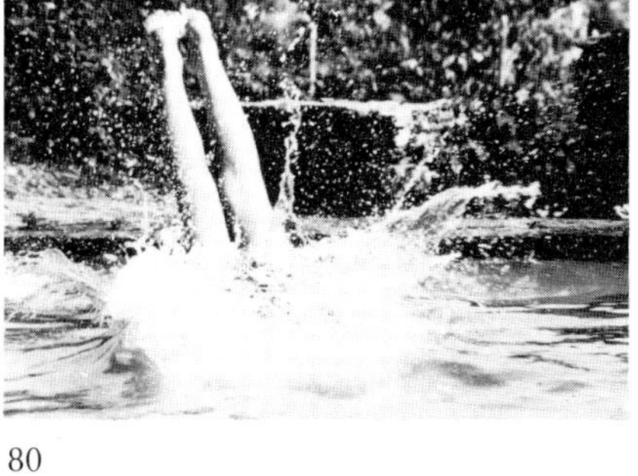

There are two main types of picture sequence. The first type is a series of photographs taken in very quick succession of a particular sort of action: the example shown on the left is a child diving into an outdoor swimming pool, showing a step-by-step analysis of the action. Any sort of physical activity can be recorded in this manner. To achieve the fast shooting rate which is required for this sort of sequence, a motor drive or winder must be fitted to the camera, with a minimum winding speed of two frames per second. The subject must be pre-focused as there will be no time to make focusing adjustments once the sequence has begun and the subject must be framed and the camera set to run continuously while the motion is in progress. When the results have been processed, the best frames can be selected to make up an interesting action sequence.

The second type is the story sequence, again consisting of a number of photographs set out in a series telling a simple story. Story sequences can be photographed without a motor drive, as the shooting rate will be considerably slower. Best photographed with more than one child, the story sequence will describe a minor event photographed over a period of a few minutes. There are various ways of achieving this; one is to 'set up' a situation into which the children are introduced and their reactions and actions recorded to make up the sequence. The example of a story sequence which is shown opposite was made by giving an apple to one child and not to the other.

The use of a zoom lens is highly recommended when shooting a story sequence as the action may range backwards and forwards from the photographer's fixed camera position. Similarly, using a lens of this type, a good mix of long, medium and close-up 'reaction' shots can be used, to tell the story in a more varied and visually interesting way.

The action sequence of the boy diving (left) was photographed with a Pentax camera, using a 80–200 mm zoom lens set at maximum focal length. A shutter speed of 1/1000 sec was used to freeze the motion, and a shooting speed of 5 frames per second selected. For the sequence, alternate exposures were chosen to show sufficiently different stages in the action. The camera was pre-focused on a point just behind the estimated position of entry into the water, ensuring an adequately focused image throughout the sequence.

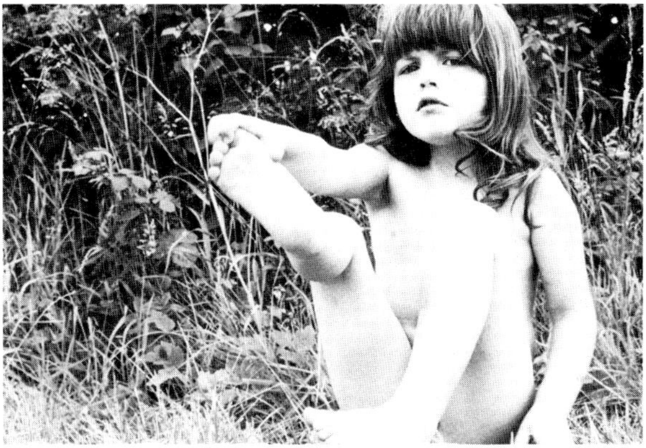

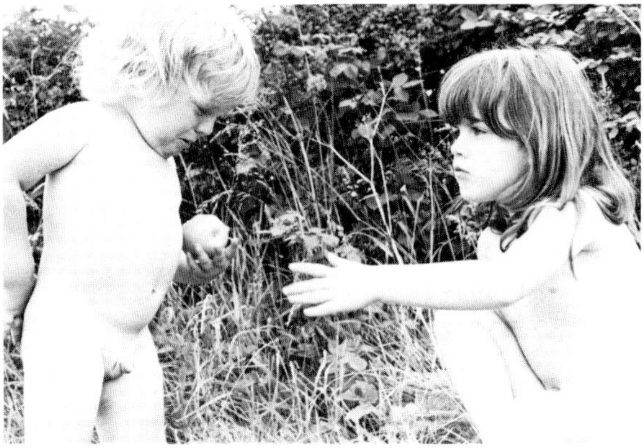

This story sequence (right) was set up in anticipation of the children's reactions, knowing that giving an apple to one child and not the other would cause an immediate incident. The story starts with the girl unaware of the situation, captures her expression as she demands the apple from her brother and finally shows the happy compromise of sharing it. Unfortunately, no one can entirely predict how children will react in a certain situation, and even such a simple story treatment can sometimes go quite wrong when the models do not oblige.

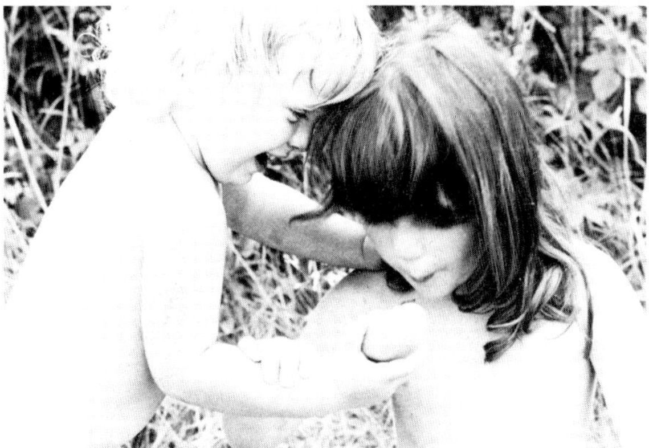

Sports and Games

Photographing sports and games outdoors presents no special problems when the light is good. Freezing, panning and peak of motion shots can all be attempted with success. When the light is poor, and in indoor situations, it is a different matter. To freeze action, electronic flash must be used but this will often destroy the mood and atmosphere. Instead, periods of minimum movement must be photographed, or the techniques of panning, controlled blur and peak of action used.

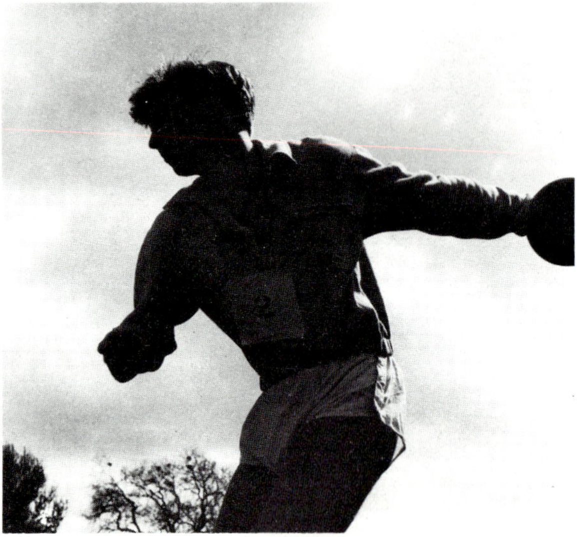

This teenage discus thrower was captured at the peak of action (left). By under-exposing the figure, a dramatic silhouette effect has been achieved against the backdrop of a moody sky.

In this action picture, photographed at 1/500 sec, notice how the facial expressions of the players contribute towards the feeling of action and concentration (below).

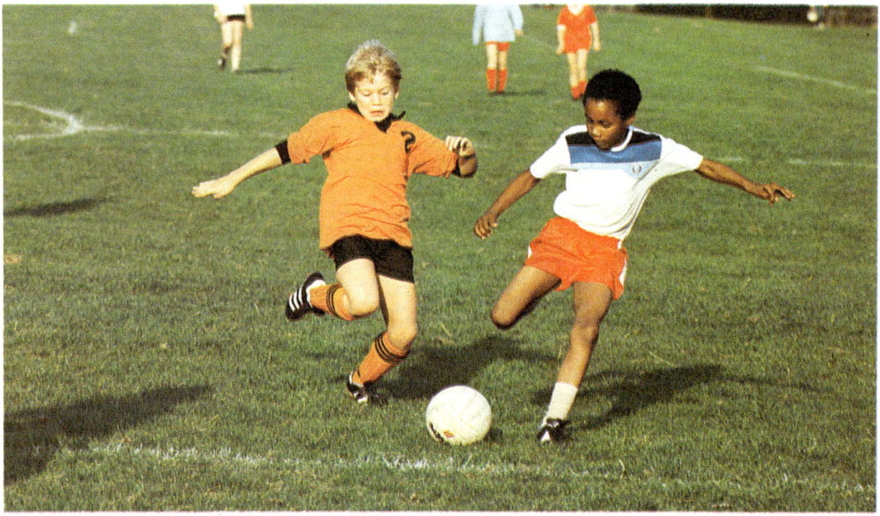

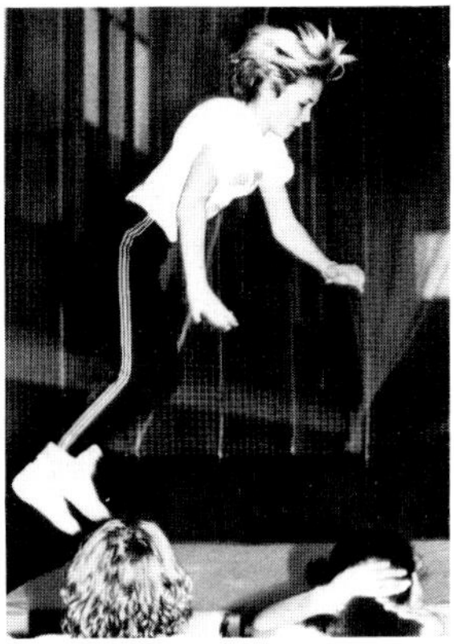

Indoor sports are difficult to photograph, and an electronic flash will almost always be required to freeze the action (above).

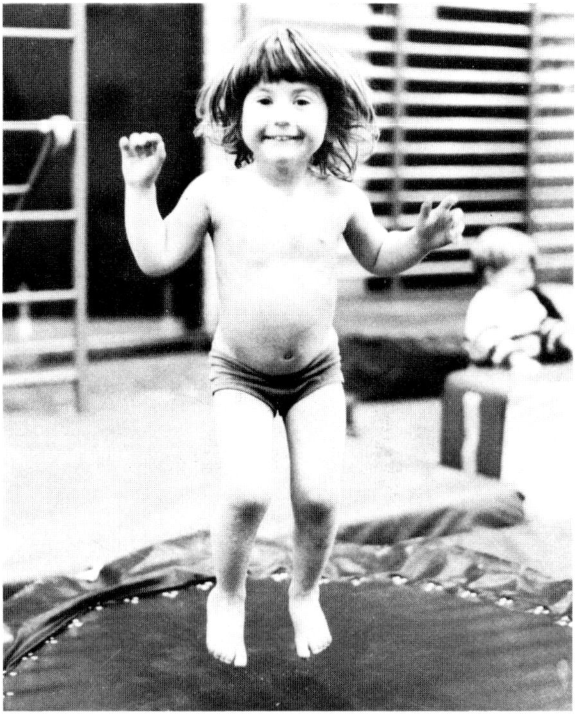

Photographed by natural light in a toddler's gymnasium, the action has been frozen by using a shutter speed of 1/125 sec at the point of peak movement (right).

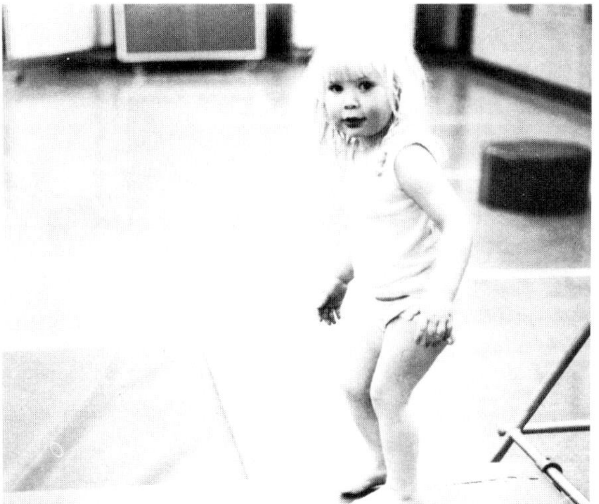

Because of the constraints and low level of artificial light, it will often be very difficult to freeze the action of indoor sports and games at the peak of motion. Instead, photographs will often have to be taken either immediately before or after the main action, when movement is at a minimum (right).

Action Pictures with Simple Cameras

It is quite possible to take good action pictures with a simple camera, provided that certain precautions are taken. The major problem with simple outfits is the lack of controllable fast shutter speeds. There are two basic types of simple camera. Very cheap models will have a shutter with one fixed speed, usually in the region of 1/40 or 1/50 sec. This is simply not fast enough to freeze motion, but is just about right for panning shots, and the most modest camera can be used for this technique with great success. It is important to remember when using a small, light camera that the equipment must be kept steady when performing a horizontal pan, and that the camera must not be jerked in a downward direction at the moment of exposure. A simple camera can also be used successfully to take true action shots, when using the 'peak of action' technique described on page 70.

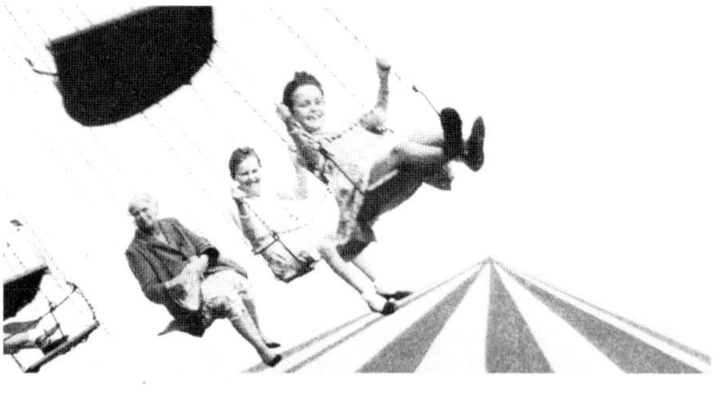

This photograph was taken with a simple cartridge-loading camera with 'programmed' shutter (left). There was sufficient light to ensure a shutter speed capable of freezing the motion of the roundabout.

This panning shot, taken with a speed of 1/60 sec, is typical of the result that can be expected from a simple, single-speed camera when used with the same technique (below).

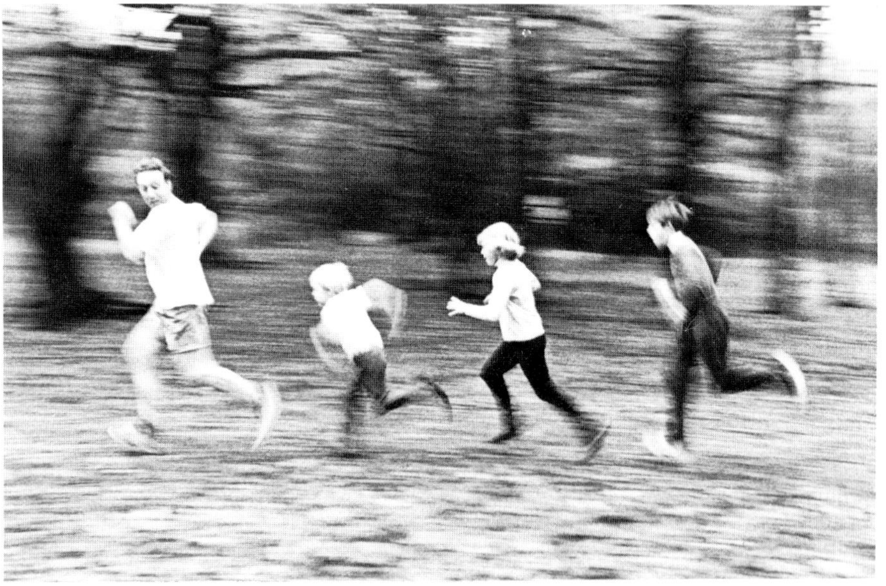

The freedom and joy of childhood were captured in this picture (right) with a simple camera using the panning technique. When using this technique it is most important to move the camera only in the direction of the subject's motion. Any vertical camera movement will spoil the result.

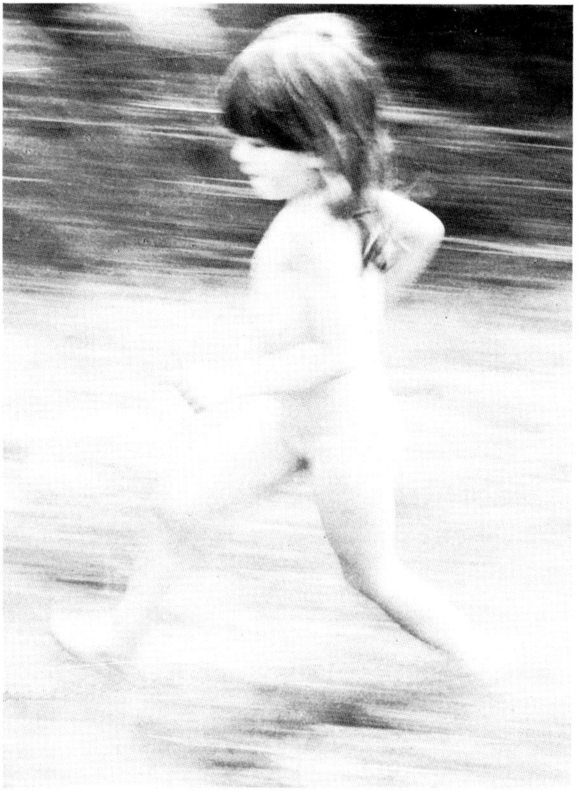

More sophisticated simple cameras have what is known as a programmed shutter. This may well be capable of producing a speed as fast as 1/400 sec, which is quite adequate to capture almost any action. The problem when using a camera of this type is that there is no indication to the photographer that such a speed has been selected. It is safe to say, however, that an automatic camera is most likely to select a fast shutter speed when lighting conditions are strong, and even more so when loaded with a fast film. Under these conditions, a programmed automatic camera will be perfectly capable of freezing most fast-moving subjects. At other times, it is safer to assume that a medium to slow shutter speed has been selected, and follow the example of the fixed-speed simple camera, and restrict your action photography merely to panned and 'peak of action' work.

Both types of simple camera can either be fitted with an electronic flash, or will already carry an integral unit. Flash can be used both indoors and out as a means of catching action although flash photography outdoors tends to have a very unnatural feel about it, especially when there is some daylight present.

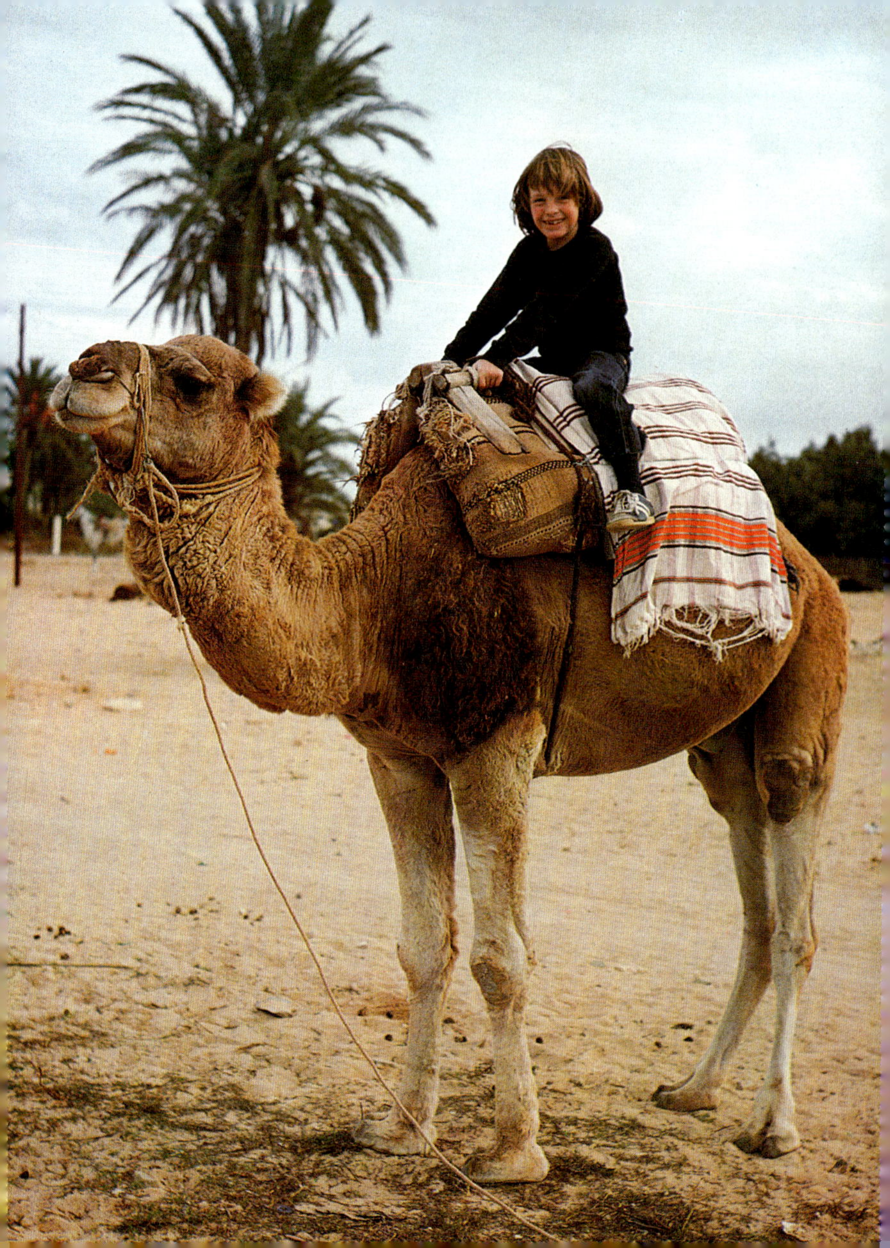

TRAVELLING WITH A CAMERA

Until the advent of the cheap box camera at the turn of the century, photography was largely a pursuit of the privileged classes. British photographers, amateur and professional, travelled far and wide, mainly to Africa, India and the East, producing a vast quantity of lantern slides and stereoscopic pairs for eager audiences enthralled by tantalizing glimpses of unknown lands, people and costumes. Now that travel is easy and relatively cheap, the modern photographer has more opportunity to take his family abroad, and is able to photograph his children in new and unusual locations, while compiling an exciting record at the same time.

Before taking a camera abroad it is obviously very important to make certain provisions and preparations to ensure the best possible results in situations that will often be unrepeatable. In a holiday period, the camera will be in use more regularly than at any other time, so it is vital that certain checks and precautions are made before departure.

When travelling or on holiday, when the camera will be carried most of the time, the photographer will be able to capture many situations of an unexpected or unusual kind. On such occasions, the children will be thoroughly absorbed by the newness of the situation and the quick-witted photographer will be rewarded with spontaneous and lively pictures.

Very few photographers with an interest in children will want to restrict their picture-taking to their own offspring. Especially when travelling, with a camera to hand, you will see other people's children in situations that are interesting or attractive, and wish to photograph them. In such cases there is absolutely no reason why you should not take a photograph, as long as it is done with diplomacy and tact, and no offence is caused to the child or his parents. There are instances, especially in foreign countries, when photographs of unusual costume or circumstances can make an invaluable addition to the record of a trip. Even if this is not the case, it is often difficult to resist photographing an unknown child in a perfect photographic situation. Shooting this type of subject is like a type of reporting, and professional photographers have coined a name for it, 'photo-reportage'. This photographic approach is described in more detail on pages 92–5.

Shooting on Holiday

When travelling with a camera it is better not to over-burden yourself with unnecessary equipment, so in planning a trip you should be absolutely strict with yourself and decide what apparatus is essential and not be tempted to take anything extra. Too many photographers take every single item of their equipment and get loaded down with the weight of it all, often spoiling what should be an enjoyable expedition. Another point worth remembering is that shots can often be lost while you are searching inside a loaded case for a particular item. With a minimum of equipment the photographer will feel freer and ready to shoot at all times.

For overseas travel it is advisable to check on the customs requirements of the countries to be visited. Some countries impose limits on the amount of photographic equipment that can be imported by the visitor, and although the allowances are usually quite generous, the owner of a comprehensive outfit might find himself over the limit. In most countries, such restrictions are not strictly enforced, but it is not altogether unknown for a particularly zealous customs officer to impound certain items of equipment for the duration of a holiday or even to ask for a cash guarantee to ensure that they are re-exported by the owner.

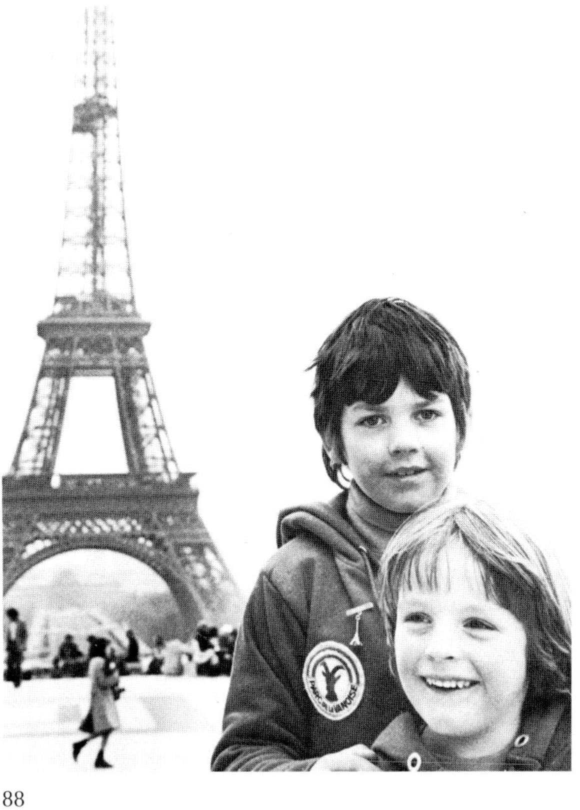

By placing the children against a well-known backdrop, the location becomes immediately recognizable (left). When used in the family album such a picture can act as an introductory shot to establish the setting for further pictures taken in the same city or town.

When on holiday, children will often become so preoccupied with new situations that they will forget the presence of the camera, enabling the photographer to shoot natural and spontaneous pictures without his subjects' knowledge (right).

It is best to take a good supply of film with you and use up any surplus at a later date rather than run out. It is usually more expensive to buy film abroad and there is always the possibility that your favourite film will not be available in that particular country. Even when the correct film is available, there is a likelihood that it has been stored on a shelf under conditions of high temperature or humidity which can be detrimental. In hot conditions, colour film should ideally be stored in a refrigerator to preserve it at its best.

Before you set out on a trip, check all your camera equipment to make sure that it is functioning correctly. Almost all cameras require batteries for exposure metering, and many rely on battery power for all functions: exposure, focusing and film transportation. If there is any doubt about the age or life expectancy of the batteries, it is a good idea to change them before you go. The same applies to flash units: as a precautionary measure, the batteries should be replaced or recharged.

When the equipment has been checked mechanically it should be cleaned. Camera interiors should be dusted with a soft brush or air-blower, with care taken not to touch or damage the delicate blinds of focal plane shutters. The viewfinder glass should be polished with a soft cloth and special attention paid to the lenses. These should be cleaned with great care, using either a special solvent or impregnated tissues. The best method, however, is to breathe softly on to the glass and polish gently with a clean cotton handkerchief. With either method, remove any loose dirt first, to avoid grinding it into the lens coating.

The best way of carrying camera equipment is to pack it in a single case which you should keep with you at all times. It is not advisable to pack apparatus in a suitcase as there is not only the risk of theft but also of rough handling at airports and railway stations. If you are travelling by air your hand luggage will almost certainly be checked through an X-ray security machine. Even though you may be assured that the machine is safe for film, ask if loaded cameras and packs of film may be inspected by hand only; this can be arranged at most air terminals. One passage through an X-ray machine may

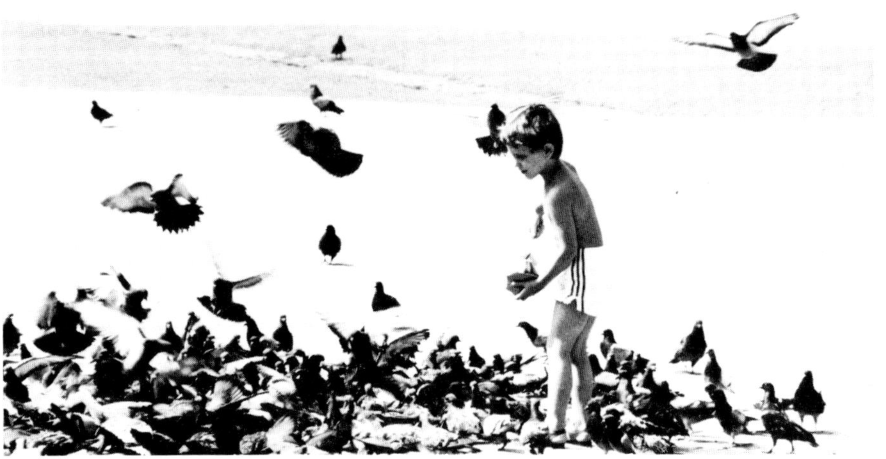

Shooting on Holiday 2

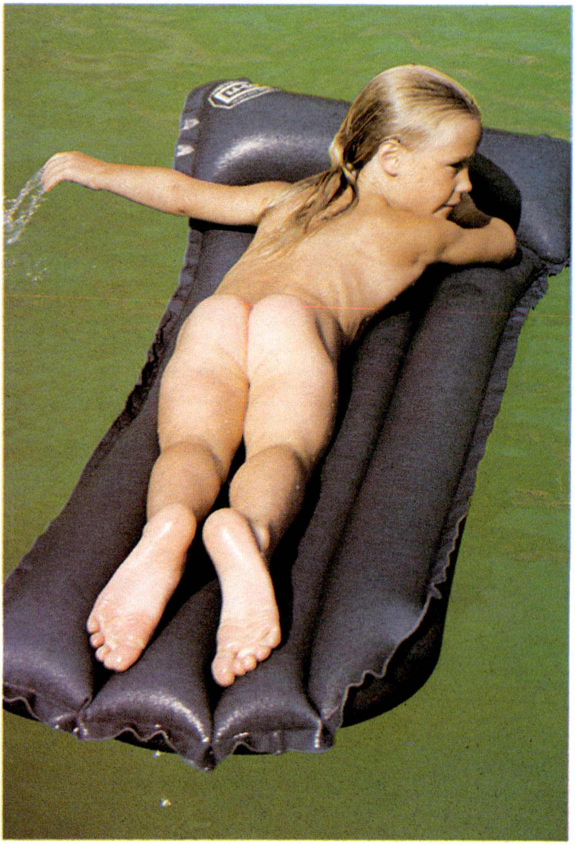

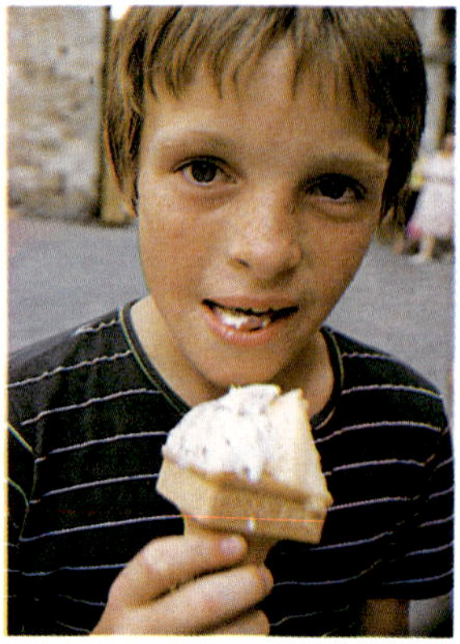

Simple activities such as eating ice-cream lend themselves to close-up treatment, which adds variety to the holiday record (above).

Swimming-pools are an ideal location for holiday photography, capturing the feeling of bright light and heat (left).

well not damage films, but the effect is cumulative and two or three treatments may spoil your pictures. Lead-lined bags are available for safe transportation of film through X-ray machines, but their value is dubious, as a security officer can turn up the radiation level to penetrate the lining, and there has been at least one legal battle where a photographer has claimed the loss of his film supposedly protected by a bag of this type. It is therefore safer to remove the film from your luggage and submit it to a visual inspection.

Final tips for travellers concern the safety of equipment. Constant exposure to heat is harmful to cameras, and they should be kept cool whenever possible. When travelling by car cushion your equipment in such a way as to prevent vibration which can damage the mechanism. Above all, do not run the risk of having your camera stolen. Never leave it lying anywhere unattended and open to view, even for a minute, and even when you are wearing it hung on your body beware of camera-snatchers.

Taking photographs on holiday will broaden the horizon of every child photographer. New surroundings and activities will give the camera-owner fresh enthusiasm and will enable him to take photographs which are unattainable at home. Many holidays are taken at the seaside, which is an ideal photographic location (see pages 64–7), but numerous other opportunities will present themselves. Children camping, riding on donkeys or camels, eating ice cream, or taking part in organized sports at a hotel, all make ideal subjects for the holiday camera.

Sight-seeing is a favourite occupation on holidays in both the countryside and the city. Almost any photograph taken on such an excursion will be enhanced by including the figure of a child somewhere in the composition; a view of a famous cathedral, for instance, can be dull and boring without figures, but with a child standing in the foreground the scene will come alive, the buildings will acquire scale and, most importantly, the photograph will become a personal record of a particular day. Even when the children depicted in such a shot have their back to the camera and are unrecognizable, they will still aid the composition of the picture, adding scale, colour and the human factor.

When photographing children as subjects in foreign surroundings, it is best to leave plenty of space around them in order to locate the picture in a particular place. The style of architecture, type of landscape, costume and appearance of the people, even posters on a wall, will all help to identify and tell a story. When visiting places of interest with well-known landmarks, what better than to photograph your child against a famous backdrop? The Eiffel Tower is only one example among many.

Photographs taken on holiday must naturally reflect the spirit of the occasion. They must tell the viewer, either by the location chosen or the activity depicted, that the people involved were having an enjoyable or interesting time. Making full use of strange, even exotic locations and brilliant weather conditions will immediately make the pictures different from shots taken in everyday surroundings at home. In turn, your subjects should look happy and carefree and as though they are enjoying themselves thoroughly.

When photographing children abroad, leave space around them to show part of the surroundings in order to locate the shot. This picture was taken in the back streets of Montmartre in Paris (right).

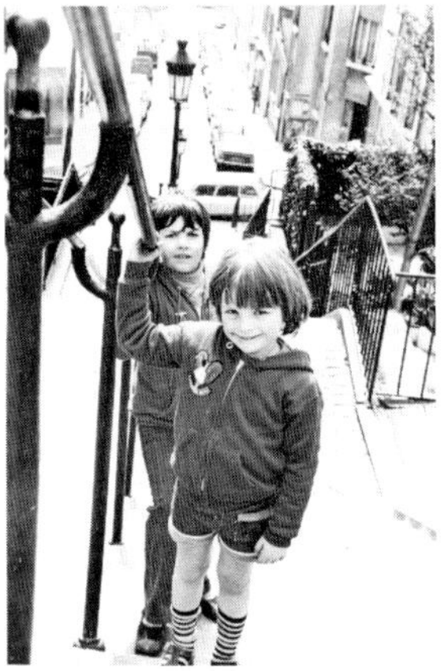

When photographing scenes, the inclusion of a child will add scale and human interest. Often it is better to have the child turned away from the camera, otherwise his or her presence becomes too important, and detracts from the scene as a whole (far right).

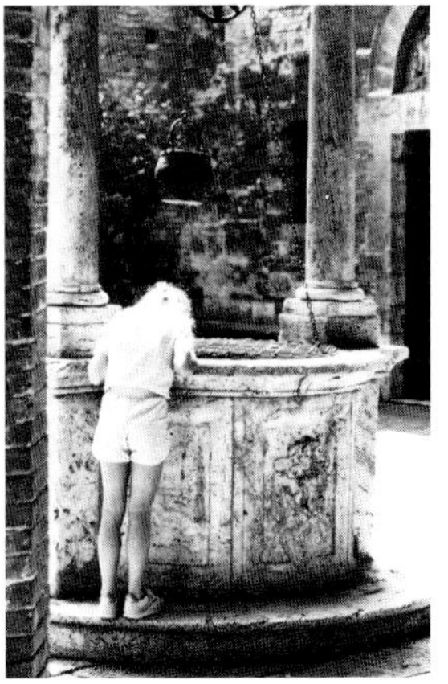

Photo-reportage

It often happens that the photographer on his travels, either at home or abroad, will encounter children other than his own in an ideal situation to be photographed. Something will attract his attention – it might be a particularly beautiful child, or a child doing something interesting or humorous – in any event, he will recognize the ingredients of a good photograph and wish to record it. This type of photography is called 'photo-reportage'.

The first thing he has to decide is whether it is important that the child is unaware of being photographed. If a candid shot is required it will have to be taken quickly, with the camera raised to the eye and the photograph taken with the minimum delay. In many cases, however, it will not matter whether the child is aware of the camera or not.

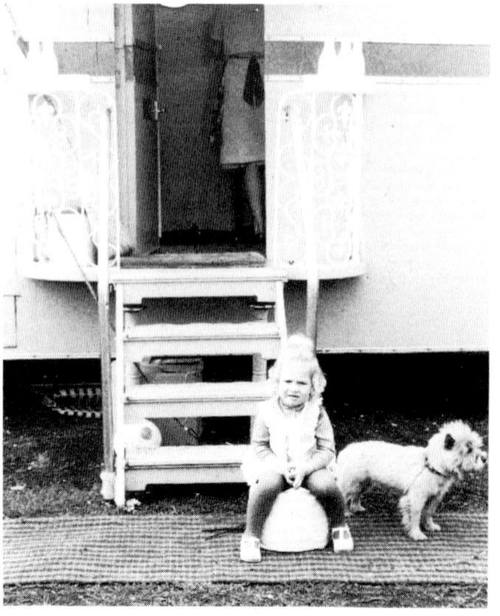

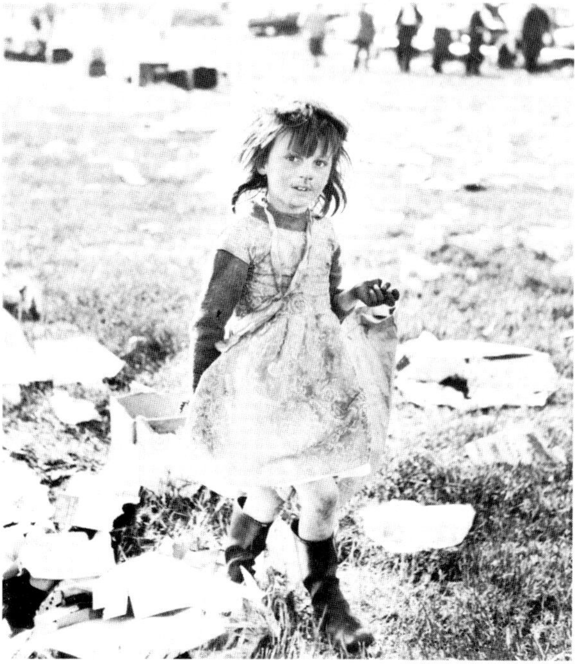

The pictures on this page are chosen from a set of circus and fairground children. This shot (above) was taken not only because the child and her dog were interesting, but because the incongruity of the wrought-iron railings of the caravan intrigued the photographer.

Another fairground child waiting while her mother beats the drum on a side-show rostrum (right); the girl was photographed, with her mother's nodded assent, by a direct approach with no attempt to disguise the camera's presence.

Photographed by evening light, after the racing on Derby Day, a fairground gypsy child scavenging among the litter and debris of the day's activities (left).

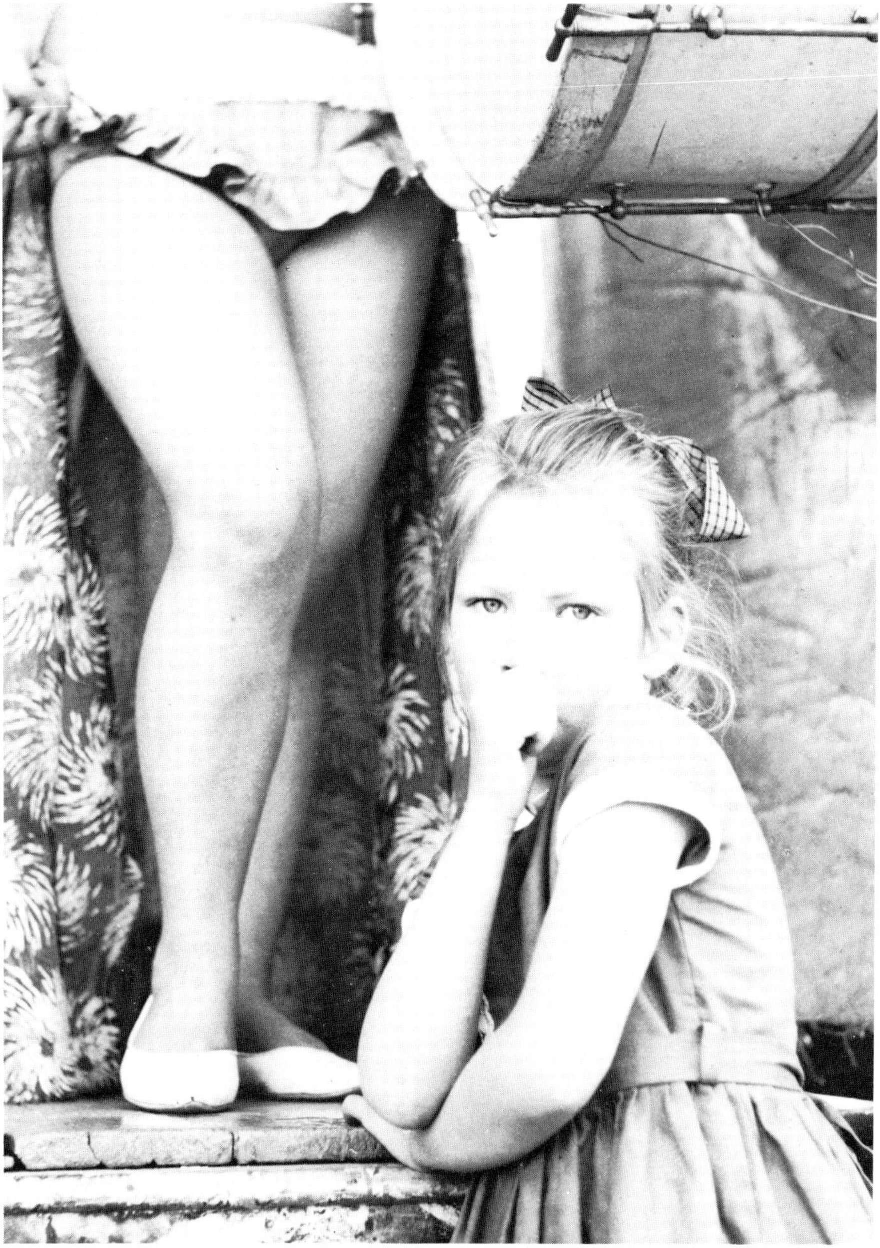

Photo-reportage 2

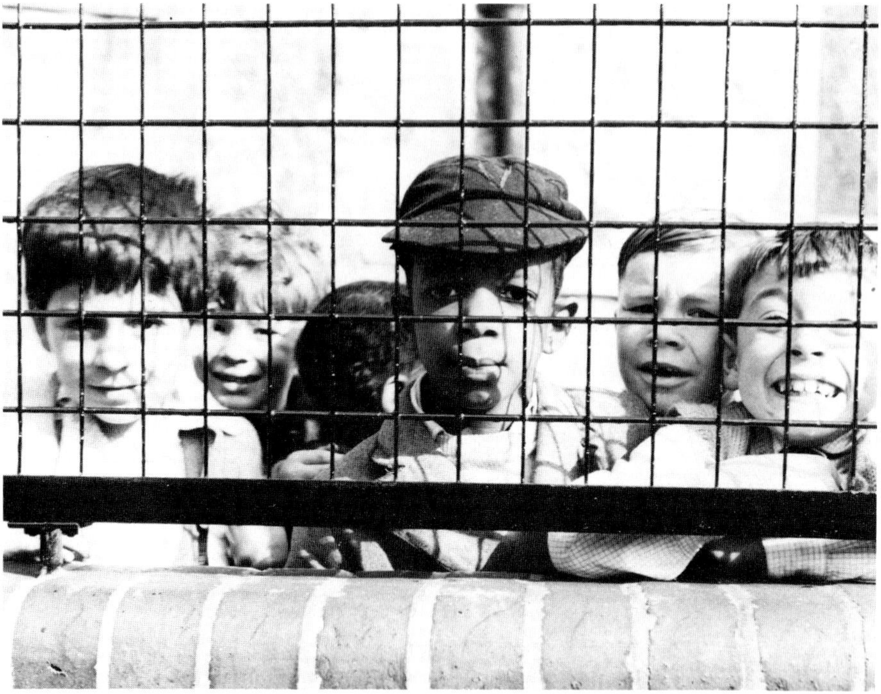

If you find yourself in such a situation, particularly in a foreign country where there may be a language barrier, it is very important that you do not frighten the child. When he notices your camera, smile at him to show that you are friendly and mean him no harm. If he smiles back, half the battle is won. You may then explain in words or signs that you want to photograph him, and if he nods assent, continue. On no account pursue a child who is worried or shy about the situation, as you will not get a good picture and will only upset the child. If the child's parents are in the vicinity it is only courteous to explain what you want to do and to ask for their permission. If they agree, you will gain their cooperation and the further confidence of the child.

The experienced professional 'reportage' photographer who is taking pictures of children for journalistic purposes will work in another way. By learning to stay in the background and make himself inconspicuous, and by working quickly and quietly, he will be able to take a series of photographs without his subjects' knowledge. If he is noticed, he will skilfully integrate himself into the scene, join in the activity and gain the children's trust. He will soon become a 'friend' and be able to photograph from inside the group.

Photographing a child in his own environment where he lives and plays will not only tend to make him feel more at ease and less nervous of you and your camera, but can also provide insight into the way of life of that community.

In this shot (left), taken with a direct approach, the schoolboys were aware of the photographer's presence and reacted to the camera characteristically. The strength and interest of the picture lie in the different ways that the children have decided to respond to the photographer and his camera.

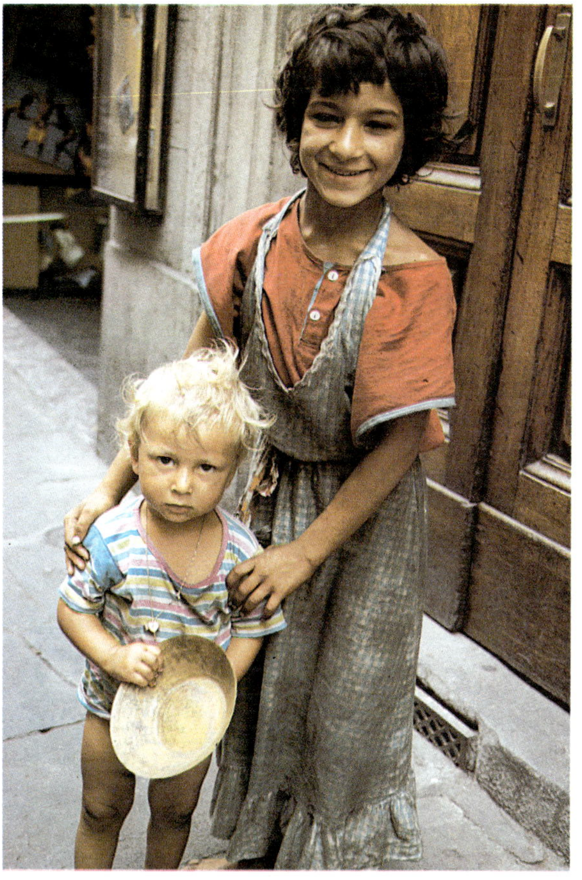

When photographing abroad, and especially in more exotic countries, there is a great temptation to shoot indiscriminately at people without regard to their feelings. This occurs mainly because of the suspicion that any attempt to communicate one's ideas to the subject would be totally misunderstood. Two opposite reactions are shown here: in one case the result of a tactless approach, where the mother is upset by the intrusion of the camera and attempts to shield her child (below). In the other picture (above) the photographer has restored goodwill with the parent, and has gained her consent and cooperation in photographing her children.

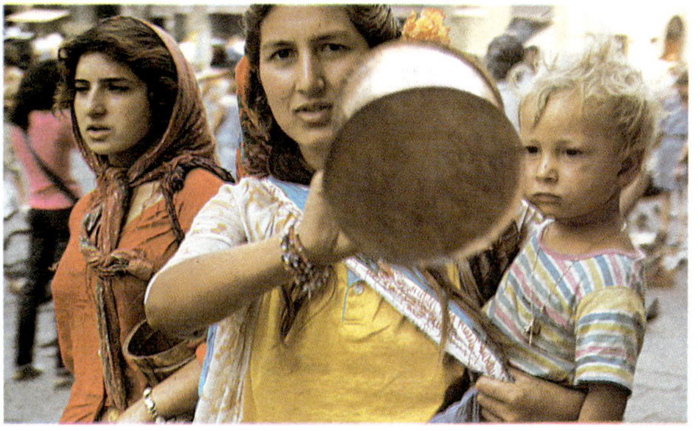

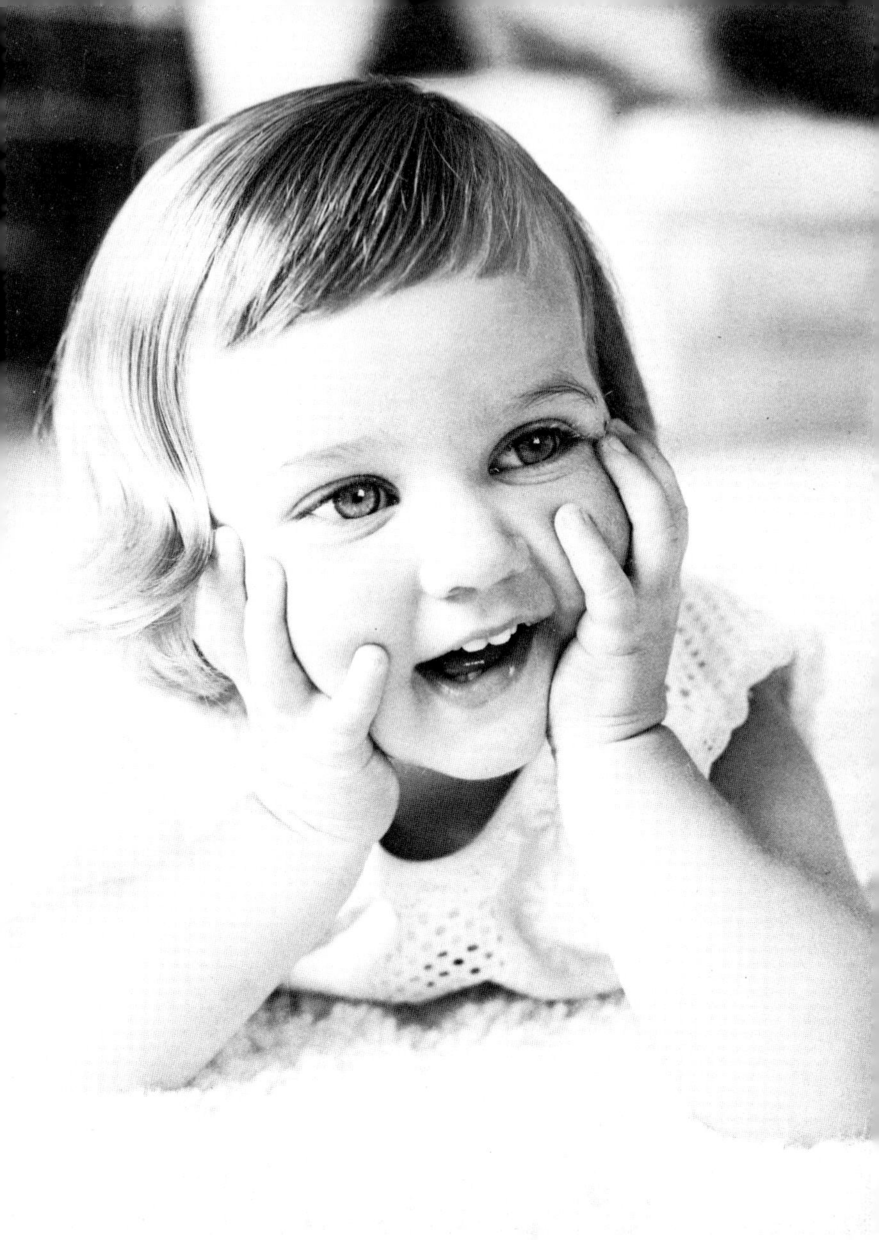

THE SITTING-ROOM STUDIO

All children have a certain spirit of adventure and love to go out and explore thei[r] immediate environment, whether it is the garden, playground or local park, bu[t] it is nevertheless in their own home that they feel most relaxed and self-assured. Within the security of familiar surroundings a child will happily enjoy being photographed, making the house an ideal location for a successful and stimulating photographic session.

The home can be the place for relaxed, informal portraiture, or the background against which scenes of the child's everyday life can be recorded. Event[s] such as mealtimes, helping in the kitchen, or bathtime and bedtime for younge[r] children can all be captured for the family record.

From a technical viewpoint, the major difference between an indoor and outdoor location is the relatively low level of ambient light. For the modern photographer, however, given the availability of very high-speed colour and black-and-white films and the wide choice of electronic flash units, this is no longer the problem it once was. Daylight from windows is a convenient and natural light source which can be used very effectively in many circumstances. I[t] can even be controlled and modified by means of reflectors.

The photographer working inside the home is not dependent on the prevailing weather conditions: he can shoot come wind or shine, irrespective of the time o[f] day or night. At first sight, indoor photography may seem problematical to a less-experienced photographer, but it is really no more difficult than shooting out o[f] doors, and is often very much more satisfying.

The enterprising photographer may wish to erect a temporary studio set-up in the home to enable him to take more formal pictures, and this can be done quite easily, without undue expense, to produce results of a professional quality. The small amount of extra effort involved is well worth it as the ability to work indoors adds considerably to a photographer's scope.

Using Window Light

The main difference between shooting indoors and outdoors is the level of ambient light available. During daylight hours, there is usually a useful quantity of light transmitted through the windows of a room. The intensity of light is obviously variable, depending on the size of the window, the weather conditions and the time of day, but on most occasions there is sufficient light for photographic purposes.

The strength of the light is greatest at the point nearest to the window, and drops away quite rapidly towards the middle of the room. From a photographic point of view, the ideal position from which to shoot is quite close to the light source. Window light is at its best when outside conditions are bright or lightly clouded, which gives a pleasantly soft quality of light. Situations where direct sunlight is shining through a window are better avoided, as this provides a harsh effect, often with the shadows of the window bars falling across the subject. Under softer conditions, using a fast film, exposure levels will usually be quite good enough to enable hand-held photographs to be taken. Care should be taken, however, to ensure that subject movement is kept to a minimum as the shutter speed will probably be relatively slow.

One characteristic of window light is that in most rooms it will be very directional. This is to say that as there is only one light source, the illumination will be coming from one direction only. Subjects will therefore be strongly lit on one side and mainly shadowed on the other. On general scenes this is often quite acceptable, but when shooting close-ups of children, and portrait studies, the effect can be too dramatic. In some cases, of course, this can be intentional, but for girls and younger children a softer treatment is usually more acceptable.

When the subject is positioned as near as possible to the window, with the head at right angles to the glass, the nearest half of

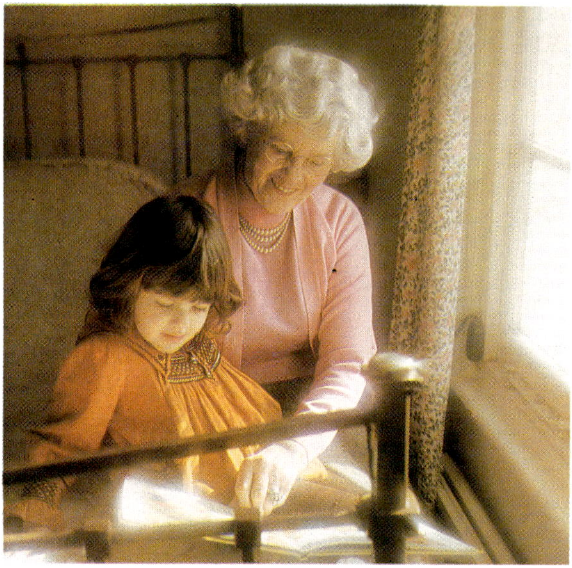

The grandmother and child were photographed using window light as the main source of illumination (left). A small flash unit was used to fill in the shadows and soften the appearance of the picture.

Using direct window light, the girl was photographed utilizing a reflector to produce a balanced effect (right). The boy was photographed without a reflector, and the effect is starker and more dramatic (far right). Both shots were taken at the same location within minutes of each other, and the same exposure used in each case.

the face will be fully illuminated, while the opposite half will be largely in shadow and lower in intensity. The way to achieve more balanced lighting in these circumstances is to use a reflector in the form of a large, white or metallized piece of card near the subject's face, but out of the camera range, to reflect light back into the dark areas. The degree of 'fill-in', as it is known, is dependent on the angle at which the reflector is held and the distance from the subject. It must be manipulated until the required balance of light is achieved. If necessary, several exposures may be made with more or less fill-in in order to establish the best result. When bracketing different exposure levels in this way it is a good idea to make notes, for future reference.

An alternative method of filling in window light is to aim a small synchronized flash unit at the opposite wall of the room. The light reflected back to the subject is usually just enough to fill in the shadows and provide a pleasing balance of light and shade. This method can of course only be used with cameras which have separate flash units.

On bright days and using the light from a large window, even simple cameras with a limited exposure potential can produce effective pictures indoors. If the camera has a choice of settings for either sunny or cloudy conditions, it should be set to cloudy, even if it is a clear day outside, as this enables the camera to operate at its largest aperture. It is also advisable to use a fast film if possible. Photographs taken by window light will have a feeling of subtlety missing from those taken with the direct, integral flash unit of most simple cameras. If there is any doubt about the sufficiency of the light, or if a red light shows in the camera before the exposure is made, then a mix of daylight and flash may be used, which will be pleasanter than flash alone. When this technique is used, the flash head should be covered with a white handkerchief or tissue to lower its output.

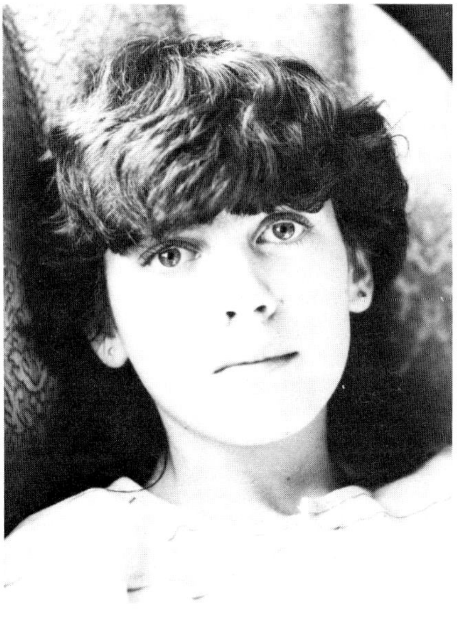

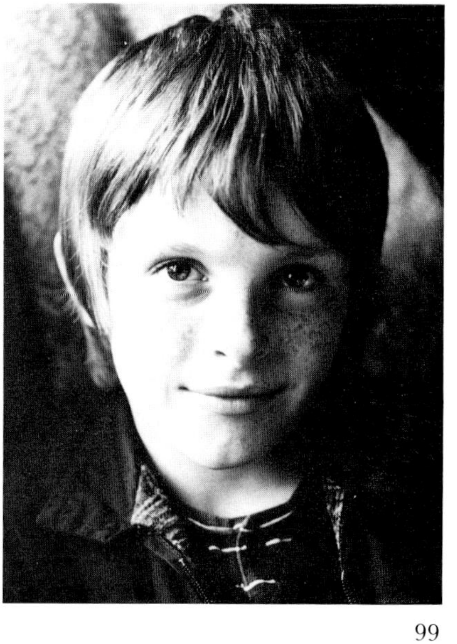

Lighting Techniques

Although window light is a pleasant and useful source of illumination for photography in the home, its use is restricted to daylight hours and to rooms with a generous window area, and such conditions will not always be present when you want to take a picture.

As a result of recent advances in film technology, emulsions of very high speed are now available, with both colour and black-and-white films with a speed of 1000 ASA and over. These enable the photographer to work with a high degree of success in considerably lower lighting conditions that ever before: the manufacturers claim that it is even possible to take a portrait by the light of a single candle. Provided that the camera is fitted with a lens with a fairly wide aperture it is now quite possible to take photographs in any room with a reasonable level of domestic lighting. Photographs taken under such conditions will capture accurately the feeling of the location, something that a flash photograph will usually destroy. However, it must be remembered that the positioning and characteristics of domestic lighting are not always perfect for child photography. Some types of lighting cause concentrations of light or 'hot-spots' which can burn out the features of a child. Care must be taken to select an area where the light is even, yet still intense enough for photography.

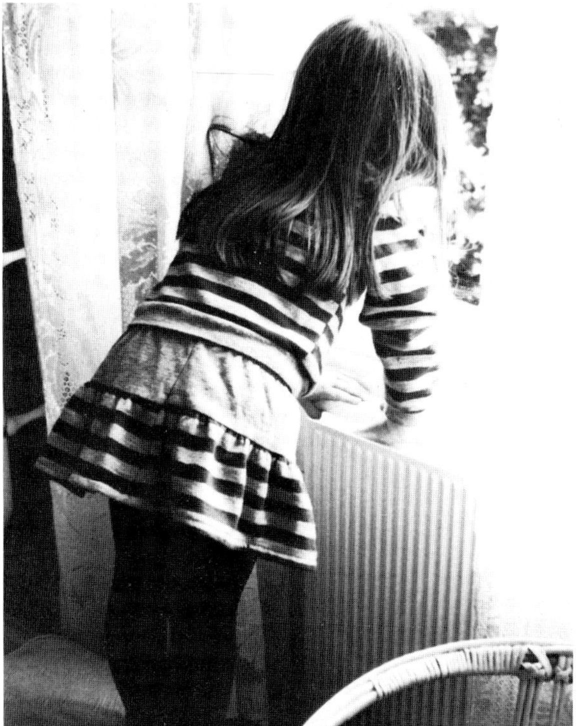

This picture (right above) was taken using the bounce flash technique giving a soft, almost shadowless form of light. Care must be taken when working in colour, as the reflecting ceiling or wall must have a neutral hue.

An unusual use was made of window light, with the window itself appearing in the composition (left). When shooting towards windows, always make sure that the camera, or additional light source if used, cannot be seen as a reflection in the glass.

By using a flash unit with a reflective umbrella, a soft light of a more directional quality can be used (right below). Umbrella lighting gives more modelling and feeling of depth than normal bounce techniques, and is widely used by professional photographers.

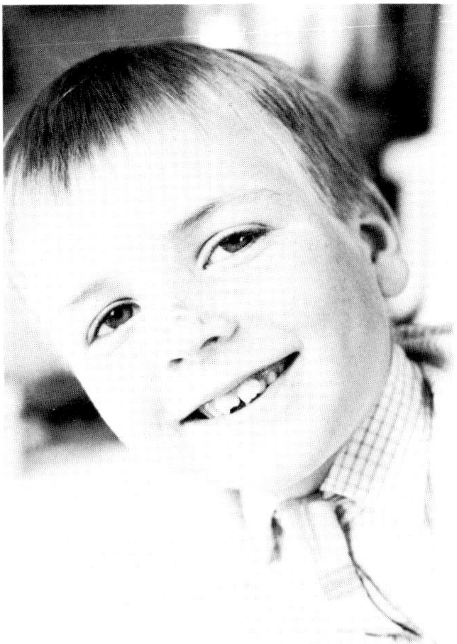

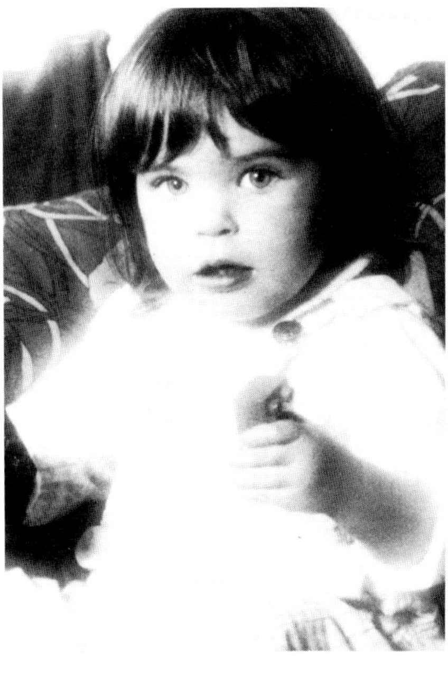

Under such conditions, the camera lens will have to be set at a wide aperture and a fairly slow shutter speed engaged, so the subject will have to remain fairly static for focusing to be accurate. When shooting colour transparencies it is important to use a film which is balanced for tungsten lighting. If a daylight-type film is used with domestic lighting, the colour transparencies will have a yellow cast. For the same reason, when shooting in colour, it is not advisable to mix daylight and artificial light together, as the colour rendering will be disturbed, with daylight becoming too blue, and artificial light too yellow.

Photographs taken by ambient artificial light will convey a realism missing in a flash photograph, but for subjects where some movement is envisaged it is wiser to use flash. The flash technique which is most commonly used by amateur photographers is the 'on-camera', direct method with the flash either mounted on or integral with the camera. Although the results of this method are satisfactory, especially for close-ups, the effect is rather unnatural with hard shadows and a dark, under-lit background. A better method is to bounce the flash light from the ceiling by angling the flash unit upwards. This gives a wider spread of light and a more normal effect with softer shadows. Another method is to use an umbrella; this has a special lining which reflects the light to produce a wide spread of even, soft light, particularly suitable for portraits. These two methods can only be used with cameras which have separate flash units, so that owners of simpler cameras with integral flashes will be restricted to the direct method.

It is worth remembering, when using direct flash, that subjects wearing dark- or medium-toned clothing will record better than those in whites or pastels. This is because direct flash tends to destroy detail in light tones, especially when films are printed on automatic enlarging equipment.

Making a Home Studio

If you want to take more formal studies indoors, a simple home studio can be set up in only a few minutes. The first requirement is a background, and for most purposes this should be plain. Unless the room you are going to use has a suitably plain wall, the best solution is to buy a roll of seamless paper from a photographic supplier. The rolls come in a variety of colours, and the usual width is 1.5 metres (5 feet), but larger widths are also available. The easiest way of suspending the roll is to run a loop of cord through the centre core, leaving plenty of slack, and to hang it from a picture rail or curtain rail by a hook. If you are going to concentrate on head-shots, the paper need only hang to floor level, but for full-length studies and shots of smaller children sitting on the ground, it must continue on to the floor.

As regards lighting, the favourite method for studio portraiture is electronic flash in conjunction with umbrella reflectors. The advantages are the short duration of the flash, allowing fast movement to be frozen, and the small size and portability of the flash units. The umbrellas and stands are collapsible, making the entire lighting system light and compact. All the equipment can be bought at most larger photographic stores at fairly reasonable cost. More expensive, mains-run units are available, but these are designed primarily for professional use. Their main advantage is that they have a tungsten modelling light, which helps to gauge the exact effect of the light on the model.

An interesting effect can be obtained with one umbrella flash, positioned so that the light falls on the subject in one plane.

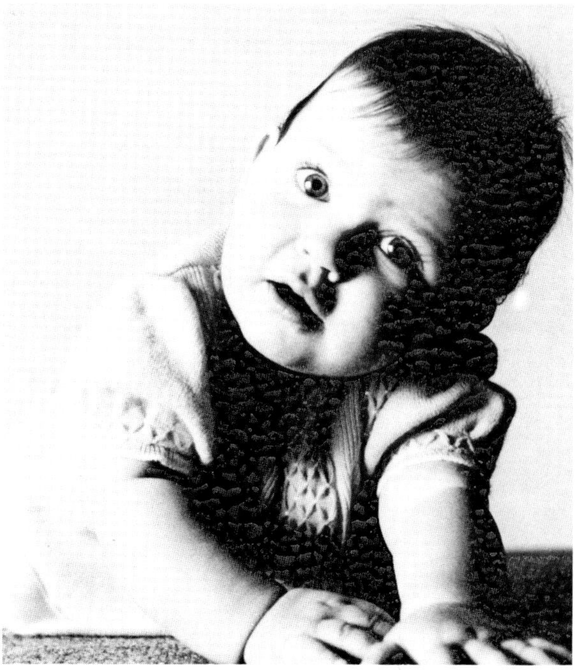

A single umbrella flash was used to take this photograph (left). The low camera angle gives the subject natural proportion. As a general rule, all small children should be photographed from their own level to avoid the effect of a big head on a small body.

This mother and child study (right) is typical of the results that can be achieved in the home studio using umbrella flash. The background was a roll of plain white paper, and one flash unit was used to light the subjects at an angle of 45°.

If, for example, the light is placed at an angle of 45°, a greater volume of light will fall on the nearer side of the face than on the other. For a more balanced light, a second umbrella can be used on the opposite side, either placed at a further distance or with lesser power. A third flash head can be used to illuminate the background, if required. Only the main flash is linked to the camera by the synchronization cable, the others being triggered remotely by means of a 'magic eye' or slave cell.

The set-up described here is very portable and easy to operate. It will produce professional-looking results from the start, although you will need to experiment a little in order to establish the best position for the lights for any particular effect. It is preferable to use computer-type flash units, but these must have detachable sensors, or ones that can swivel. On conventional computer units the sensor cell is positioned forward of the flash unit and would not work correctly with umbrellas.

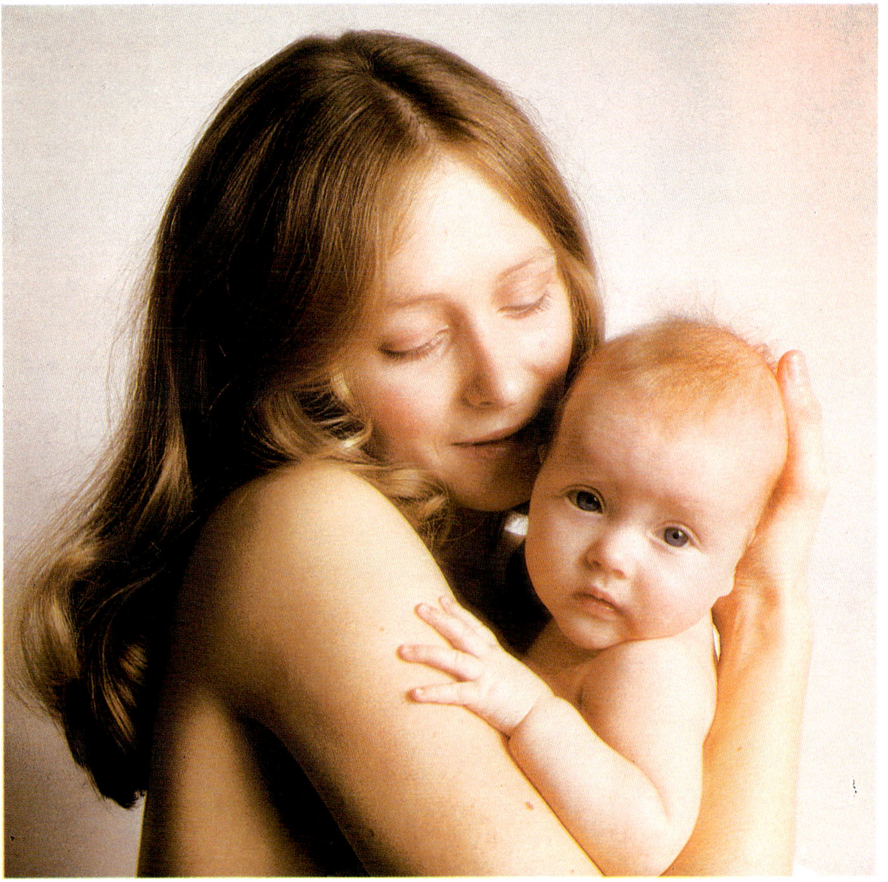

Photography Around the Home

The child photographer will find that there is no shortage of good material around the home, and that once he starts looking, even the most everyday activity can be turned into a stimulating and enjoyable photographic session for all concerned. Bathtime is just one possibility as young children in particular really enjoy the fun of splashing about in the bath, especially if there is enough foam and bubbles. There will be plenty of scope for many delightful pictures for the family album, starting with the first bathtime of a new baby. The bathroom is an ideal location for using bounce flash, as the room is usually small, with light-reflectant walls.

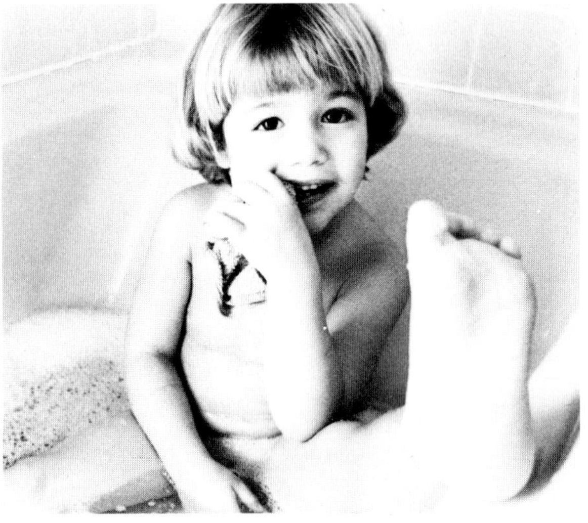

Young children are usually happy and relaxed at bathtime, which makes it ideal for photography as there will be plenty to keep them occupied (left above). Resist all attempts by the model to spray you and your camera with bathwater and do not use any form of mains lighting as this would be dangerous.

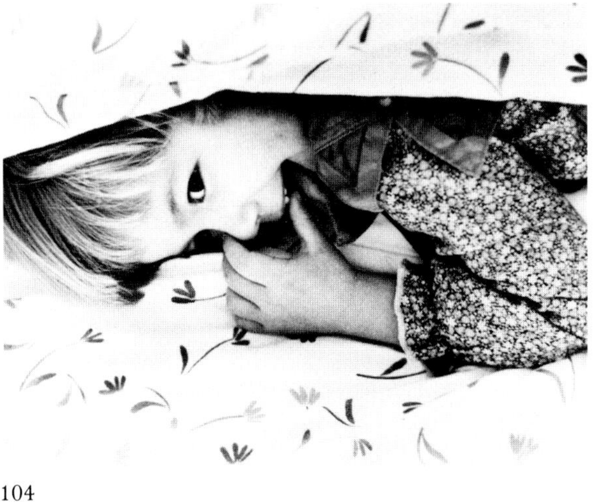

A game of peek-a-boo is a good way of making a child interested in a photographic session. In this case, the child hid under a duvet, and every time she lowered the cover and peeped out, a picture was taken (left below).

The bathroom is an ideal place for bounce flash photography as the room is usually quite small, with light-coloured, highly reflective walls (right). The bath itself also acts as an efficient reflecting medium.

The bathroom is of course only one example among countless others as entertaining and attractive pictures of children's fun and games can be taken all over the home, in every room. Children derive much fun from helping with household chores – baking, dusting, washing-up – all of which can provide charming shots. Photographs can be taken with or without the child's cooperation and knowledge, and the choice of lighting technique made on the spot according to the circumstances. If you want to take a portrait, very effective and subtle effects can be achieved by using window light, with a reflector to produce evenly balanced lighting (see page 99).

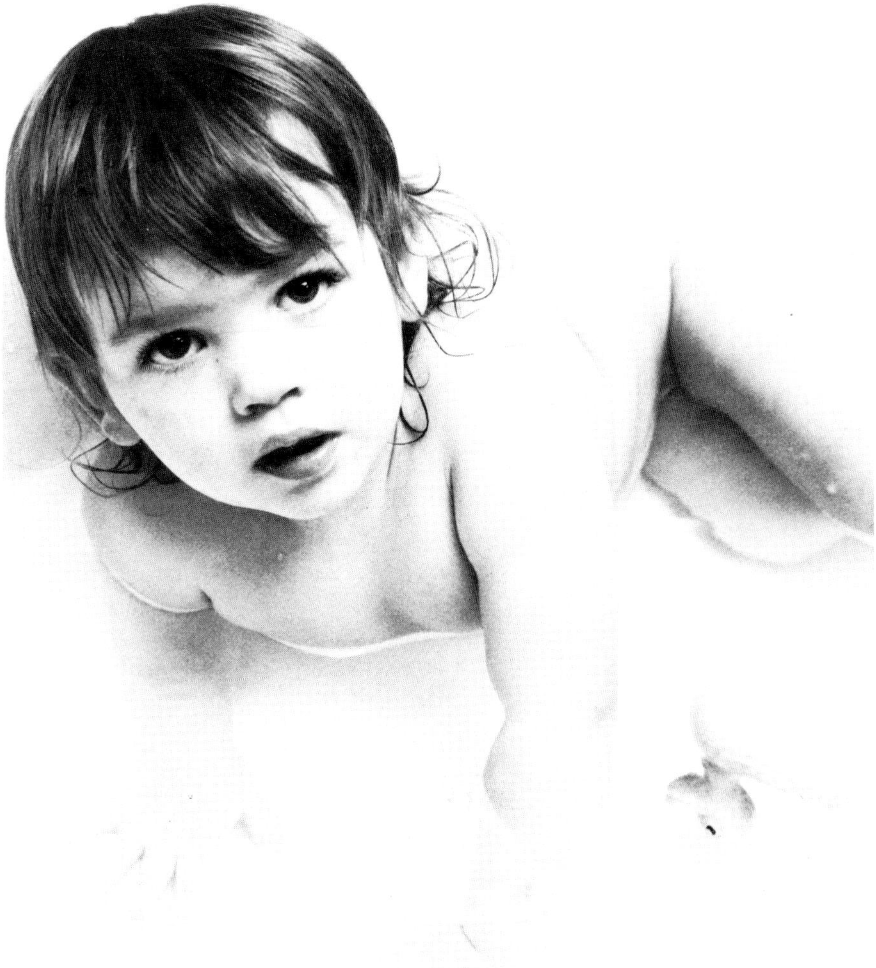

Photography Around the House 2

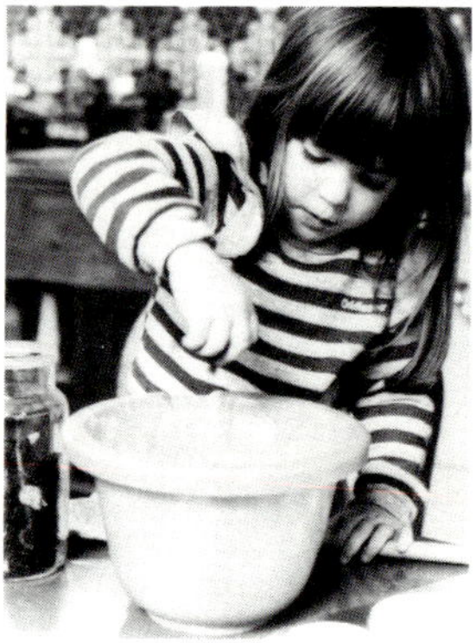

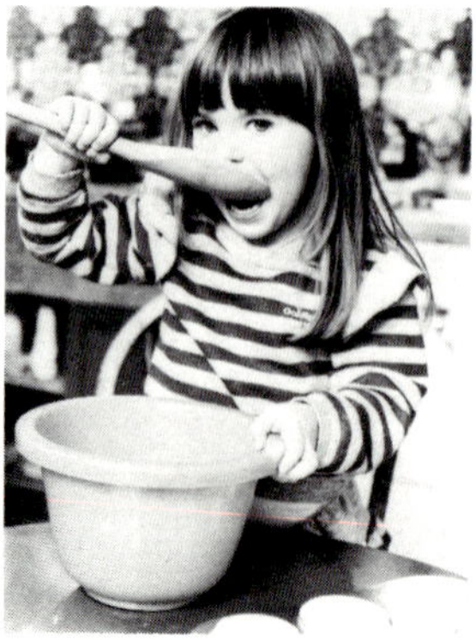

When a child is doing something of interest she will be much too busy to take any notice of the camera. This is a good ploy for taking natural pictures (left and far left).

The help of another person is invaluable in directing the subject's attention away from the camera (below).

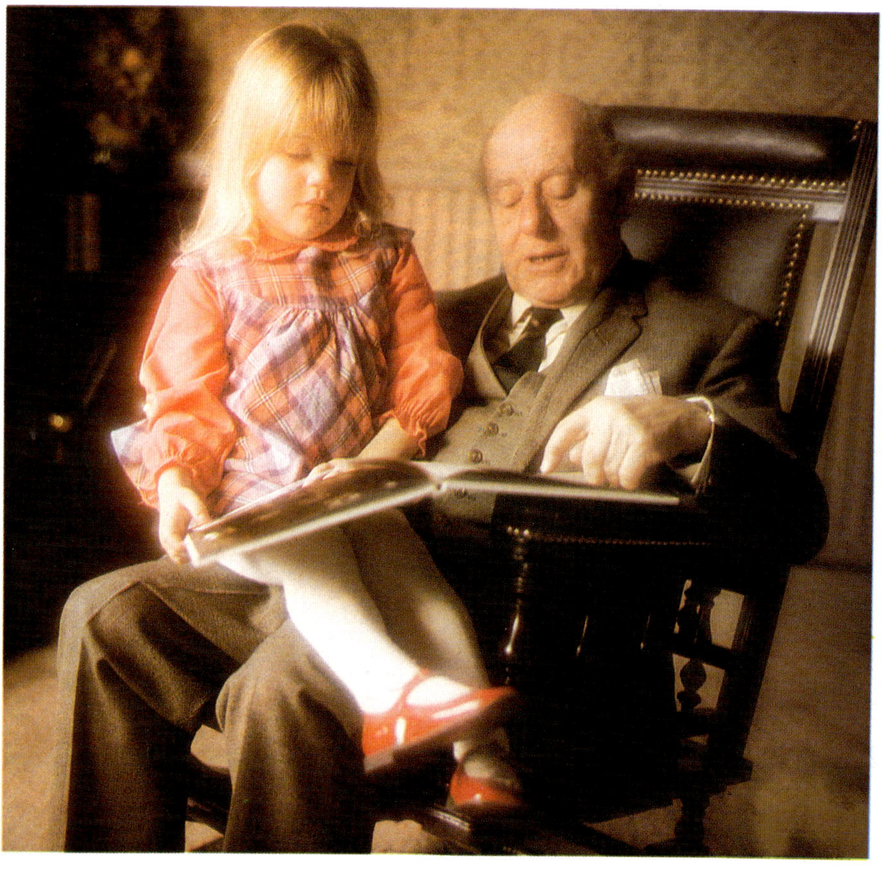

In this unconventionally framed portrait, the background wall and decoration have been used to locate the model, while at the same time giving the picture a feeling of light and space (right).

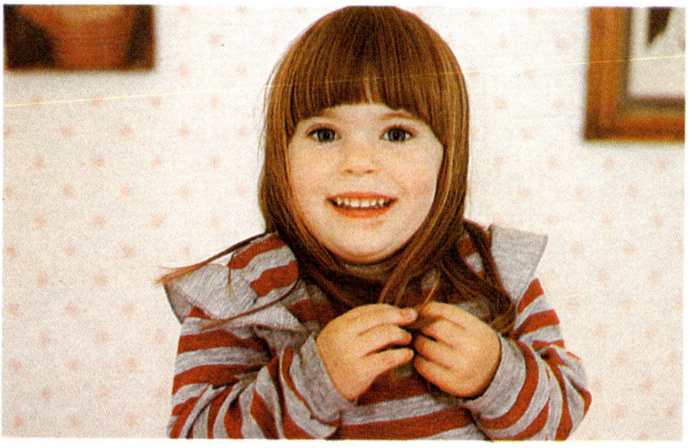

Shots of this nature must be seized when the opportunity arises, and use made of the ambient light (in this case daylight) if there is not time to fit a flash (right).

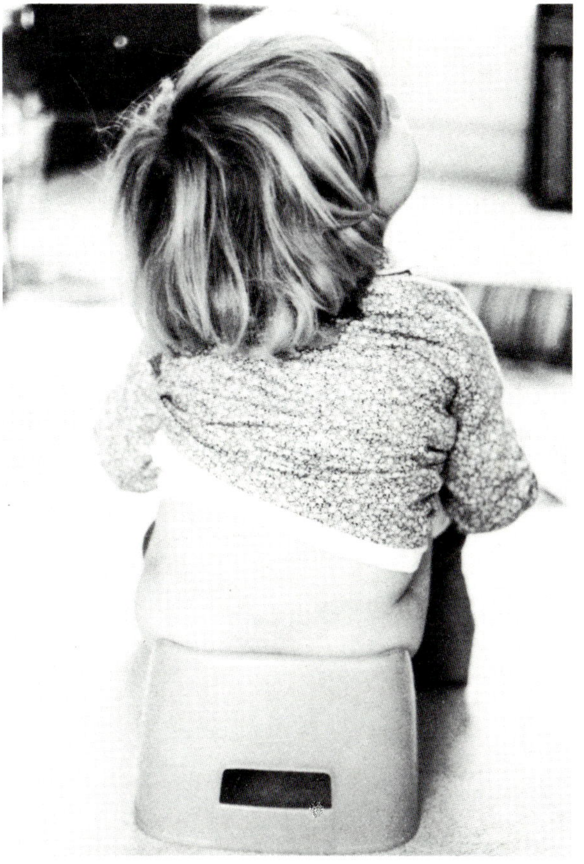

Whenever possible, choose a fully lit area when shooting close-ups as a fairly small aperture will be required to give good depth of field (below).

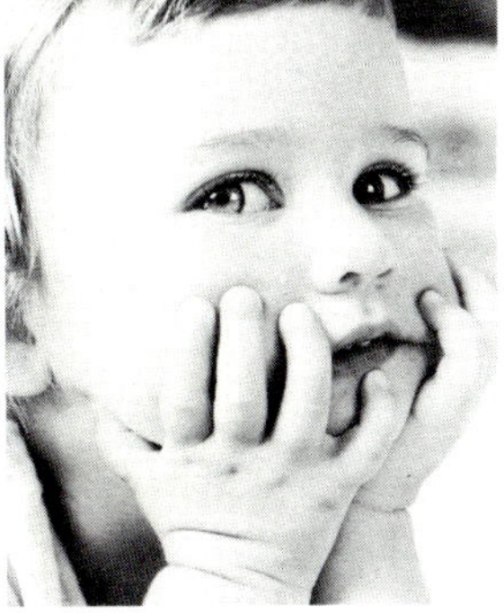

Equipment for Shooting Indoors

Although most cameras can be used indoors, with reasonable success, some types are better suited to this sort of work than others. Because most indoor photography, without flash, will be carried out in quite low lighting conditions, it is a good idea to use a camera which has a lens with a wide maximum aperture. It is also important that the camera should have an accurate focusing system, as most indoor subjects will be photographed at quite close distances. This is especially important when a lens is being used at or near its maximum aperture as depth of focus is much more critical in these circumstances.

The two types of camera which fulfil these particular criteria are the 35 mm SLR camera and the compact camera with automatic focusing. The SLR is probably the most suitable as the focusing system is extremely accurate and standard lenses with a very wide aperture are available. Another advantage is that a wide-angle lens can be fitted to the SLR, which is very useful for shooting indoors where condi-

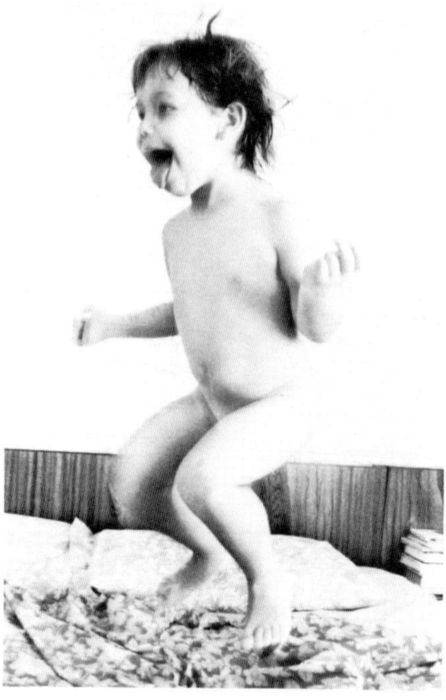

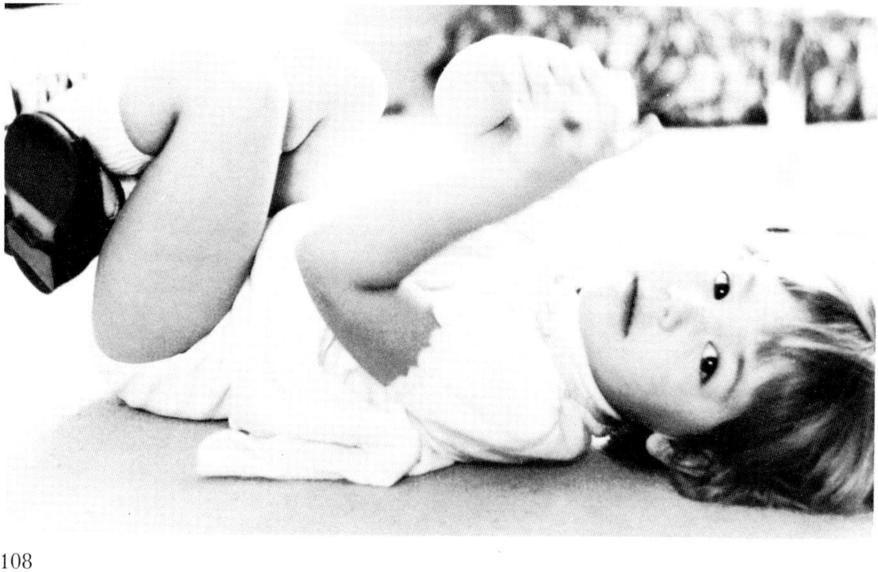

An auto-focus camera is ideal for shooting a moving subject indoors, when the direction of motion is unpredictable and depth of field will be fairly limited owing to the use of a wide aperture (left).

For stationary subjects such as this, slower shutter speeds can be selected, but the camera must be mounted on a tripod for steadiness (right).

Towards the centre of a room, window light loses intensity rapidly, necessitating the use of a fast lens at its widest aperture. A high-speed film would also be an advantage (below left).

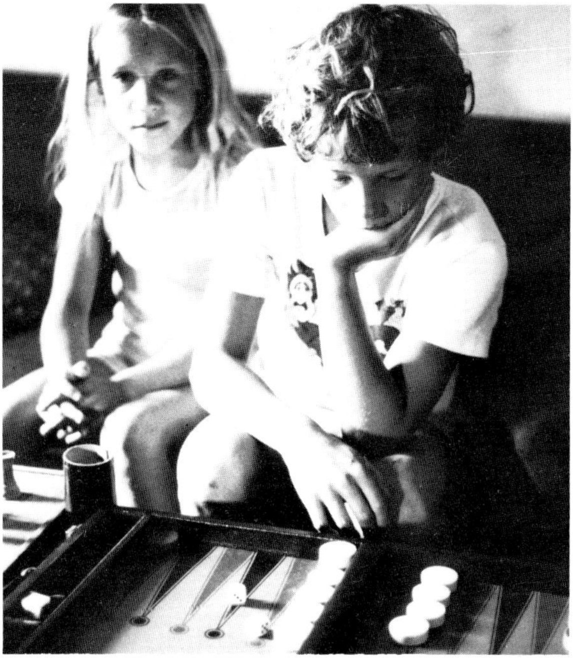

tions can be rather cramped. The compact camera also has the ability to focus with perfect precision, and as the system is automatic, this makes it ideal for use indoors when the light is low, when reflex focusing can be difficult. The lens of a compact camera usually has a quite wide maximum aperture and, with automatic focusing, can be used wide open with complete confidence. It is possible to take indoor shots with other types of cameras but, unless there is strong window light, they will be better suited to flash work.

The SLR is by far the best choice for use in a home studio. When shooting portraits at close distances, accurate framing of the subject in the viewfinder is very important, and this is most easily achieved on the focusing screen of a reflex camera. Another advantage of the SLR is that it can be fitted with a variety of lenses. A telephoto lens of medium focal length will be necessary in order to achieve the best perspective, and lenses of this type require critical focusing. In studio conditions it helps to use a tripod so that the photographer can concentrate his attention on the sitter and not be hampered by the weight of the camera and the lens. The use of a roll-film SLR or twin-lens reflex camera mounted on a tripod for easy handling will produce superb results in a home studio owing to the larger negative size and the high-quality lenses which they accommodate. The improved quality will only be noticeable, however, when prints of a considerable enlargement are made. For smaller prints, of album size, the improvement will not justify the significantly higher price of such equipment.

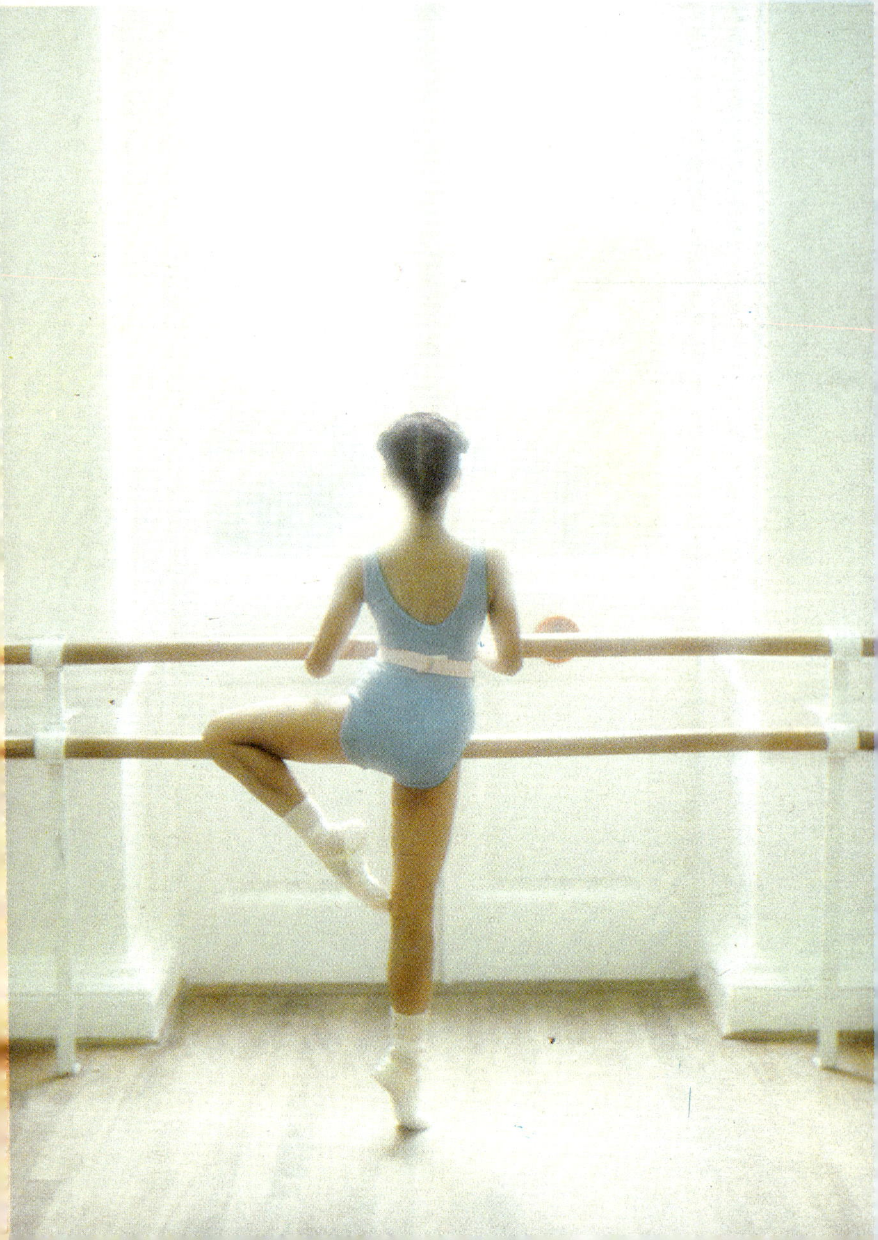

AVAILABLE LIGHT PHOTOGRAPHY

The term 'available light photography' is usually applied to situations where the photographer utilizes the light which already exists in a chosen location, irrespective of its suitability for photographic use. Furthermore, in most cases, the ambient light is of a fairly low level. Although from the technical aspect available light photography is sometimes problematical, its use is often essential in order to convey a particular mood or atmosphere. Exploited to its best advantage, as in the work of famous photographers such as Bill Brandt and W. Eugene Smith, it can produce results of almost theatrical drama and impact.

Modern high-speed films have made photography in low light conditions considerably easier, and there is the added possibility of 'pushing' the film at the processing stage to gain a further increase in sensitivity. Successful available light photography does not only require the use of a very fast film, it will also usually be necessary to use a camera lens with a wide maximum aperture. This means that a simple camera cannot be used for this type of work, even with the fastest film available. With a simple camera, flash must be utilized under low light conditions, which will destroy the mood conveyed by the existing source.

Because of the technical constraints, photographs taken by available light have a characteristic look or feeling about them. The results are necessarily grainy, because of the high-speed film, and also more contrasty, especially when push-processing has been used. Using a wide-aperture lens means that depth of field will be limited. For these reasons, photographs can sometimes have a rather 'raw' feeling, not always entirely suited to child subjects, where a certain delicacy of tone is preferred. Often, however, if it is a case of having a grainy picture or none at all, a photographer should not miss a potentially good shot for fear of technical shortcomings in the result.

Problems of Low Light Conditions

Shooting in low light brings the photographer up against almost every possible technical restriction, and when there is a degree of action involved, the problems are compounded. The first requirement for this type of photography is fast film, available for colour prints, colour transparencies and black-and-white. In all three types, a 400 ASA film gives a good compromise between speed and quality, and will be adequate in many situations. When the ambient light is particularly low, or when a considerable degree of movement is anticipated, a faster 1000 ASA type is more suitable. However, there will be an inevitable sacrifice in terms of grain and image resolution, further emphasized if the film is push-processed to provide even greater sensitivity. In available light photography there must always be a compromise between the need for a clear, sharp lens image and a technically acceptable film quality. Thanks to modern high-resolution film technology such a compromise is usually quite satisfactory.

The best lens for this type of work has a wide maximum aperture. A fast lens enables the use of higher shutter speeds, to lessen the possibility of subject or camera movement, but in certain situations a wide lens aperture and a slow shutter speed will have to be used together. In this case it is worth looking for some means of support for the camera, such as a chair back, low wall or pillar, on which the camera can be rested and steadied. Another possibility is to use a monopod, a collapsible one-legged support, to stabilize the camera. Obviously, when working from a fixed position, a standard tripod can be used to eliminate camera shake completely.

Subject movement is more of a problem, and under most conditions it is unlikely that a sufficiently high shutter speed can be used to freeze fast action. A panning or controlled blur technique must be used instead, unless it is possible to capture the movement at a near-stationary peak. To freeze action under adverse light conditions often requires push-processing of an extreme level, giving results which are technically unacceptable.

As regards the choice of lens, it should have a maximum aperture of at least f2.8. On cameras with an interchangeable lens facility and a range of lenses, the standard

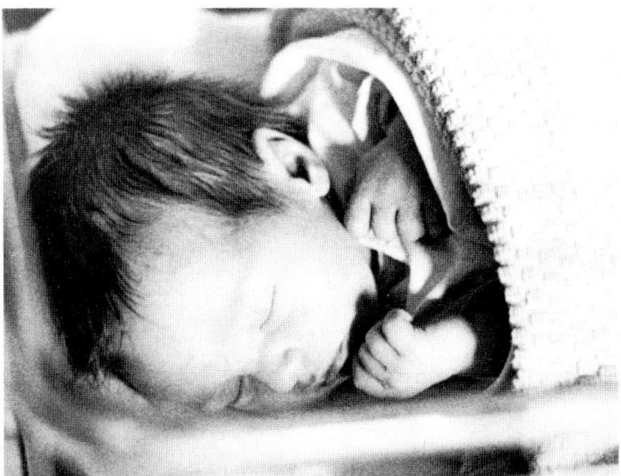

The very first picture of a newborn baby will be taken by available light, probably in a hospital or nursing-home. Because flash will not be permitted, a fast film must be used to cope with the subdued lighting of the nursery (left).

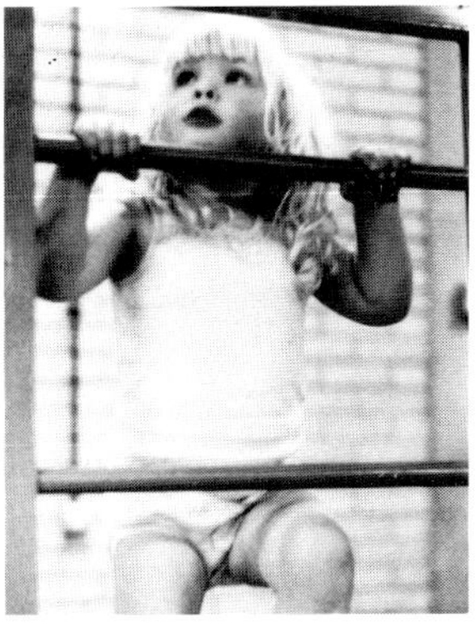

When shooting under very low light conditions, such as this indoor playroom, a certain loss of technical quality must be tolerated in order to get a photograph at all (above).

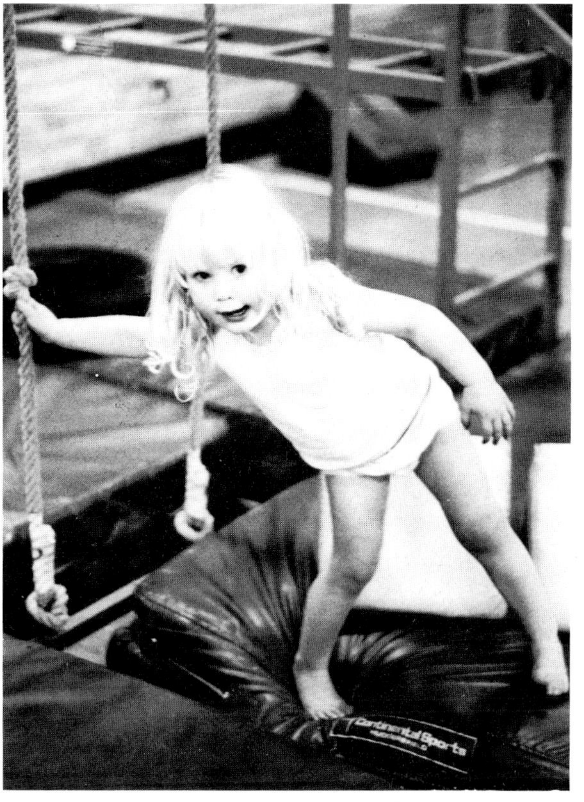

Focusing is most critical under low lighting conditions, as the lens will often be used wide open and depth of field will therefore be very limited (right).

lens will have a wider maximum aperture than most accessory lenses. Zoom lenses especially have a fairly modest maximum aperture and are therefore often not suited to shooting in available light. By comparison, many standard lenses have an aperture of at least f2 and are often as fast as f1.2, eight times faster than a normal zoom lens. For this reason, a standard lens is the most suitable type for low light conditions. When a telephoto effect is required, it is often better to use a small section of a negative taken with a standard lens, as opposed to using a longer, slower lens and risking both camera and subject movement. Because lenses will be used at a wide aperture, depth of field will be limited, and focusing must be carried out with great accuracy.

Child photography in available light encompasses many activities: at school in plays, concerts, indoor sport, and out of school at dancing lessons and the gymnasium. There are many occasions when younger children will be photographed in less than ideal lighting conditions, the very first possibly when your baby is just a few hours old in the hospital nursery, where flash is not allowed, and the lighting is of necessity subdued.

The Ballet Class

A ballet class is a good example of a subject which, by virtue of its particular atmosphere or style, lends itself to the technique of available light photography. The combination of low light levels inside the studios and the problems involved in photographing the dancers in motion provides a challenging exercise in both skill and imagination. The series of pictures shown here illustrate the effects which can be obtained by the use of high-speed films in conjunction with push-processing, a range of lenses and varying shutter speeds, to produce successful images.

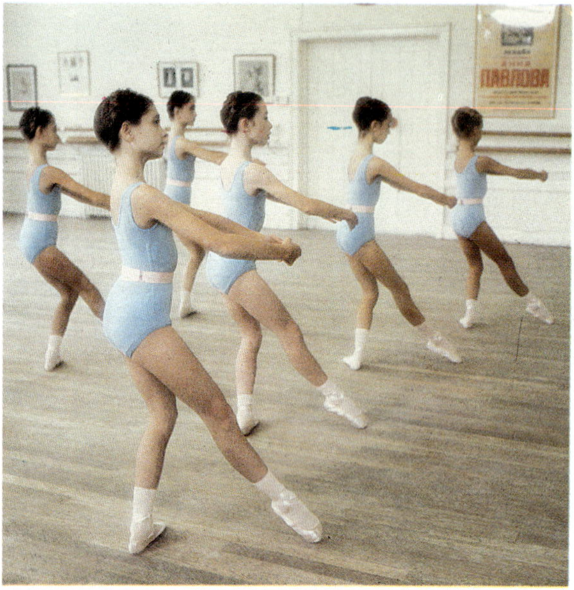

Ektachrome 400 film, pushed to a speed of 800 ASA, was used for these pictures of a ballet class. They were taken with a hand-held Hasselblad roll-film reflex camera, fitted with an electric motor for ease of use. The ambient light from the window of the dance studio was the only source of illumination (left).

Most of the exposures were made at the relatively slow speed of 1/60 sec, at or near maximum lens aperture. To resolve the problem of subject movement, the exposure was made at the peak of the action, with the limbs fully extended but momentarily stationary (right).

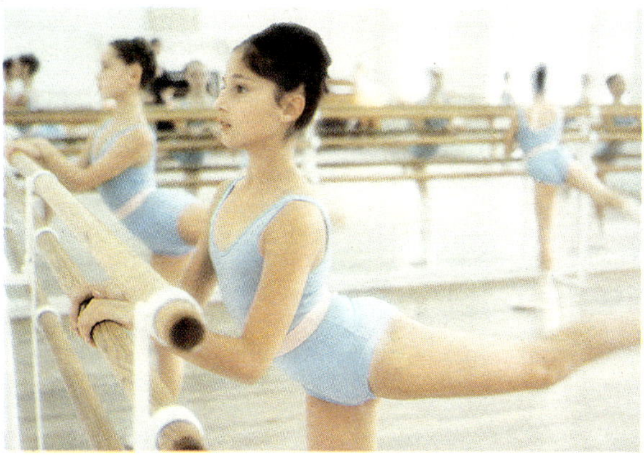

To portray the dancers in a gentle manner and also as a means of keeping the over-all contrast down, a Softar diffuser was used over the camera lens (left).

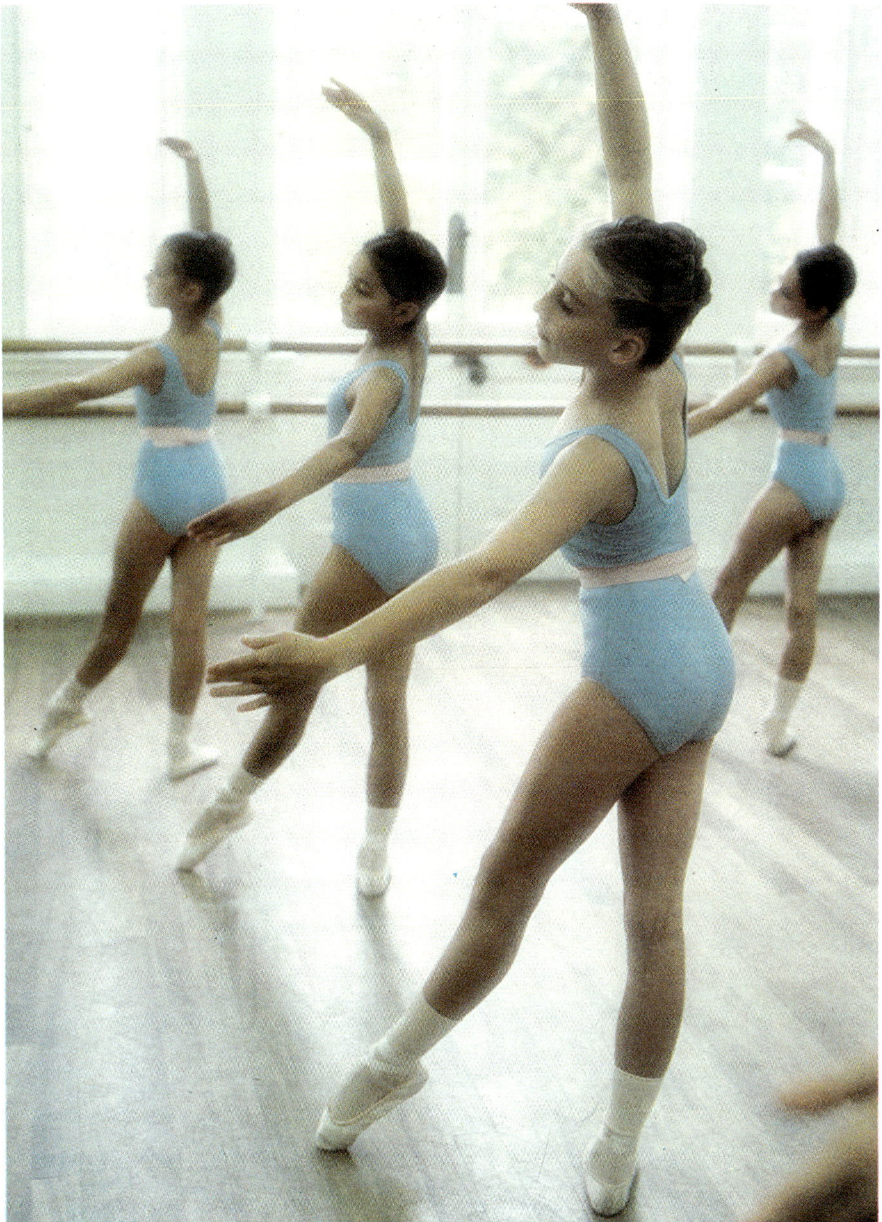

The Ballet Class 2

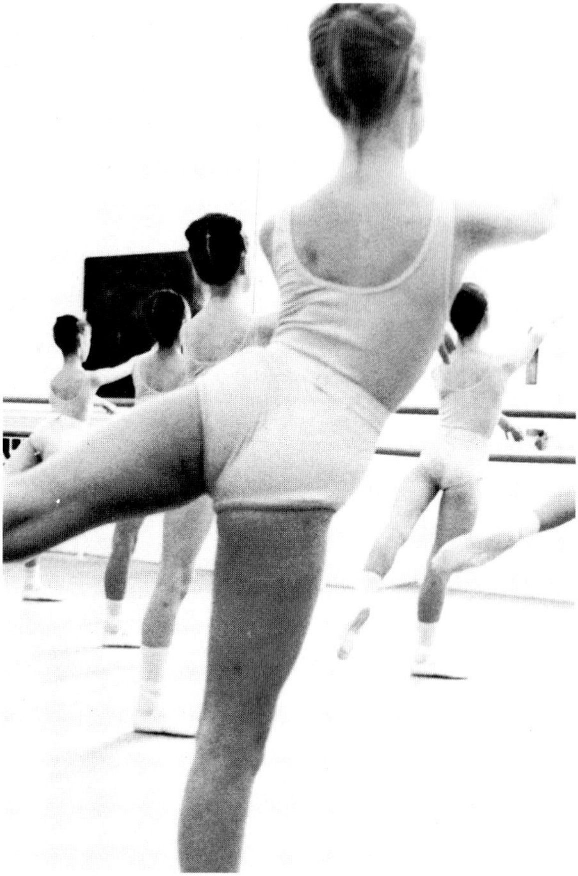

The black-and-white photographs on these pages were taken on Kodak Tri-X film, pushed to 800 ASA, matching the colour materials. By using a 400 ASA film and extending the development time, the extra sensitivity was achieved without undue increase in grain or contrast.

By using a 35–70 mm zoom lens, a range of angles and perspectives were obtained without having to make frequent lens changes, allowing wide-angle shots and medium close-ups to be taken from the same camera position. When it was not possible to shoot at the peak of action, the medium shutter speed registered motion in the form of a slight blur, just enough to give the impression of movement.

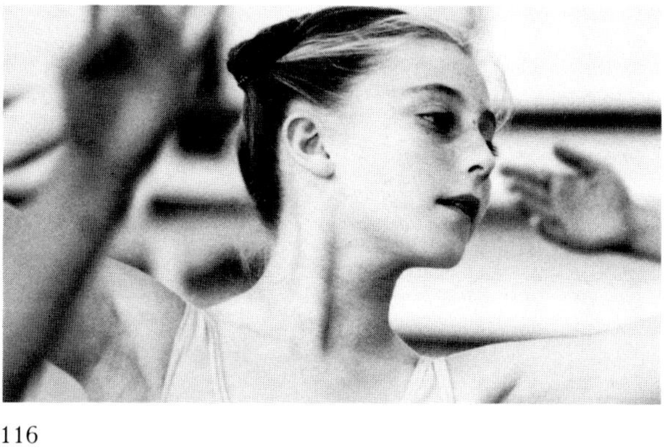

As the outside light was changing constantly during the session, the light level had to be monitored regularly, and this was done with the TTL metering system of the camera.

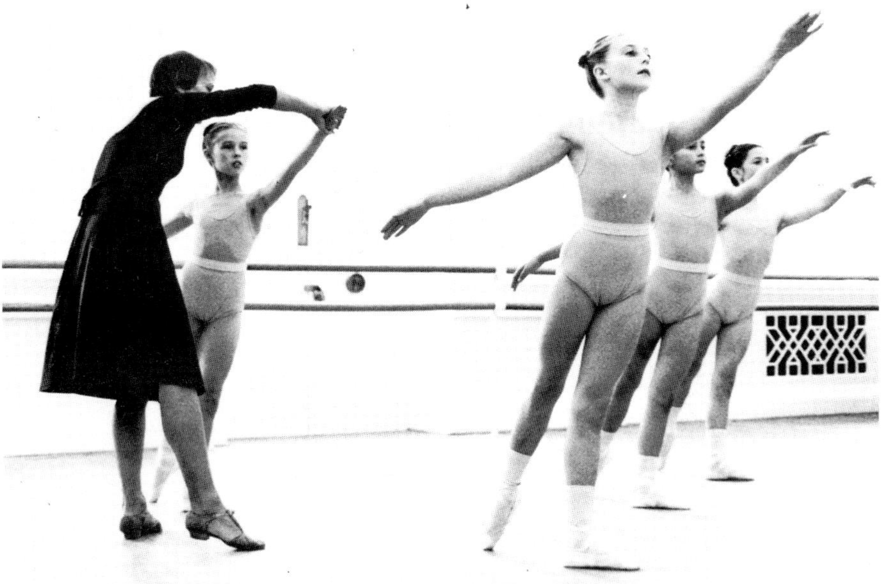

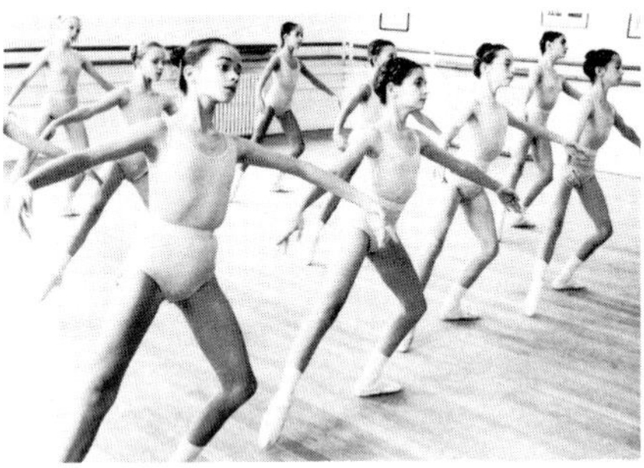

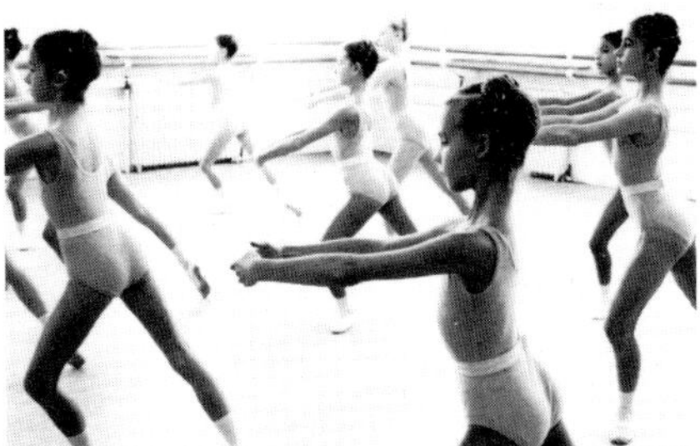

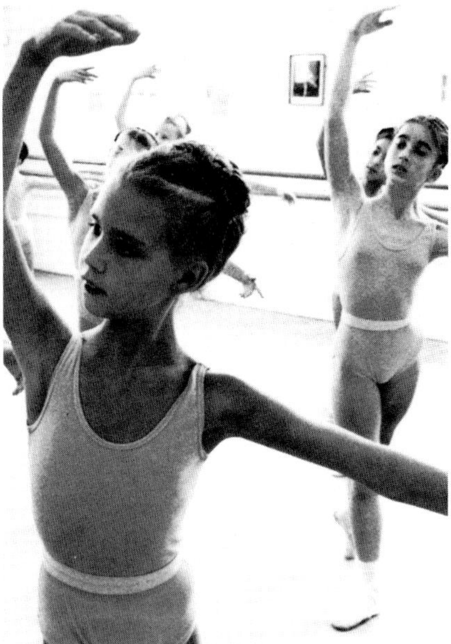

A Birthday Party

A birthday party is an event which every parent photographer will want to record for the family album, and this can often be done with good results in a very natural way by using available light rather than the more usual flash. It is a good idea to check the lighting level in the room where the party is going to be held before the event takes place. Take a meter reading of the light at the appropriate time of day, and if the level seems to be sufficient, then all should be well. If you have any doubts

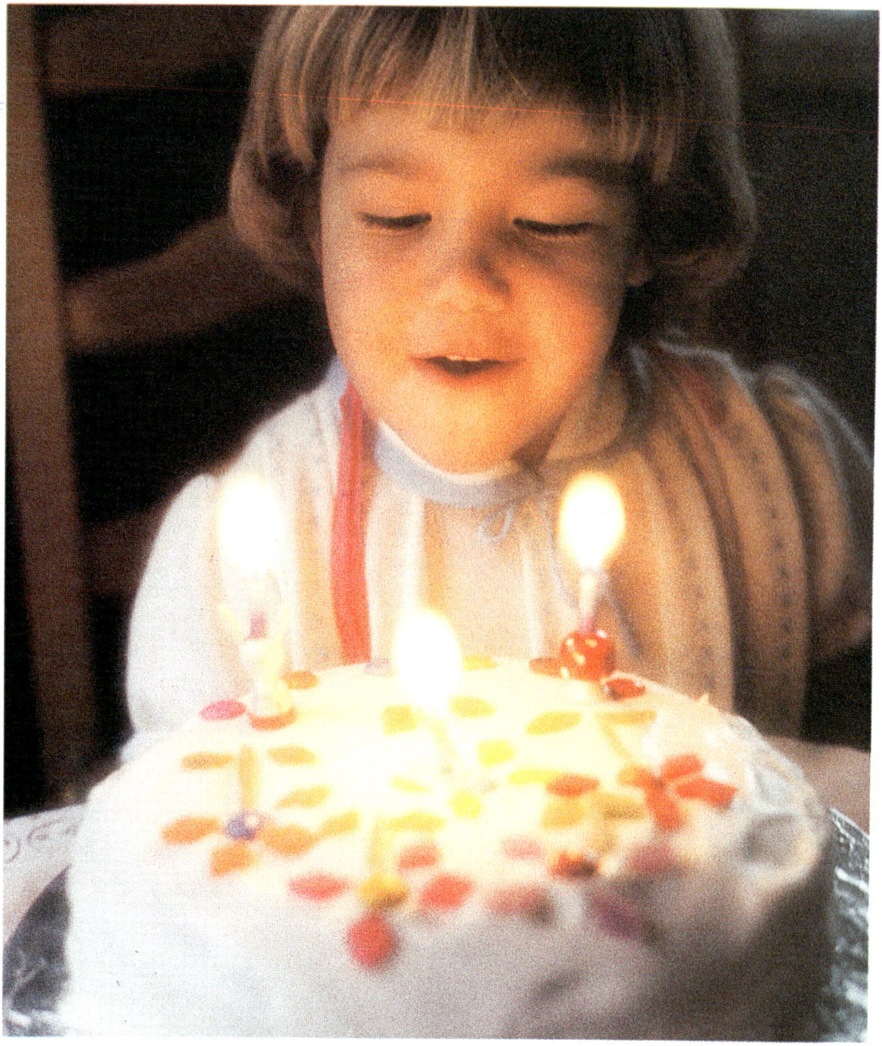

Whenever possible, it is best to take a wide-angle view of the assembled birthday party, including all the guests. In this way a complete record of the memorable day can be made in one shot, with the birthday girl or boy prominent in the picture (right).

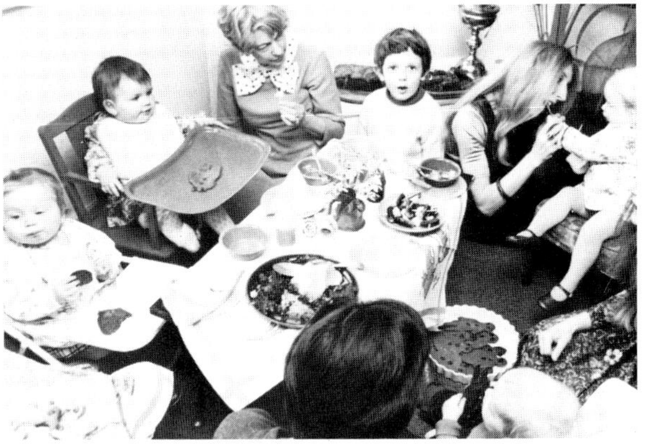

A picture of the birthday cake is an essential for every album (left). Try if possible to shoot the scene using only the light from the candles. This can be done by using a fast film, in this case 3M's 1000 Reversal. Flash will kill the magical light from the candles, destroying the feeling of the picture.

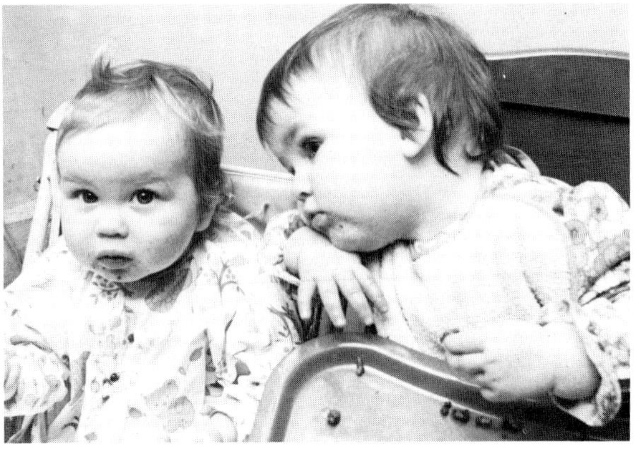

Having taken a general view of the proceedings, concentrate on shots of individual children or groups of children (right). Try to catch them spontaneously and unaware of the camera, and looking as though they are having a good time.

about the intensity of the light, even when using a fast film, then it would be better to play safe and use a bounce flash technique instead.

Parties for very young children are usually fairly static affairs, with the main activities being eating, drinking and tearing open the presents. As children grow, however, parties become more and more active, culminating in the teenage discos. If there are going to be organized games, a certain amount of action and movement must be expected, offering great scope for entertaining pictures.

For most parents, the photographic high spot will be the birthday tea-party itself, and above all the activity around the cake. The child's face behind the candles is an ideal subject for the available light technique, and there will be enough light from the candles alone to record the scene on a fast film. Use of flash would destroy the soft light from the candles, and even cause the flames themselves to vanish. Obviously, the level of illumination from the cake will depend on the age of the birthday child: the more candles on the cake, the easier the task of the photographer.

Indoor Sports and Special Events

Most indoor activities involving children can be recorded by available light, including active sports and events such as school concerts and plays. In most cases, the illumination will be provided by artificial light, and for a natural rendering when shooting in colour, film balanced for an artificial light source must be used. In the case of sporting activities there will rarely be sufficient illumination to freeze the action, so either a panning effect or controlled blur technique will have to be used instead. Even with the fastest film types of 1000 ASA and more, it is unlikely that a shutter speed shorter than 1/125 sec will be possible.

In many instances, the artificial light which is set up for theatrical or sporting events is patchy and varies in intensity over relatively small areas. For this reason, it is preferable to use a camera with a through-the-lens (TTL) metering system, as the intensity of the light can be measured within the precise area of the camera's field of view.

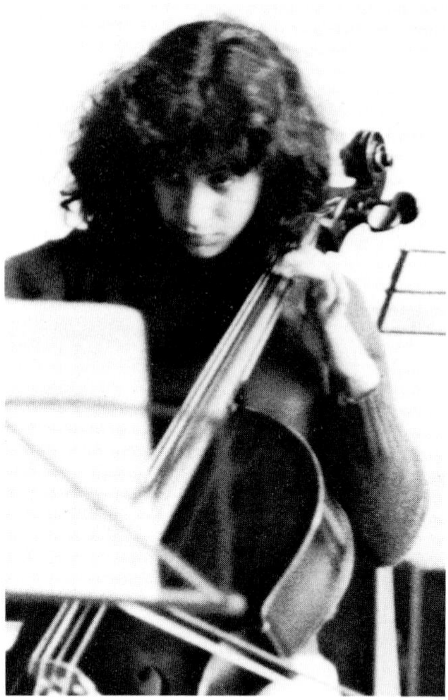

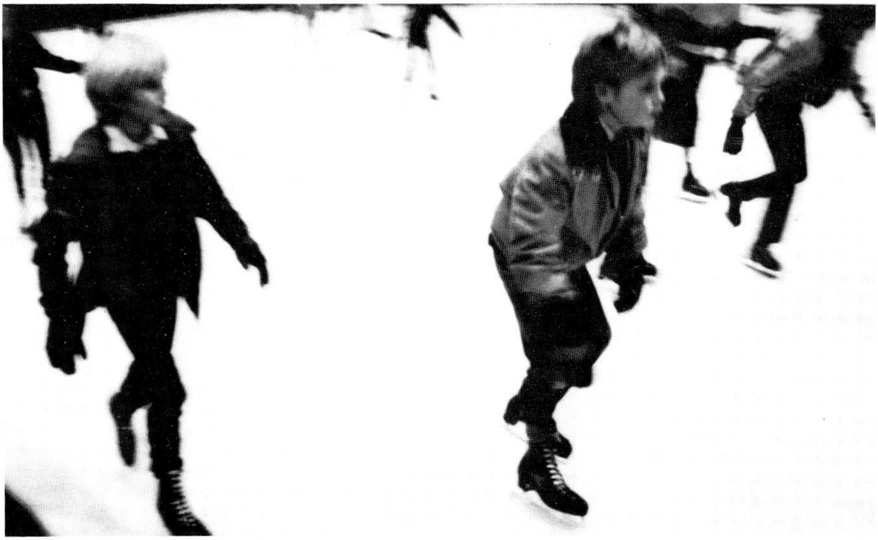

A school concert will often take place in very dim lighting, and even with a very fast film and a wide-aperture lens the exposure will be near the limits for subject movement (left). On these occasions, a certain loss of quality is inevitable, which is better, however, than no picture at all.

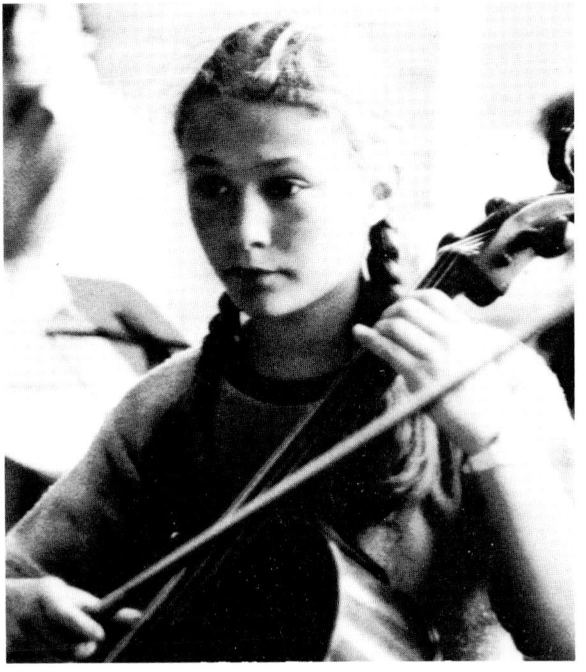

Taken under the same conditions as the photograph opposite, the appeal of the subject and the effect of natural lighting make up for the loss of technical quality (right). A sharper result would have been achieved using flash but the atmosphere would have been lost.

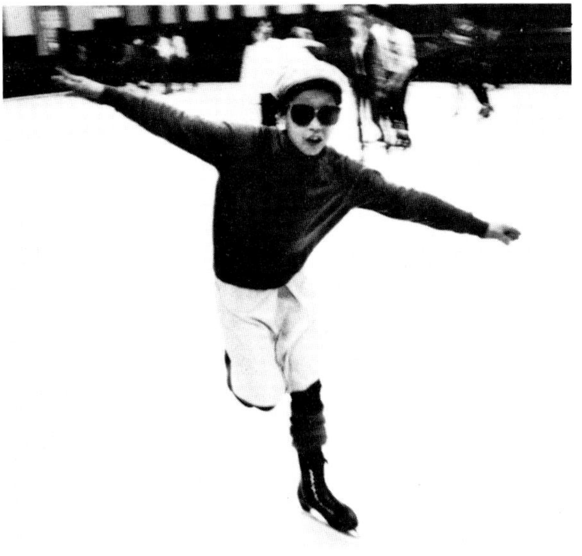

Photographs in indoor skating rinks are very difficult to take as there is a lot of action and usually very little light. Without using flash, the only technique that will capture the feeling of motion is a panning or controlled blur method (left). If it is possible to utilize a speed of 1/125 sec or faster then the freezing technique can be attempted and this will be considerably easier when the action moves towards the camera (right).

Indoor Sports and Special Events 2

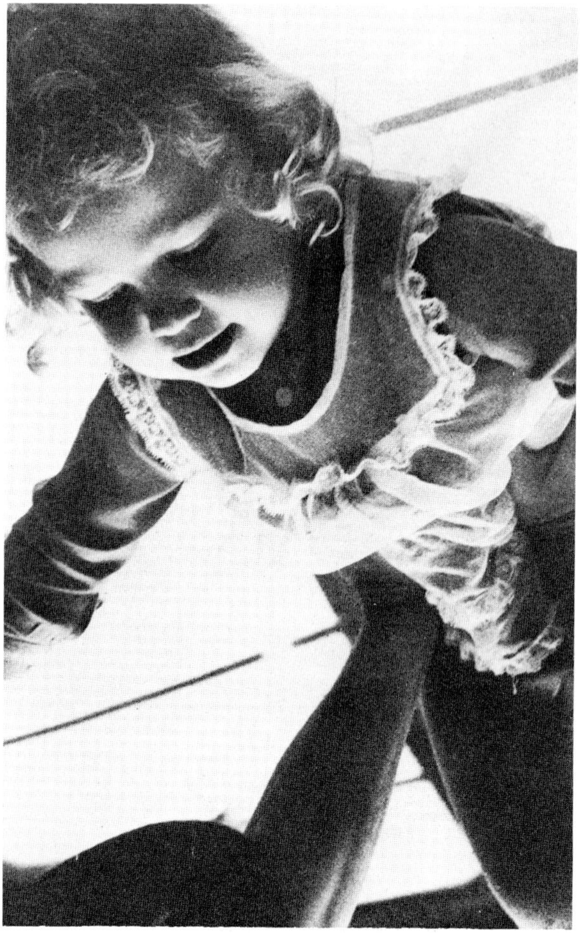

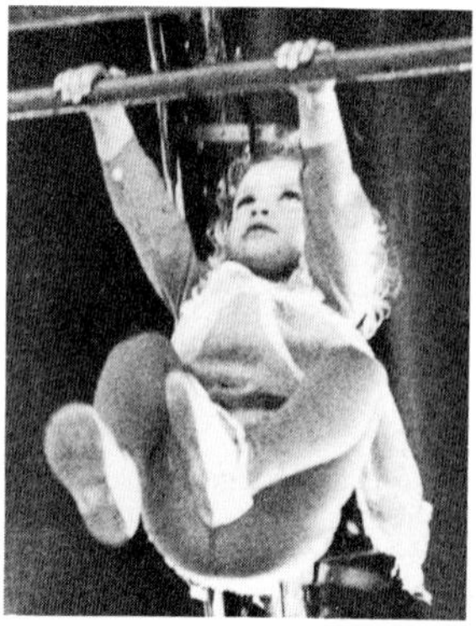

The motion of this young trapeze artist was caught at the height of her swing to avoid blur at a slow shutter speed (above).

When shooting indoors by artificial light, a film balanced for electric light must be used (right). A daylight material would give a yellow colour cast under such conditions.

Taken with a very fast film, Royal-X Pan, this shot of the circus child learning the art of trapeze was photographed solely by the daylight penetrating the canvas of the big top (left).

It is important to remember that working with available light often results in a photographic image which is technically less than perfect. Very few pictures taken under such conditions are perfectly sharp, for example, but the sacrifices made in terms of definition and tonal scale are more than offset by the increased feeling of atmosphere and realism present in the photograph.

Many of the most dramatic and classic photographs taken under poor light conditions would make a photographic perfectionist gasp with dismay when looked at purely from a technical standpoint, yet these images are incredibly powerful and capture fully the feeling of a particular happening or occasion. In many situations it is well worth risking a shot, knowing that technically it will be less than perfect.

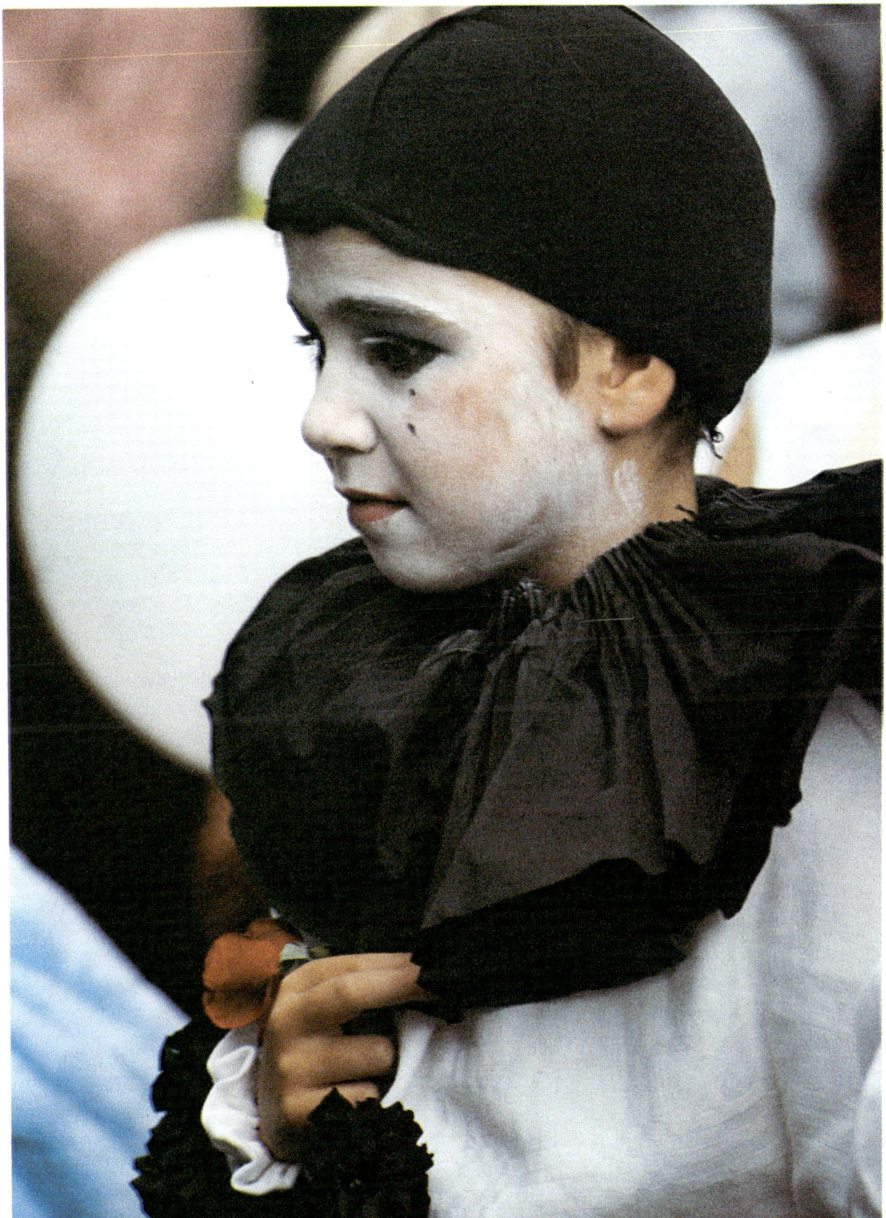

High-speed Films

A high-speed film is essential for available light work. Fast films are produced in two main groups, 400 ASA and 1000 ASA. The first group of 400 ASA films is particularly useful as they are also suited to everyday photography under all types of lighting conditions. Although these films are grainier than medium-speed films of, say, 100 ASA, their quality is still very good, and under medium magnifications results will be almost indistinguishable from those of the slower type. The films are available in both colour and black-and-white emulsions, and all types can be push-processed to two or three times their rated speed, by extended development or special processing techniques. However, the results of push-processing will not always compare favourably with the use of a higher-speed film processed normally.

There are several daylight-type colour transparency films available at this speed, such as Kodak Ektachrome 400, and almost all laboratories will push-process the film by 1, 2 or 3 stops if required. There is only one film type balanced for tungsten light, 3M's Reversal 640T, with a nominal rating of 640 ASA. All the major manufacturers produce colour negative film in this range; their speed can be uprated by push-processing, but very few laboratories are prepared to do this, and it is usually considered to be a technique for the home processor. There is a danger of distorted colour values when colour negative film is greatly uprated.

Several black-and-white films have a rating of 400 ASA. The speed can be doubled by extending the development time, in a normal process, and it can be further increased by the use of special developers. However, such treatment will often boost the levels of contrast and grain. Two special variable-speed films are available, Ilford XP1 and Agfapan Vario-XL, which can be used at between 125 and 800 ASA according to the particular requirements of the individual photographer. These two films use a special developing technique, similar to a colour negative process, in which the final negative image consists of photographic dye instead of developed silver. The grain and tonal range of these films are considerably better than those of conventional materials rated at comparable speeds.

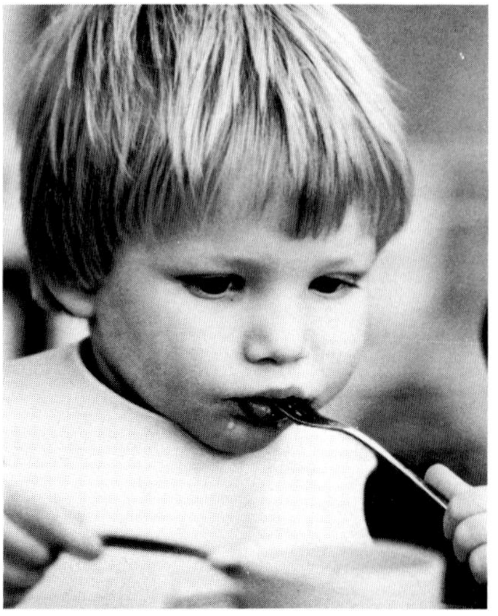

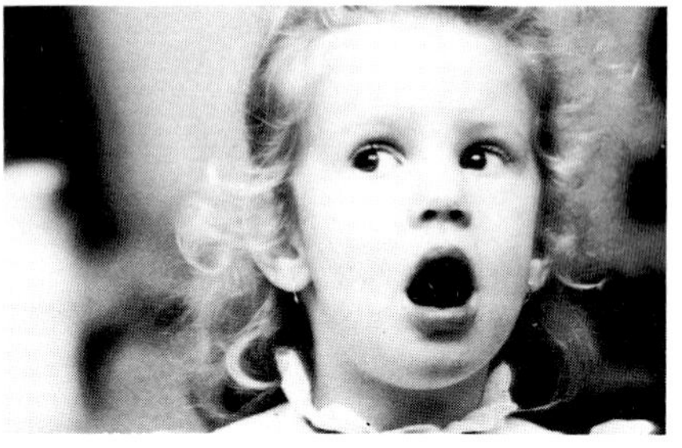

The second group of 1000 ASA films is designed exclusively for use in very low light conditions, and are not generally suitable for normal circumstances except for special effect. These materials are grainy,

Even when using the fastest film materials, depth of field will often be very restricted in available light situations. This is often advantageous, however, as it lifts the subject-matter away from the background (left).

Artificial lighting used for theatrical events is often very harsh and patchy. When photographing in such a situation look for a part of the stage where the light is relatively soft and even (right).

Activities such as carol singing frequently take place under very dark conditions. A slow speed must often be used and, to avoid facial movement, the exposure must be made at the peak of the action – in this case with the singer's mouth wide open (left).

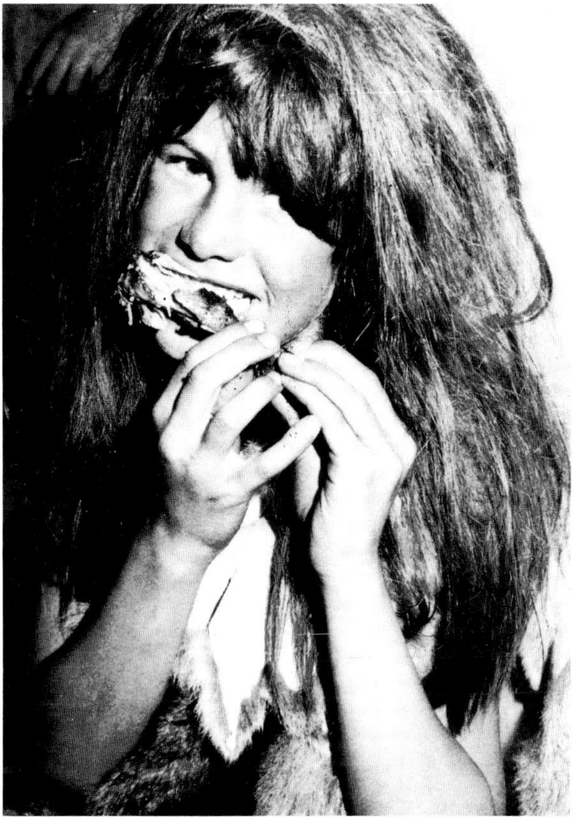

but when required this characteristic can be exploited. Very fast films also have poor resolution, being incapable of recording very fine detail. However, recent developments, especially in colour negative films, have brought great improvements. Emulsions utilizing innovations in silver crystal technology are capable of results comparable to earlier 400 ASA materials. These very fast films are sufficiently sensitive for most applications, used normally, but when a loss of quality can be tolerated, they can be uprated to at least twice their nominal speed by special processing.

The choice of materials is more restricted in this group. 3M's 1000 ASA colour reversal film is balanced for daylight, but there is no direct tungsten equivalent, although 3M's 640T film can be push-processed to at least 1300 ASA. The only colour negative film at this speed is Kodak's new Kodacolor VR 1000. Two black-and-white films are available, both from Kodak: Royal-X Pan (1250 ASA) and Recording Film 2475 (1000–4000 ASA). Films of such extremely high speeds tend to be very grainy indeed, and produce results of a very distinctive tonal nature.

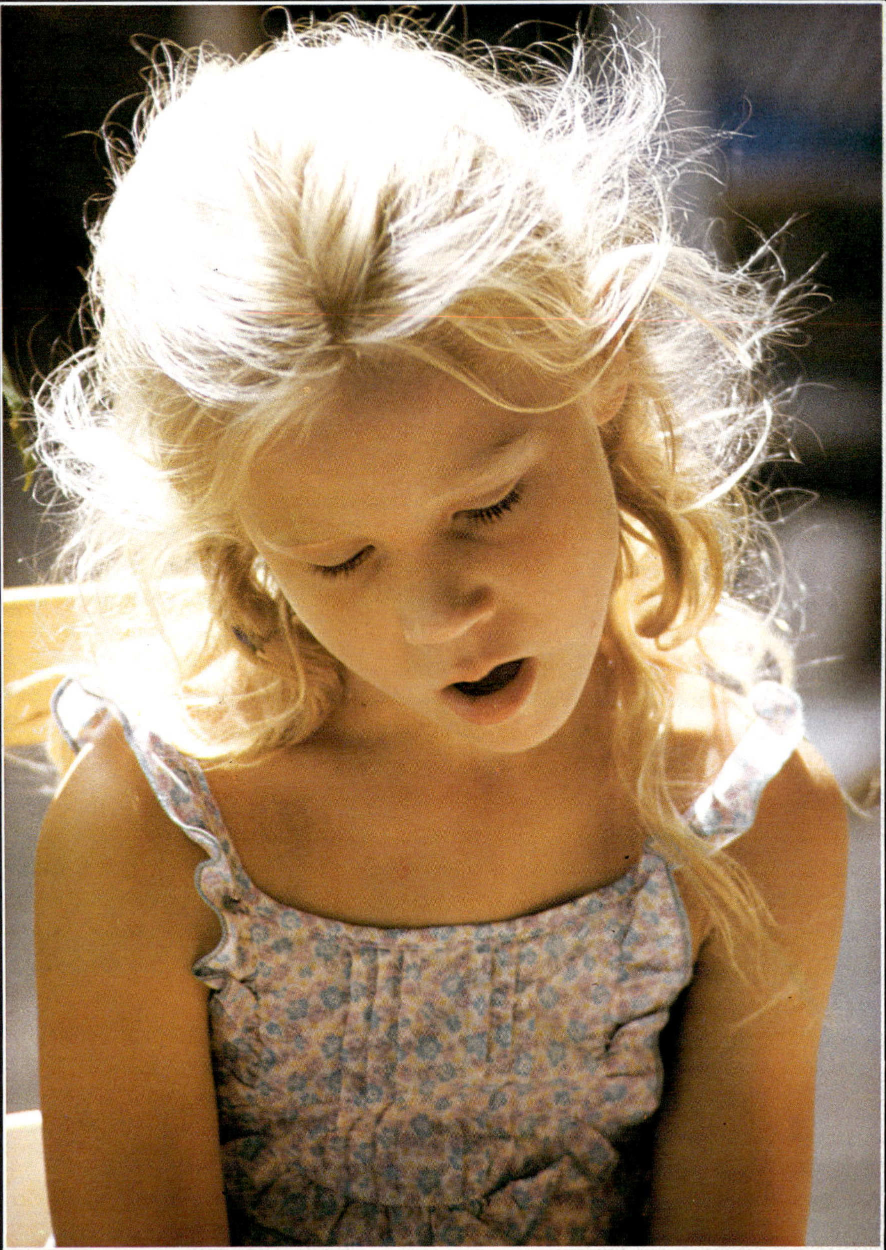

EXPOSURE

Exposure calculation plays an important part in the success or failure of a photographic image. 'Correct exposure' means the admittance of a measured and controlled quantity of light to the film in the camera, sufficient to record all tones in a subject to a required level. Exposure is controlled in two ways, by the lens aperture which regulates the amount of light received by the film, and by the shutter speed which controls the length of time that the film receives this light.

Lens apertures are calibrated in f-stops, calculated by dividing the focal length of the lens by the diameter of the aperture. The smaller the f-number, the more light is admitted through the lens. Shutter speeds are expressed in seconds or fractions of a second. For example, 1/1000 sec is a short exposure and is known as a fast speed, while 1/15 sec is a long exposure and is known as a slow speed. Exposures of longer than one second are usually referred to as time exposures.

When calculating exposure, the sensitivity or speed of the film in use must also be considered. All film has a speed rating, denoted by a numbered scale; the most widely used scale is the ASA (American Standards Association) system. In order to determine correct exposure relative to the speed of the film in use, some kind of measuring device is required to establish the quantity of light reflected from the subject. Most modern cameras have an exposure meter incorporated in the design, though separate, hand-held meters are also available. When a correct exposure level has been established, a suitable shutter speed and lens aperture can be chosen according to the requirements of the subject-matter. For instance, an action subject will require a fast shutter speed, and a relatively large aperture to compensate. In the same way, when a small aperture is selected, a slow shutter speed will be necessary in order to bring the exposure level up to the requirement of the film.

Correct Exposure

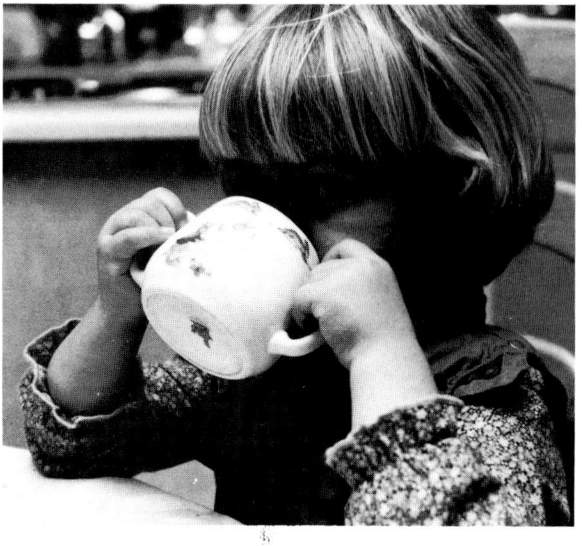

When insufficient light is allowed to register on the film during exposure, the resultant negative or transparency is under-exposed. When this occurs, the shadow areas and dark tones will merely become dense masses, with little or no detail. In this example of under-exposure, only the lightest part of the picture, the child's mug, can be considered to have received sufficient exposure (left).

'Correct exposure' is normally considered to be the minimum level required to record detail in the shadow areas of a subject. Most modern cameras incorporate some form of metering system to evaluate correct exposure, and owners of such equipment can expect a high proportion of adequately exposed photographs. Some situations, however, will be beyond the ability of a built-in meter, and certain manual adjustments must be made. There are various types of automatic exposure meter, and some give more control over the selected exposure than others.

Very simple cameras have no exposure control at all and work at a combined fixed aperture and speed, usually about 1/60 sec at f11. Cameras of this type rely upon the latitude of the film – its ability to tolerate over- and under-exposure – to produce a result of reasonable quality under fairly good weather conditions. Some simple cameras have a choice of lens aperture, for cloudy-bright or sunny conditions, thus extending their range slightly.

More sophisticated inexpensive cameras, including some 35 mm compacts, have an automatic system where the apparatus selects a shutter speed and aperture combination suited to the conditions; on these models, a red indicator light shows when there is insufficient light. The major disadvantage of these cameras is that although they are much more flexible, the photographer cannot select a particular speed or aperture for a specific purpose, such as photographing movement or gaining maximum depth of field.

The best form of exposure control is a manual metering system; this enables the photographer to select either the speed or aperture he desires, and manipulate the opposite control until a signal informs him that the correct exposure combination has been achieved. Two alternative, more convenient forms of this system are the shutter-priority and aperture-priority methods. In these, when the chosen shutter speed or aperture is selected, the meter will indicate on a viewing screen the com-

When a photograph receives too much exposure, the lighter tones of the subject will build up into a maximum white tone, devoid of detail. When this occurs, the print transparency is described as 'burnt out'. Unless the picture is very over-exposed, the shadow areas will remain fully detailed. In this example, the child's face is burnt out, and matches and blends with the light background (right).

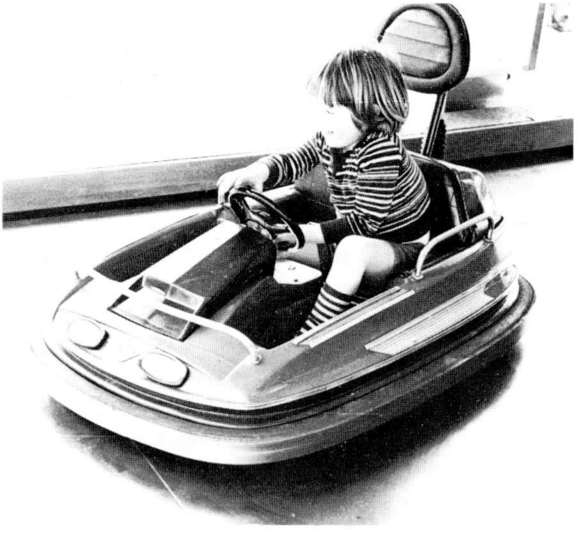

patible exposure computed by the camera. This means that the photographer is able to control one element of the exposure, and knows whether the total exposure value is suitable for his subject. Some types of more sophisticated SLRs incorporate an exposure system with manual metering and one or both of the priority systems, which gives great flexibility.

The most accurate method of measuring exposure is probably the use of a separate hand-held meter. Many cameras for professional use have no integral light-metering system, as the manufacturers know that the photographer is likely to use a separate meter. A hand-held meter allows reflected light readings to be taken from all parts of a subject and an average value calculated; this gives an accurate measurement, satisfying all aspects of the subject. An alternative method using a hand meter is to use an invercone, a white, dome-shaped diffusor, over the sensor of the instrument. The meter is then placed in the subject position, pointing towards the light source. This allows the intensity of the light falling on the subject to be measured, unaffected by different degrees of reflection and absorption. This technique is known as the incident light method and is especially useful for colour transparency work.

A spot meter is another type of hand-held meter, mainly used by experienced photographers and professionals. The meter has a rectangular or circular focusing screen in the middle of which is a small engraved circle representing a 1° view of the subject. The meter measures accurately the value of the light contained within this circle, so that small but important areas of the subject can be isolated for exposure evaluation, unaffected by adjacent areas of contrasting light or tone. Although all hand-held meters are very accurate, they are slower than the built-in type and are therefore most suitable in set-up situations, where the photographer has time to take the relevant readings and transfer them to his camera.

Through-the-lens Metering

The most popular form of exposure metering is probably the through-the-lens (TTL) system used in the SLR camera. This is available as a manual control and, in more expensive cameras, as an automatic device using the shutter-priority and aperture-priority methods. The principle behind all three types of exposure metering is the same. The camera contains two or more light-sensitive cells, such as cadmium sulphide, silicon and gallium, which measure the intensity of light entering the camera. Some models have a focal plane shutter blind with a special reflective surface which beams light back to a receiving cell, allowing last-minute adjustments to be made to the exposure just a fraction of a second before the picture is taken. The timing of long exposures is even computed by measuring the intensity of the light which is reflected from the surface of the film itself.

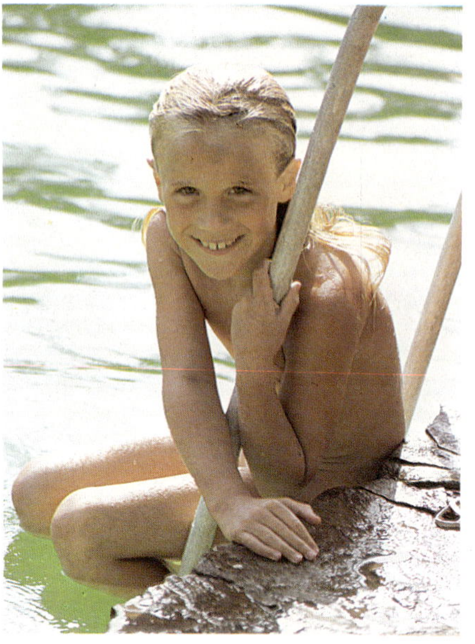

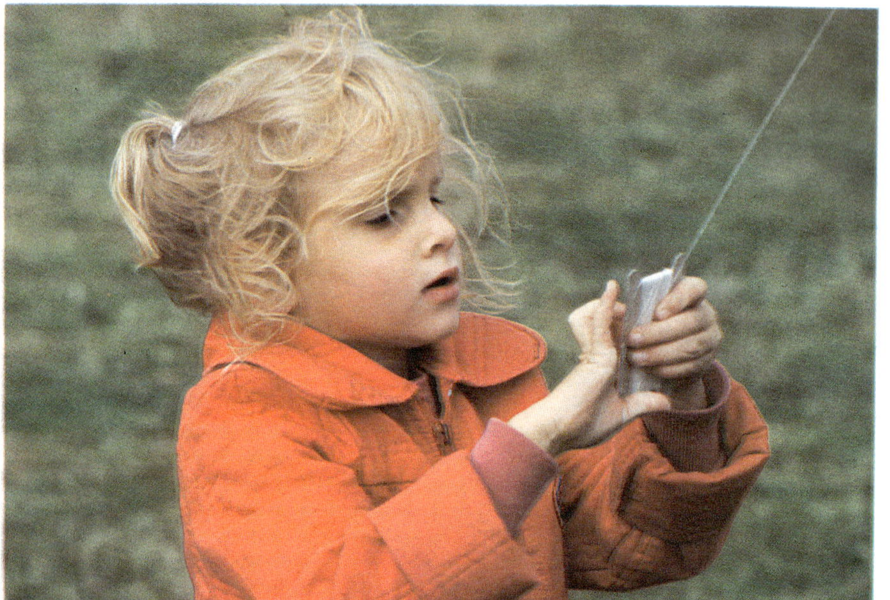

Because the model has been photographed against a very much lighter background, correct exposure will only be achieved with a centre-weighted system (left). Without centre-weighting, the exposure would have to be modified.

An ideal subject for correct exposure with TTL metering with areas of dark, medium and light tone equally distributed (right).

An even distribution of tone is particularly important for correct exposure in colour using TTL metering. The majority of tones in this shot are average, causing no metering problems (below left).

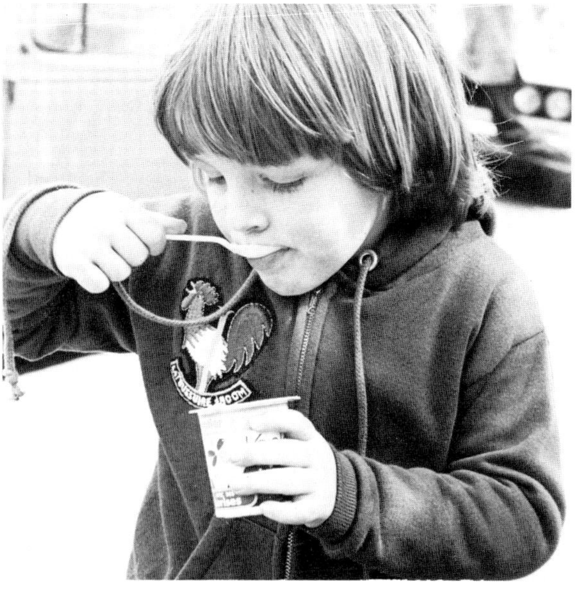

However the exposure is assessed in a TTL camera, the important point is that the measurements are made at the focal plane or its equivalent at the focusing screen, thus representing precisely the amount of light falling on the film itself. This is irrespective of the lens in use, and of any filter or lens attachment that might cut down the intensity of light transmitted.

Some TTL cameras meter light equally from the whole of the screen area, which is quite adequate when the scene to be photographed contains an even distribution of tones and light and shade. However, many shots will have the most important elements placed towards the middle of the screen image, and for this reason most cameras have centre-weighted metering, where the greater part of the measurement is made from the centre of the screen. Almost all TTL systems have an area of reduced sensitivity along the top third of the screen, so that predominantly light skies will not over-influence the readings for landscape work. Some more expensive SLRs have provision for taking optional spot readings from a small central portion of the screen.

When you use a TTL camera, remember that the whole system is geared to a scene of *average* reflectance. As long as the screen image contains a balanced range of tones, all will be well, but if there is a predominance of light or dark areas, the meter will be confused and the exposure incorrect. This will also be the case with a subject of medium tones set against a very dark or very light background, or when a shaded subject is photographed into the light.

The TTL metering system can be very accurate and quick and easy to use, but it is certainly not foolproof. For the best results it should be understood and used intelligently, and the photographer must be aware of situations in which a false reading is likely to occur.

Difficult Lighting Conditions

All cameras which have an integral exposure meter work on the principle that the subject to be photographed contains an average range of tones. It is when there is a predominance of light or dark tones in a scene that difficulties can arise. A good example would be a photograph of a child in a snow scene. As most of the tones will be light and bright, the camera meter will be 'fooled' that this is an average scene reflecting a large amount of light and will expose accordingly, with the result that the shot will be under-exposed. The opposite occurs when the model is placed in a setting of largely dark tones.

Most automatic cameras have an override facility which can be used to modify the reading shown on the viewing screen. In a situation where the subject is set against very light surroundings the override should be used to increase the exposure by one or two stops, according to the brightness of the setting. In the opposite situation of a very dark background, the exposure should be decreased by one or two stops. The exact degree of modification has to be estimated by guesswork or experience, and it is a good idea to bracket exposures, taking a range at slightly varying settings, to ensure at least one good shot.

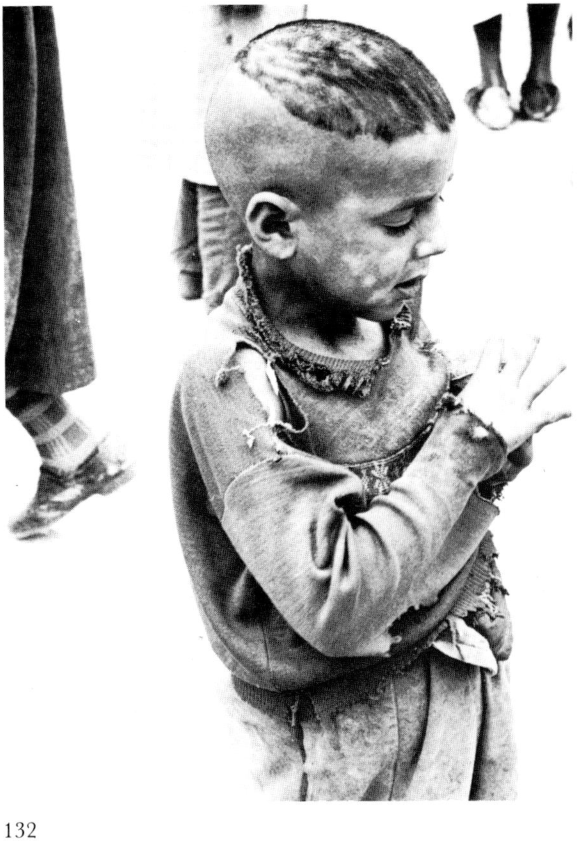

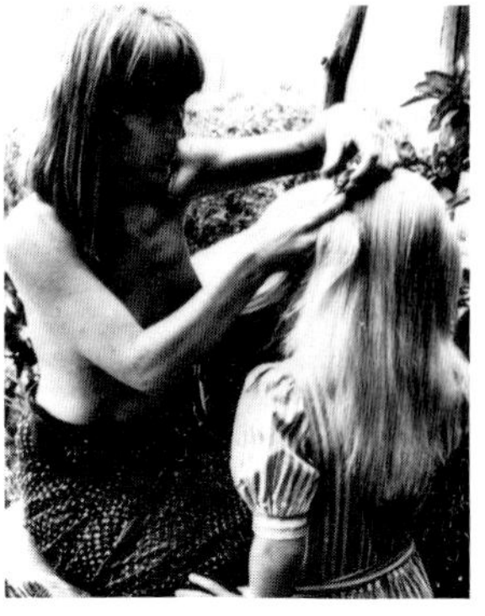

In this shot a normal reading has given a mid-way exposure, a compromise between the exposure needed to record detail in the highlight and shadow areas. This has caused some areas to be slightly over- and some slightly under-exposed (above).

In almost every case, exposure should be assessed for the main subject. Here the intensity of light has caused the sand background to over-expose, allowing the subject to stand out better (left).

Similar modifications must be made when the subject is strongly back-lit. The meter will again be misled by the predominance of bright light from behind and around the subject, and will under-expose accordingly. In this sort of situation, it is usually adequate to increase the exposure by one stop.

Some cameras with through-the-lens metering have a device which makes it possible to move closer into the subject and to take a reading directly from the child's features, with the exposure being computed and locked into the camera's memory. The photographer can then move back, to take in the whole scene, knowing that the exposure which is set is correct for the main subject. Cameras with a spot-metering system can be used in the same way to measure only the light reflected from the main subject. Some cheaper cameras have no form of over-ride facility. However, in these situations it is still possible to modify the computed exposure by using the film speed control, altering the ASA setting proportionately when more or less exposure is required, remembering to return it to its correct setting when shooting under normal conditions.

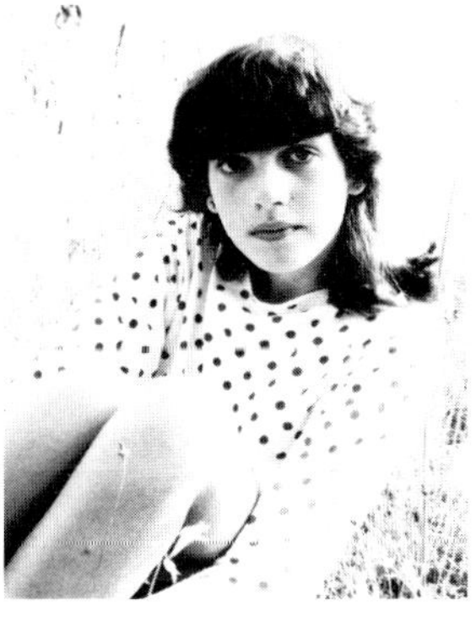

Because all the tones in this picture are light, the TTL camera will tend to under-expose (above). When there is a predominance of light or dark tones in a shot, the over-ride must be used to modify the exposure.

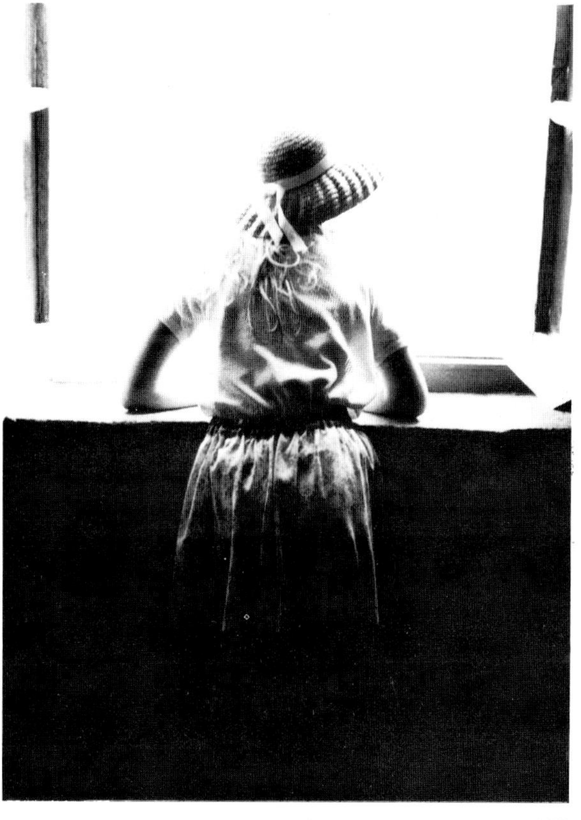

In this subject, half the scene is strongly back-lit and the rest in deep shadow (right). The only satisfactory method of assessing correct exposure would be to take a spot-meter reading or separate meter reading from the girl's blouse.

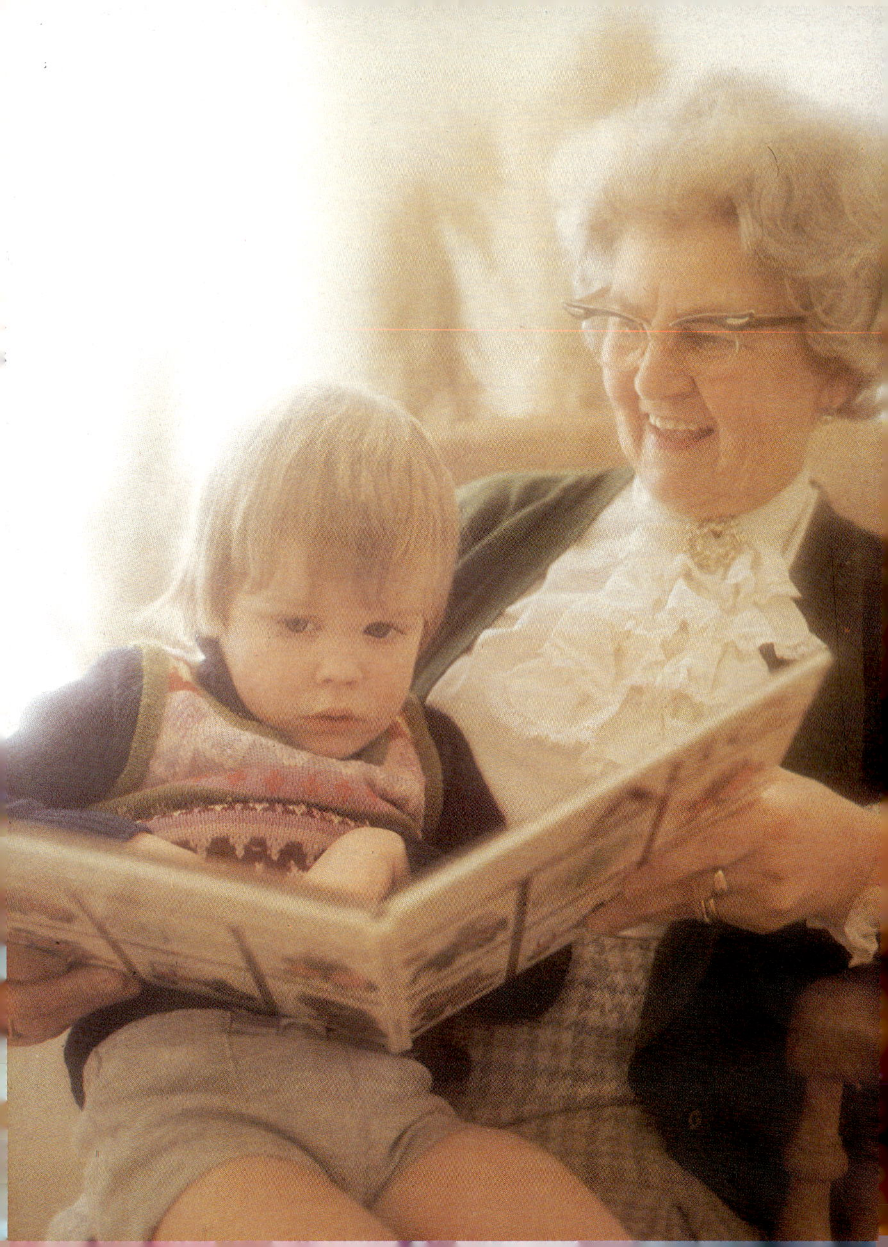

FOCUSING

A photograph is said to be in focus when the main subject is sharply defined as a result of correct positioning of the lens system. The point of focus is the position at which rays of light refracted by the lens converge to form a sharp image. When a lens is focused at infinity, the distance between the film plane and the lens itself will be equal to its focal length. When the subject is brought nearer to the camera, the distance from lens to film plane must be increased proportionally to provide a focused image. Almost all cameras have the means of varying this distance by moving the lens in relation to the film plane. In most modern cameras a helical screw on the lens barrel can be rotated to move some or all of the lens elements backwards or forwards in order to achieve correct focus.

The degree of sharpness in a photograph will depend on the focal length of the lens and the aperture chosen. By careful control of these factors, it is possible to adjust the depth of field. In close-up work, where the focused distance can be measured in centimetres rather than metres, special accessories can be used to achieve results outside the normal focusing range of the lens.

As regards the methods of establishing correct focus, in the past this has usually been achieved by visual assessment, with a manually operated control used in conjunction with a ground-glass screen or split-image rangefinder. While such methods are still commonly used today, especially in SLR cameras, a growing number of cameras, and in particular 35 mm compact models, now have automatic focusing. This obviously saves time, and is particularly useful for child photography where the subject's movements may be rapid and unpredictable; focusing on a moving child is difficult at the best of times, and in certain situations can be almost impossible. With a number of exceptions, correct focus is a matter of technical rather than aesthetic considerations, and in most instances the use of an auto-focus camera will aid rather than hinder the creative potential of the photographer.

Focusing Methods

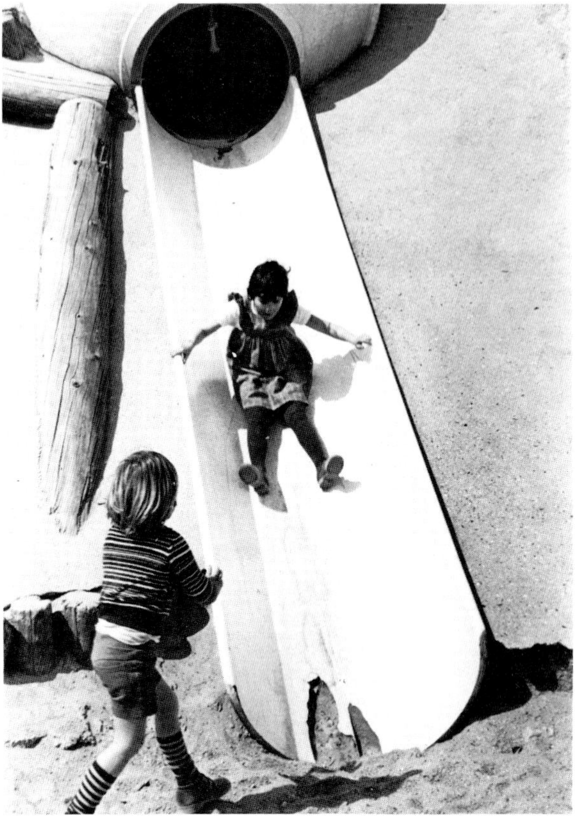

A child running directly towards the camera is very difficult to focus. The only easy way to guarantee a good result is to use an auto-focus camera (right).

The photographer will often have the dilemma of whether to choose a small aperture for increased depth of field or a fast shutter speed to freeze action. Frequently both effects will be required, and when it is not possible to load a faster film, a compromise will have to be made. In this example, a shutter speed of 1/125 sec was selected to freeze the subjects with a slight trace of blur, but enabling an aperture of f8 to be used to give the necessary depth of field (left).

Very simple cameras have no focusing control at all and the lens is pre-set at the 'hyperfocal distance', a position that will ensure reasonably sharp results at all distances between 2 metres (6½ feet) and infinity. Other types have a distance scale, which must be estimated, or a three-position 'zone' focusing system for close-ups, full-length figures or views. On simple cameras these focusing systems are usually quite adequate.

All other camera types have more accurate focusing systems. Compact cameras, without auto-focus, often have a rangefinder coupled to the focus mechanism. In these cameras, the centre of the viewfinder contains a colour-tinted secondary image, and when the subject is framed, the focusing ring of the lens is rotated until the tinted image of the subject coincides with the main image in the viewfinder; the subject will then be critically focused. Comparisons have always been drawn between the speed and convenience of the rangefinder and the reflex focusing screen. Most photographers prefer the latter, although a rangefinder is more useful in poor light.

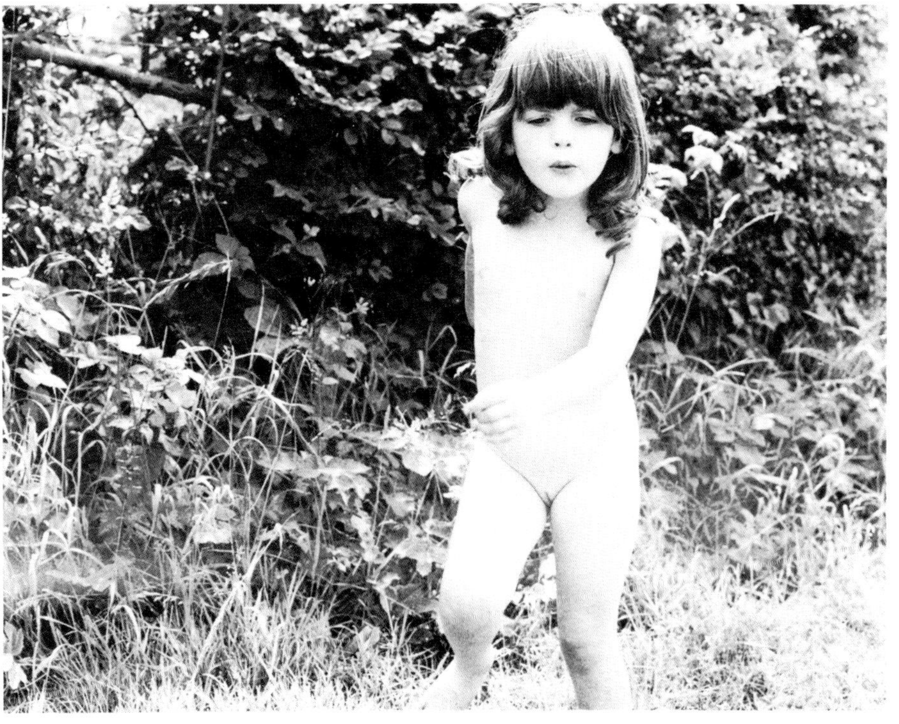

The advantage of reflex focusing is that an exact replica of the finished photograph can be seen in the viewfinder and there are no problems in close-up work. Furthermore, the depth of field at varying apertures can be pre-judged by using the manual stop-down control. Higher-quality SLR cameras can be fitted with a variety of focusing screens, such as plain glass, graticuled, micro-prism and split-image rangefinder. The rangefinder type is useful for lenses of short and medium focal length and gives the choice between rangefinder and screen focusing.

Auto-focus cameras usually work on the beam-reflectance principle. The beam may be sonar or infra-red, and the mechanism is activated by measuring the time taken for the beam to be reflected from the subject to a sensor. The sequence is normally started by pressure on the shutter release button, or sometimes by a separate button, and in most cases the adjustment is carried out instantaneously. Certain precautions are necessary. With the sonar type, it is not possible to focus through a window as the sound waves bounce off the glass, and with all automatic models it is important not to include any foreground object near the measuring part of the frame, as the focus will merely lock on to the nearest object within this area. Special auto-focus lenses are available for some makes of 35 mm reflex camera, and when appropriate these can be used instead of the normal lens with manual focusing.

Differential Focusing

Differential focusing is the means of isolating a subject from its surroundings by throwing all the extraneous details out of focus. For instance, if you wanted to concentrate attention on the face of one particular child among a group of children at different distances from the camera, you could choose a lens and aperture in a suitable combination to ensure sharp focus on the subject alone. By throwing their images out of focus, all distracting detail in the other children in the group could be eliminated and the interest concentrated on one face. Another use of differential focus is to eliminate detail in distracting backgrounds.

The technique involves reducing the depth of field to a minimum, in other words reducing the planes of sharp focus immediately in front of and behind the subject by as much as possible. Depth of field depends on three factors: the distance from the subject, the focal length of the lens, and the aperture in use. The nearer the subject is to the camera, the less depth of field will be apparent, and similarly, depth of field will be reduced as the focal length of the lens increases and the aperture is made larger. The way to apply the technique when photographing a child, then, is to use a long lens or a wide aperture, and preferably a combination of the two. As the aim is to eliminate depth, focusing on the model must be very critical. An SLR with a lens stop-down control is the best camera to use as the depth of field at different apertures can be gauged visually on the focusing screen.

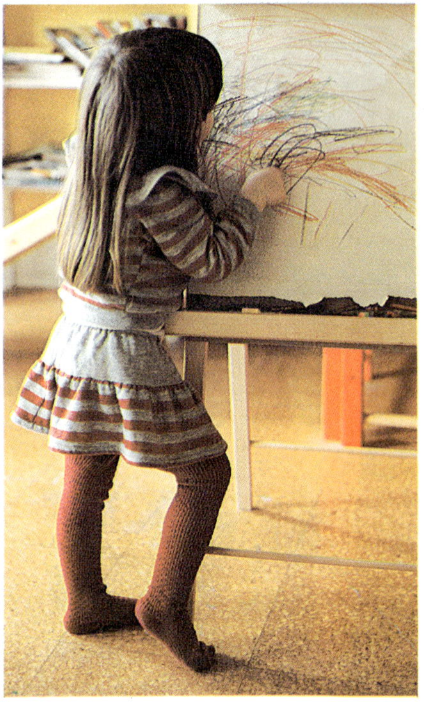

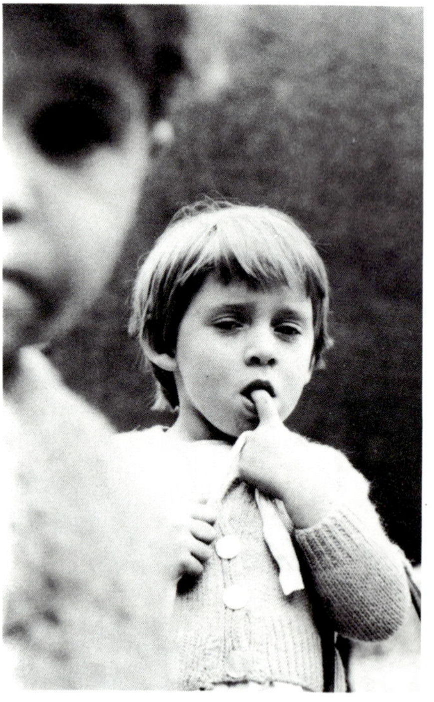

With the lens at maximum aperture, the background has been thrown out of focus, but as the depth of field in the subject area was very narrow, great pains were taken to ensure critical focus on the mother and child (right).

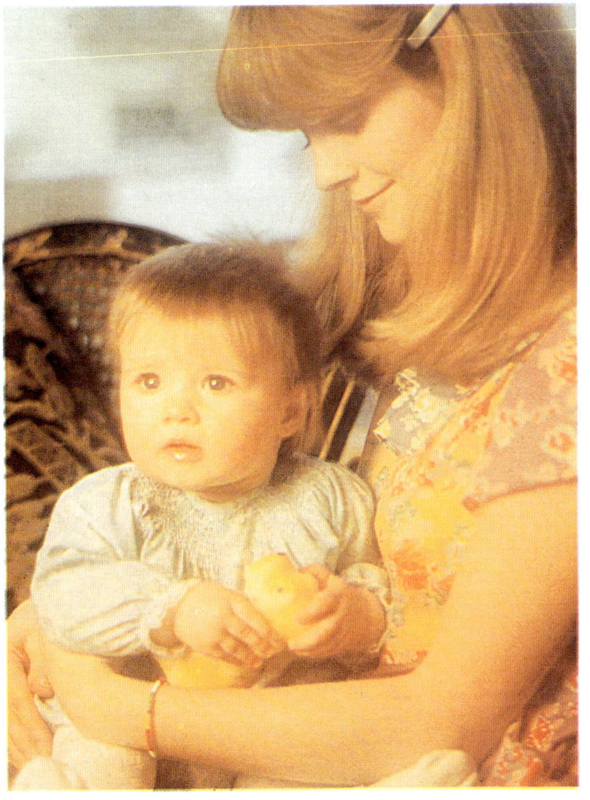

When shooting indoors by window light a large lens aperture will usually be necessary, throwing articles in the background out of focus (far left).

By focusing on the child furthest away, the face in the foreground has been recorded out of focus (left).

The image of the fighting boys has been intentionally kept out of focus to concentrate interest on the girl spectators behind them (right).

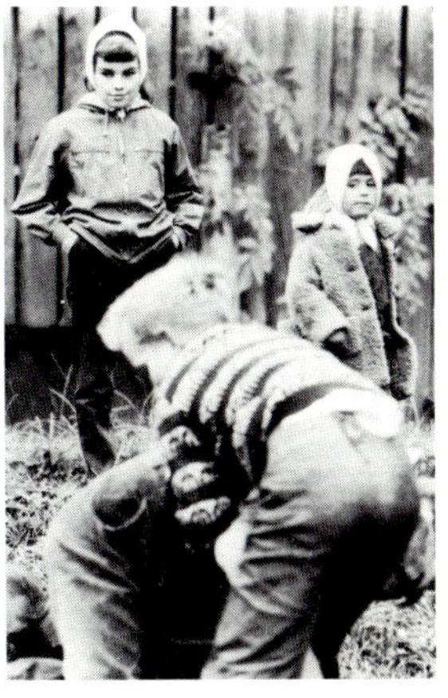

Two children were required in this photograph, but the emphasis had to be placed on the boy. This was achieved by critical focusing on him, allowing the other child to be far less clearly defined (far right).

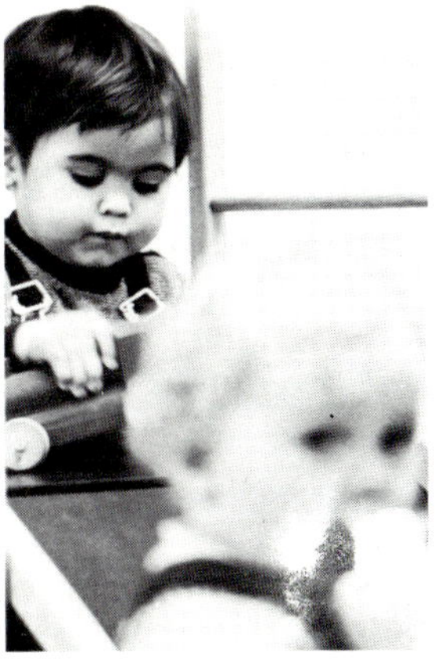

Close-up Photography

Most cameras and lenses will only focus to between 0.5 and 1 metre (1½ and 3 feet), so when you want to approach nearer to your subject, to take a close face shot of the child, for instance, you will have to use special accessories. One option is to use a special macro lens which is designed to take photographs at a distance as near as 10 centimetres (4 inches). These lenses are expensive, however, and the cost is not really justified if you are only going to do this kind of work occasionally. A less expensive alternative is to buy a zoom lens with a macro facility. These are slightly more expensive than a normal zoom but they will be more useful as a general-purpose lens. Both types require a slight increase in exposure, but this is usually

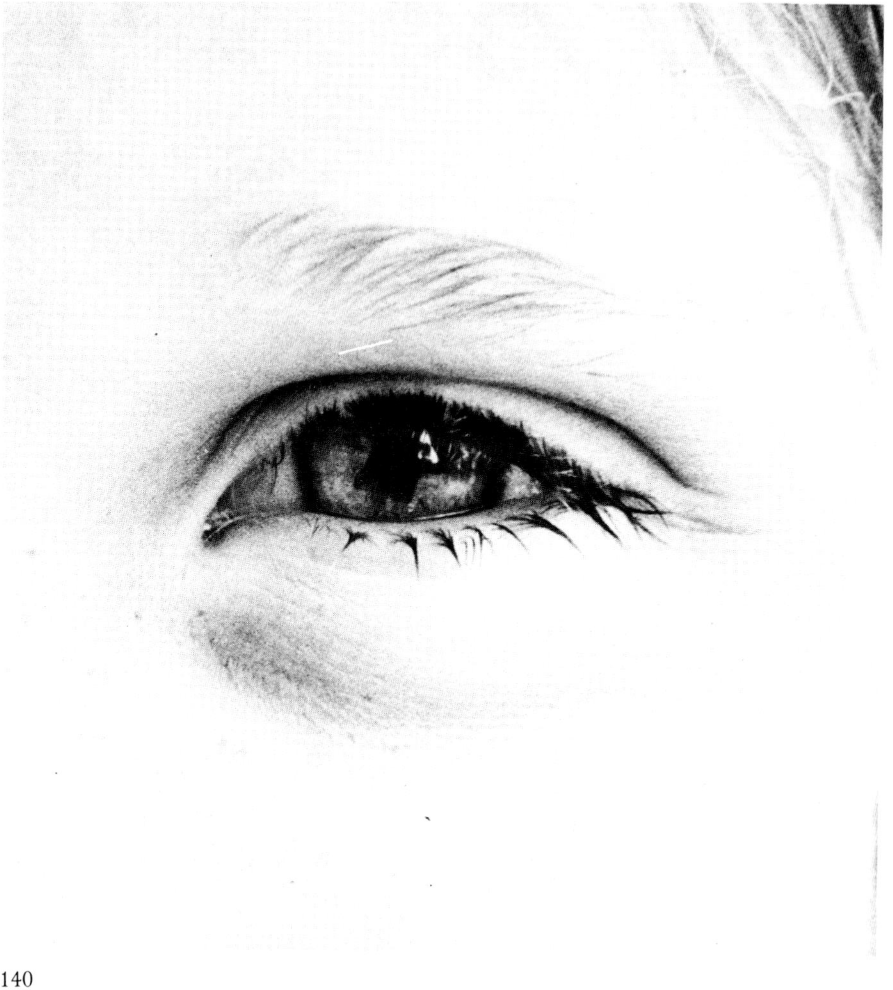

Medium close-ups of this type are best photographed using a weak supplementary lens of 1 diopter. These require no increase in exposure, and are simple and convenient to use (right).

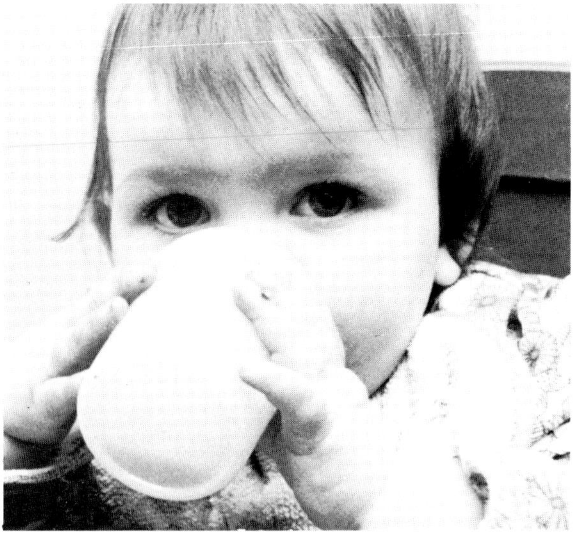

By using a special macro lens it is possible to photograph at very close distances. However, you will not usually wish to focus as near as this picture (left), and for less close, full-face shots, a zoom lens with a macro facility is useful and less expensive.

taken care of in the manufacturer's calibrations. In any event, this type of lens is likely to be used in a TTL camera, where exposure adjustment will be automatic.

A cheaper alternative is to fit a supplementary close-up lens over the normal camera lens. These are available in various strengths, measured in degrees of refraction called diopters. The most commonly used lenses are 1, 2 or 3 diopters, the higher numbers being the strongest. These lenses result in a very slight lowering of image quality, more noticeable towards the edges, and for this reason are best used with the main lens stopped down below maximum aperture.

Another inexpensive method is to use extension tubes fitted on the camera lens. These simply extend the distance between the lens and the film plane, thus allowing closer focus. The tubes are sold to fit specific cameras, usually in sets of three varying lengths. An increase in exposure is necessary, and the relevant information will usually be engraved on the tube; with TTL metering the adjustment in exposure will be taken into account by the camera meter. A more flexible method of increasing the distance from lens to film plane is by using focusing bellows. These work on the same principle as extension tubes, but the focusing range will be infinitely variable between 1 metre and about 2 centimetres (3 feet and ¾ inch) according to the model.

When photographing children at very close distances, focusing is extremely critical. It is most important that the child should remain quite still, and so you should make sure that he is seated comfortably. Any slight movement will alter the focus and, whenever the light allows, a small aperture should be used to maximize depth of focus. As in all portraiture, but especially important in close-up work, the camera should be focused on the child's eyes. It is worth remembering that even when there is insufficient depth to render all the facial features sharp, the photograph will still be acceptable if the eyes are clearly lit and sharply focused.

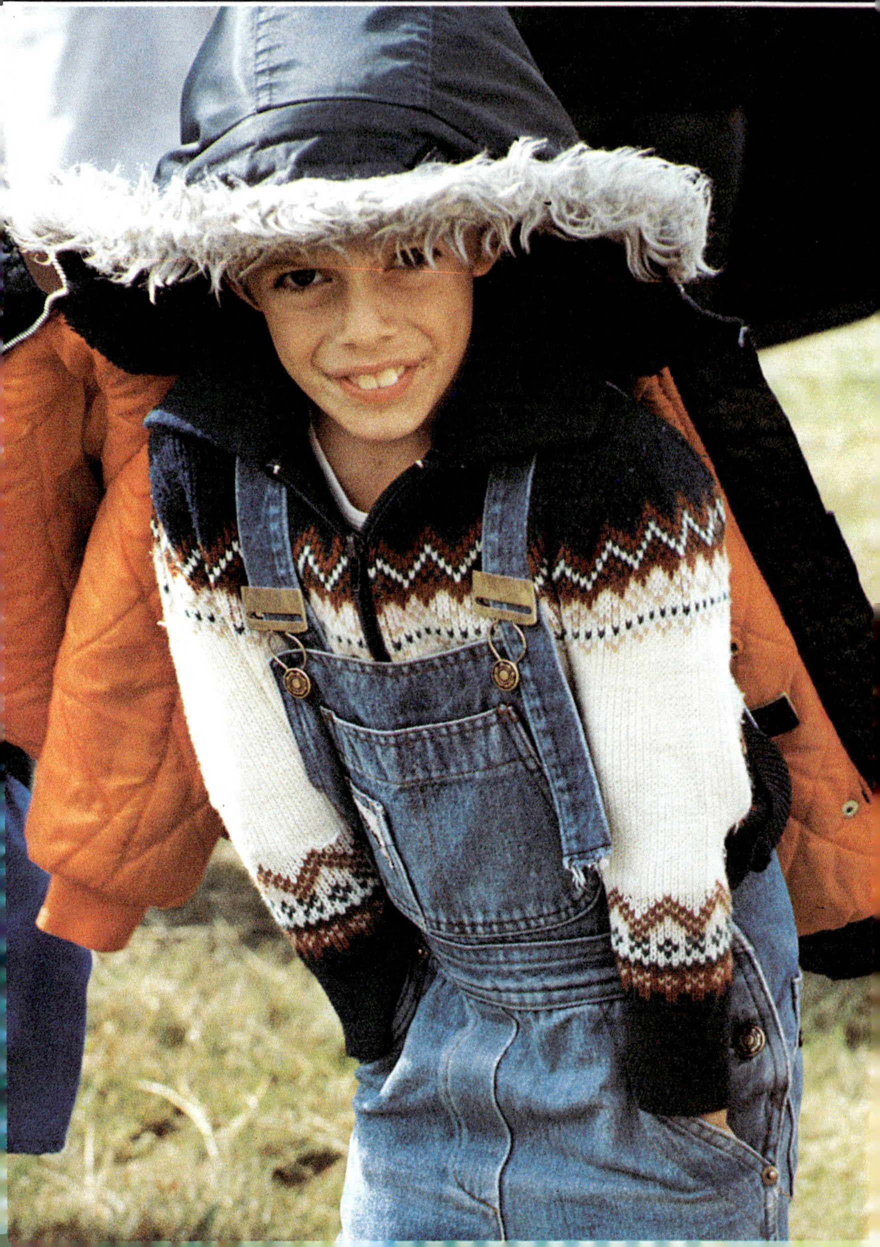

LENSES

A lens is an element of glass, which is shaped, ground and polished in a way that will allow it to refract light to form an image. For photographic purposes, an image of this type can be recorded on a light-sensitive material and developed into a permanent facsimile of a scene. In order to provide a sharp image, a lens must be scientifically designed, often with the aid of a computer, and manufactured with great precision. In order to correct the chromatic aberrations and astigmatism that can affect the performance, special techniques are used to make optical glass of a very specific refractive index.

Modern lenses produce results of very high definition, even those for the very small 110 and disc-loading cameras, and recent products have reached a state of near perfection. Simple cameras and compacts have a fixed, standard lens of a focal length considered to be most useful in the majority of situations which produces an apparent perspective similar to that of the human eye. More advanced cameras, including SLRs, have the facility of interchanging lenses, allowing the photographer to choose from a range of focal lengths, according to his requirements.

For child photography, the ability to select lenses of differing focal lengths, or to fit a zoom lens, is an immediate advantage. Children cannot, or will not, always be positioned to the photographer's advantage, nor be expected to remain immobile, and a high proportion of good child studies are taken with the photographer on the move. In such circumstances the worker using just a standard lens will be constantly striving to keep up with his subject, wasting physical and nervous energy, as well as drawing attention to his presence. With a choice of lenses he could maintain a camera position and choose a focal length as appropriate. Similarly, the choice of lens can be important when a photographer has limited space at his disposal and wishes to take in a wide angle of view.

Lens interchangeability is also desirable if a special effect is needed, and in such cases a macro or fish-eye lens can be fitted. However, it must be stressed that it is not essential to possess a wide range of lenses in order to produce successful child photographs, and that very good pictures can be taken with the standard lens supplied with the camera. Often the ability to fit an alternative lens to the camera will make the photographer's job very much easier and allow him to concentrate more fully on his subject-matter, and for that reason it is worth consideration. Creatively as well, access to a range of lenses of differing focal lengths is useful, as it allows the photographer to make use of the full potential of a situation in order to produce shots of different effect and perspective, and thus to broaden their appeal.

Lens Types

The main advantage of lens interchangeability is the opportunity it gives of selecting lenses of varying focal length, which, in more practical terms, means varying angle of view. A lens with a short focal length will have a wide angle of view, and is known as a wide-angle lens. For example, a 28 mm lens used on a 35 mm format camera will have an angle of view of 75°, which is quite wide compared to a 50 mm standard lens with an angle of view of approximately 45°. A long-focus or telephoto lens will have a narrow angle of view, 8° for a 300 mm lens; this means that it can produce a larger negative image of a subject at some distance from the camera.

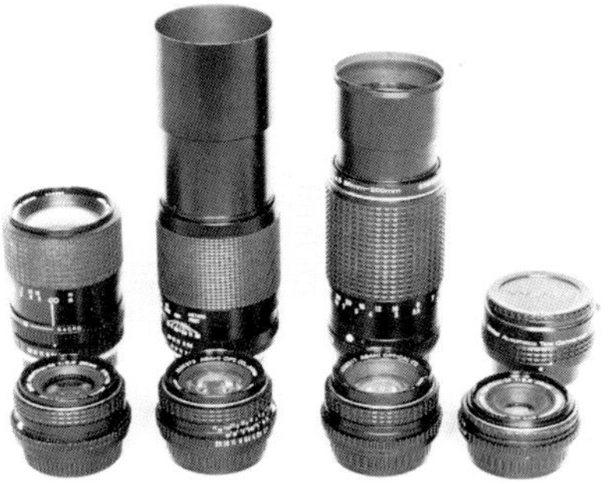

A selection of lenses for a 35 mm SLR camera. They range from 28 mm to 200 mm, with a tele-converter.

Zoom lenses have a variable focal length, usually covering a substantial range. They are most commonly available in two groupings, 35–70 mm (62°–32°) and 80–200 mm (30°–12°). The former covers a variable range from medium wide-angle to short telephoto, while the latter commences as a short telephoto, zooming to a longer one. Zoom lenses often offer a macro facility, to simplify working at very close distances.

A useful addition to the camera outfit, known as a tele-converter, can be fitted between the prime lens and the camera body, to double and, in some cases, treble the focal length of the lens. Used in the usual manner with a standard lens, it gives the effect of a telephoto lens. However, it does produce less sharp results than a prime lens, and is also subject to a light loss of two or three stops. A tele-converter is small and light and can be easily carried as an emergency stand-by; it is also relatively inexpensive and is a useful way of extending the lens range of a photographer on a tight budget.

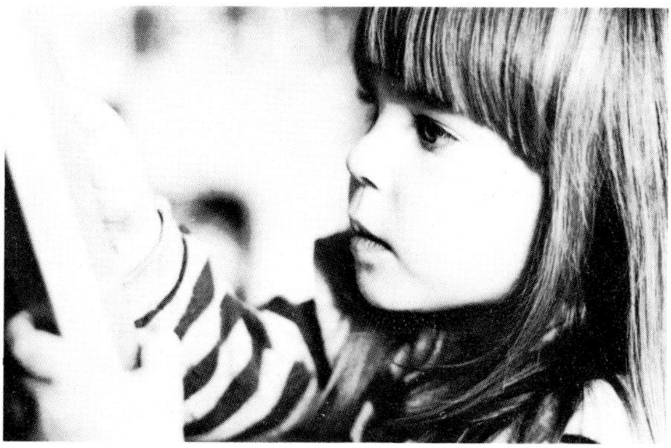

This shot was taken under very low lighting conditions using a standard lens (left). Because standard lenses have a larger maximum aperture than most other lengths they are very useful in poor light, and no camera owner should ignore the possibilities they offer.

A long-focus or telephoto lens is very useful when the subject is some distance from the camera. This picture was taken at a range of about 200 metres (220 yards), using a 300 mm lens on a reflex camera (right).

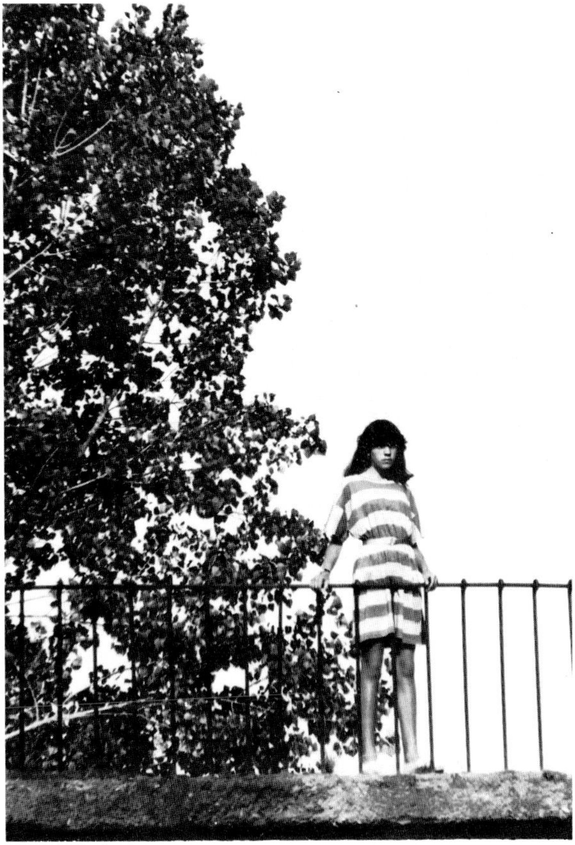

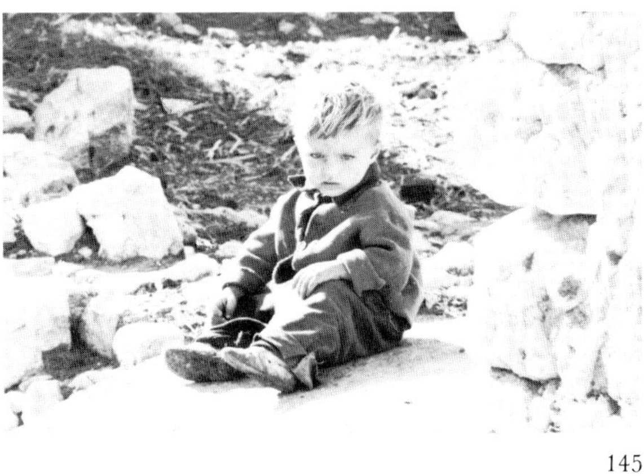

A zoom lens would have been ideal in this situation, allowing close-ups and long shots to be taken of an unknown child, without having to move closer and risk upsetting him (right). A zoom is a perfect lens for candid work.

Wide-angle Lenses

A wide-angle lens has two basic uses in child photography, one strictly practical and the other creative. In practical terms, this type of lens with its wide angle of view is especially useful when working in small rooms and tight areas: for example, you may wish to photograph a child in the bathroom, perhaps stepping into the water or testing the temperature with a toe. As bathrooms are often relatively small, it is not always possible to get far enough away from the subject to take a full-length image with a standard lens. Using a short-focus lens with its wide angle of view means that the whole figure of the child can be included, with the added advantage of a broader view of the room to establish the location.

From a creative point of view, a wide-angle lens is useful for forming 'space' around a child in a picture. Because of the broader angle of view, a child photographed with a short-focus lens will relate very much more to the background, allowing the surrounding scene to become more dominant and descriptive.

Care must be taken when photographing children at close distances with a wide-

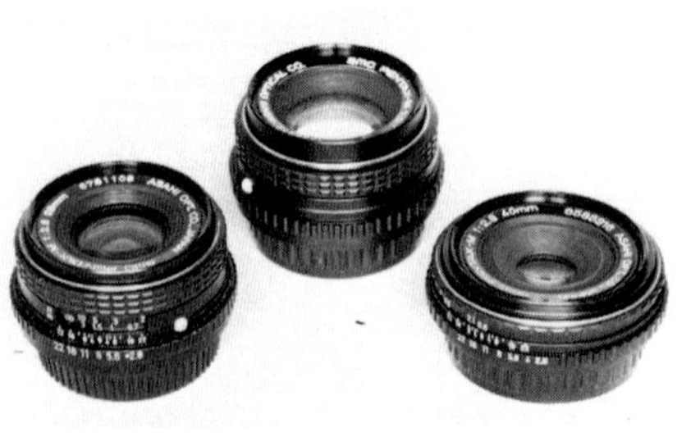

A selection of wide-angle lenses for a 35 mm camera: 28 mm, 35 mm and 40 mm.

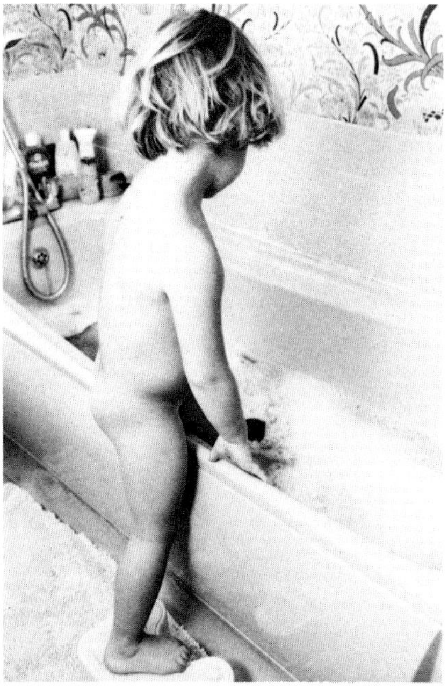

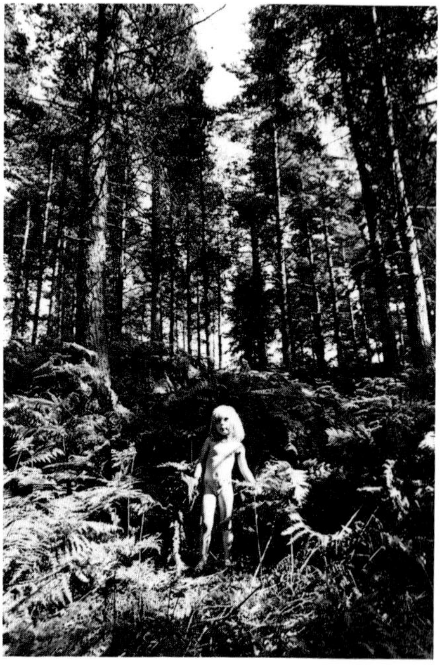

angle lens. If you approach too close, body and facial features will become distorted by the perspective characteristics of the lens. On a head-shot, for instance, the nose, a raised chin and all features nearest to the camera will appear over-large in comparison to the rest. This effect can be used deliberately sometimes and, with a low-level camera, can be exploited to give the model a long-legged appearance.

Using a wide-angle lens allows more background detail to be included. In this case the photographer wanted to show the waterfalls (right).

Two reasons for using a wide-angle lens: (opposite left) to work in a confined area, and (opposite right) to give the shot space and drama.

The railings of the climbing frame exaggerate the perspective effect peculiar to wide-angle lenses (below).

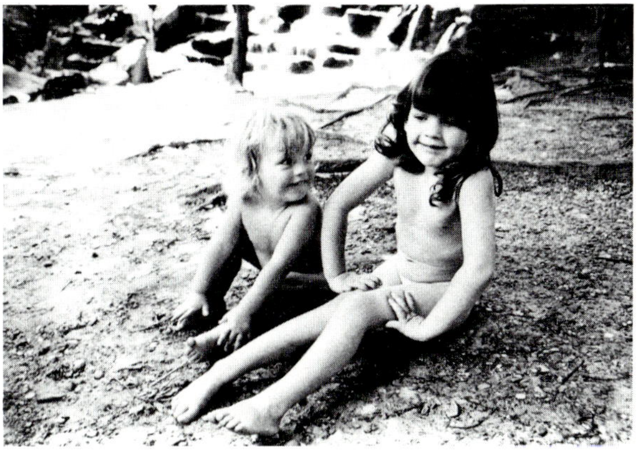

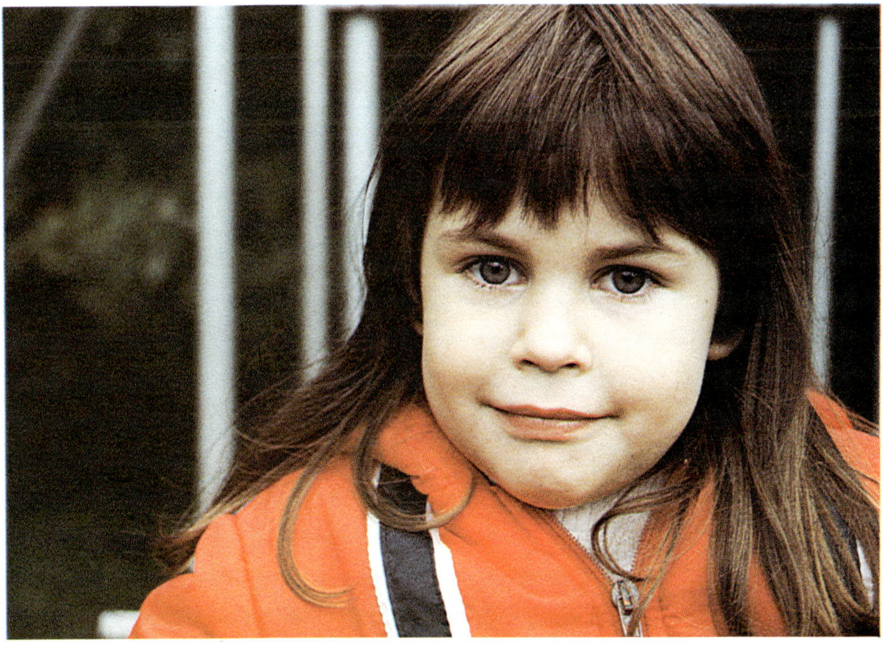

Telephoto Lenses

Telephoto or long-focus lenses are ideal for many aspects of child photography. They are perfect for portrait work as, unlike wide-angle lenses, they produce a flattened perspective effect, and when working at relatively close distances all facial features will be recorded in their natural proportions. They are also useful for sports events and other activities, as they enable the photographer to maintain distance from the child who will not be made nervous by the camera's presence.

An important characteristic of a telephoto lens is its limited depth of field, especially at wider apertures. It is ideal for isolating a child from a background by means of differential focus, and in candid work the use of a long telephoto makes it possible to work at a considerable distance, thus causing minimum distraction.

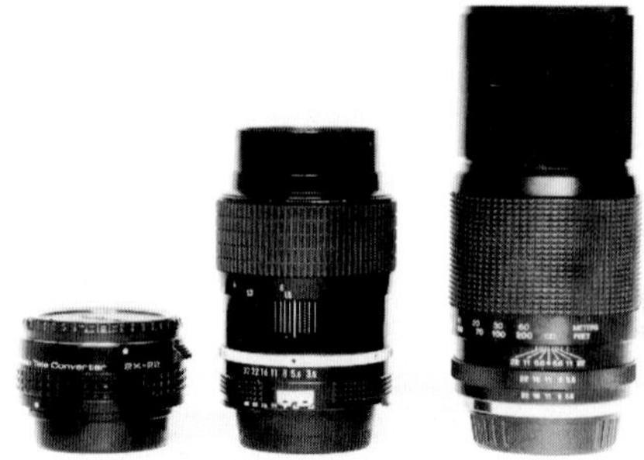

Telephoto lenses. From left to right: tele-converter, 135 mm and 200 mm.

There are, however, some drawbacks to this type of lens. Because depth of field is so limited, focusing must be very accurate.

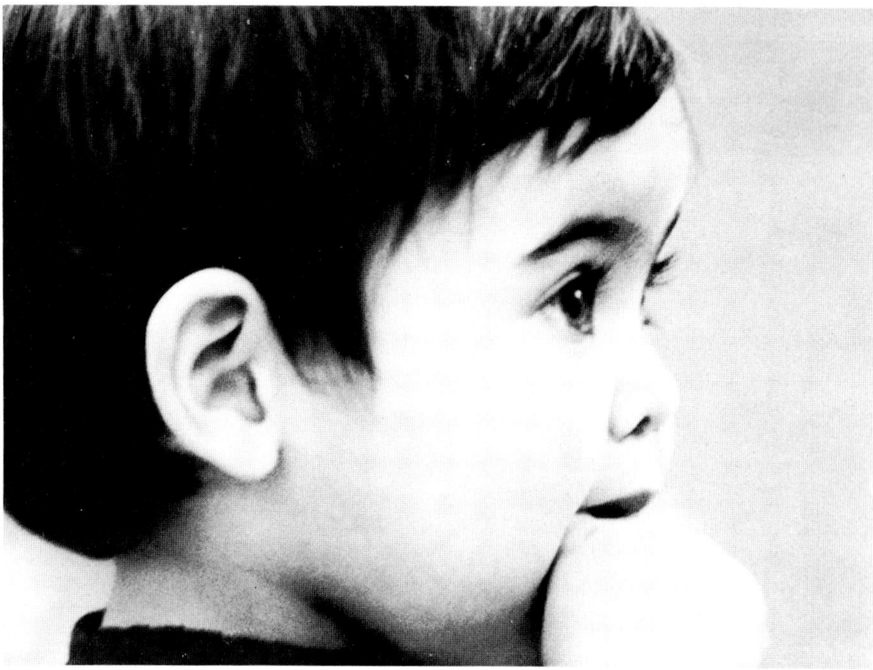

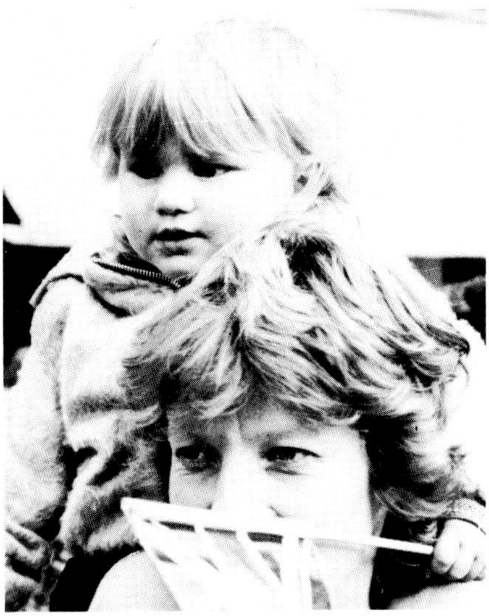

Long-focus lenses are also very susceptible to camera shake, and a fast shutter speed must be selected whenever possible when working hand-held. This of course requires the use of a larger aperture and diminished depth of field. Telephoto lenses are bulkier and heavier than lenses of shorter focal length, and when you first start using them you may have some difficulty when shooting moving subjects. The focusing system requires a greater degree of rotation of the lens barrel, which means that this operation takes longer to carry out. For this reason it is always advisable to have the lens roughly focused when attempting moving subjects so that the minimum of re-focusing is necessary when your model starts to approach the shooting area. Alternatively, pre-focus the camera and wait for the subject to move into focus.

Telephoto lenses are perfect for isolating one child from a crowd, with the added benefit that the background can be thrown completely out of focus, thus isolating him even more (above).

Although depth of field is very shallow with all telephoto lenses, and focusing needs to be done very accurately, candid shots are easy to achieve with such a lens without the subject's knowledge (left).

Using a telephoto lens for a portrait session reduces the child's awareness of the camera, so that he becomes less self-conscious and will behave more naturally (right).

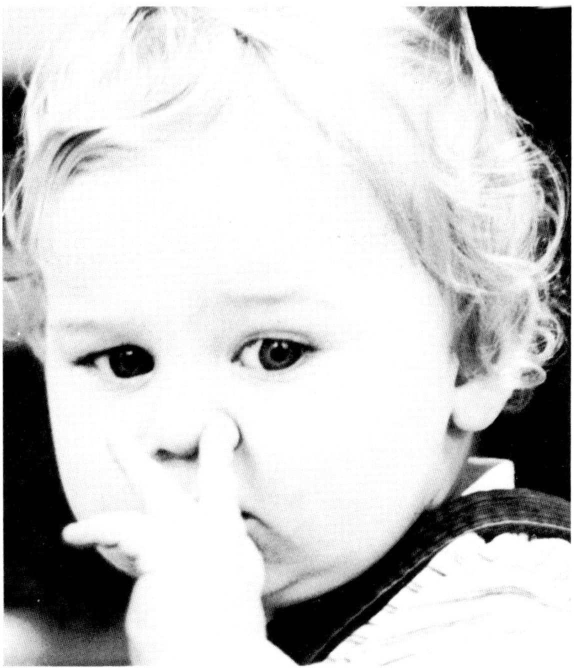

Choosing Lenses

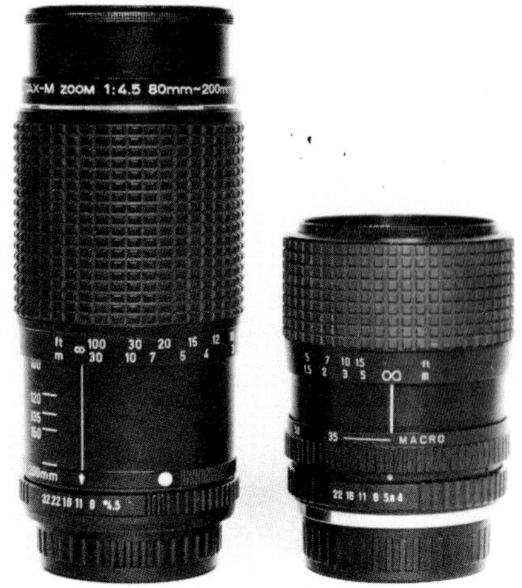

Zoom lenses. Left: 80–200 mm lens. Right: 35–70 mm lens with macro facility.

When you are choosing a set of lenses for use in child photography, the first thing you have to do is to decide whether to buy a set of prime lenses of fixed focal length, or one or two zoom lenses of continuously variable focal length covering a similar range. There will in actual fact be very little difference in cost between the two options, and the choice is merely a matter of personal priorities. Two zoom lenses will take up considerably less space in your camera bag than would four or five separate lenses, and would of course be considerably more convenient in use. On the other hand, zoom lenses do have certain disadvantages, such as greater weight and bulk, slightly inferior image quality and, as a general rule, slower maximum apertures.

It is well worth considering buying a wide-angle lens of 28 mm or 35 mm focal length, and a medium telephoto lens of 135 mm. Later on you could add a longer telephoto of 200 mm. An alternative, which would give you the same range of focal lengths, would be to buy two zoom lenses, one wide-angle to short telephoto, and another medium to long telephoto. There are single zoom lenses available which encompass the complete range of focal lengths from 28 to 200 mm but these are very bulky indeed, have a comparatively small aperture and, because of their elongated range, produce results of poor technical quality.

Whichever option you choose, do not disregard the standard lens. Although you might think that the focal length (usually 50 mm) produces uninteresting pictures, it is an excellent general-purpose lens, with a maximum aperture considerably faster than that of most other focal lengths. It will be especially useful in low light conditions when you will frequently find that your accessory lenses are too slow to use, especially zoom types.

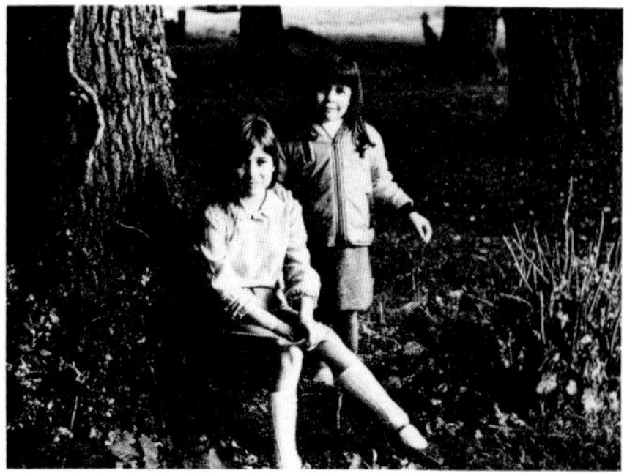

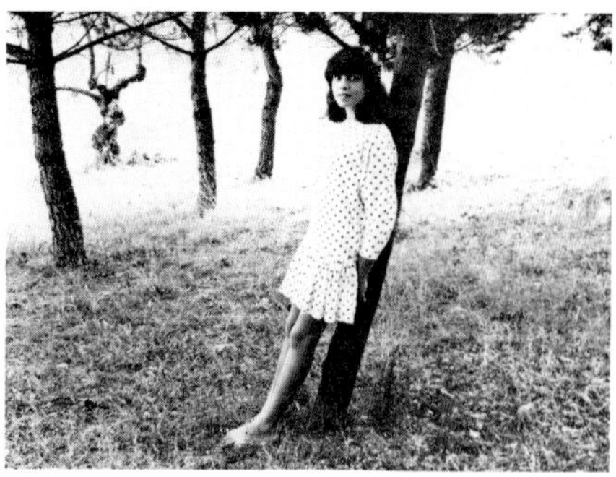

This strong portrait of a teenage girl was taken with a long-focus lens, giving a pleasant impression of the facial features (right).

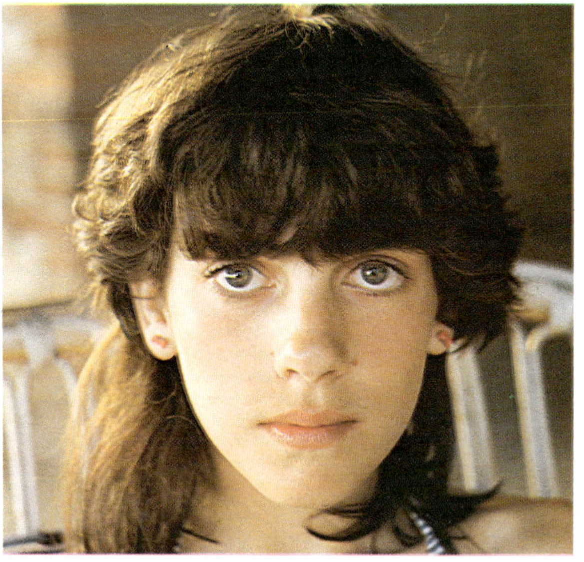

(Below) The zooming range of an 80–200 mm lens, showing (left to right) photographs taken from the same position at 80 mm, 135 mm and 200 mm focal lengths.

(Bottom) The zooming range of a 35–70 mm lens, showing (left to right) photographs taken from the same position at 35 mm, 50 mm and 70 mm focal lengths.

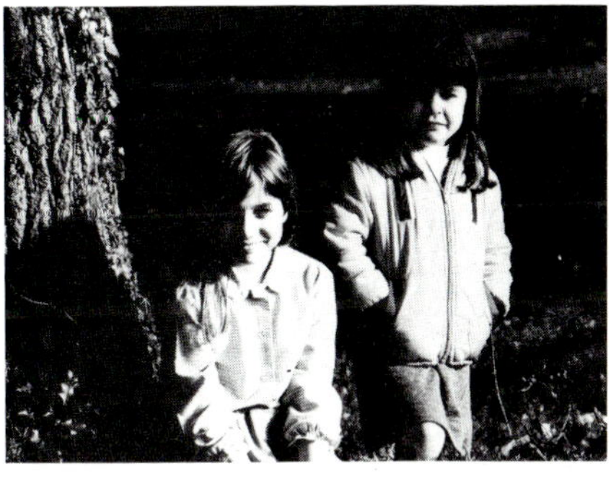

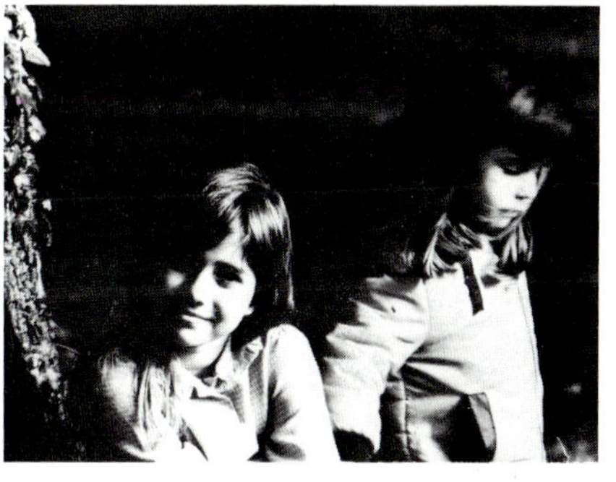

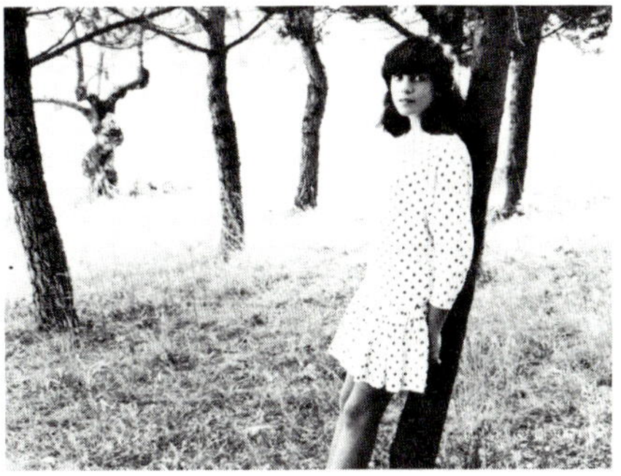

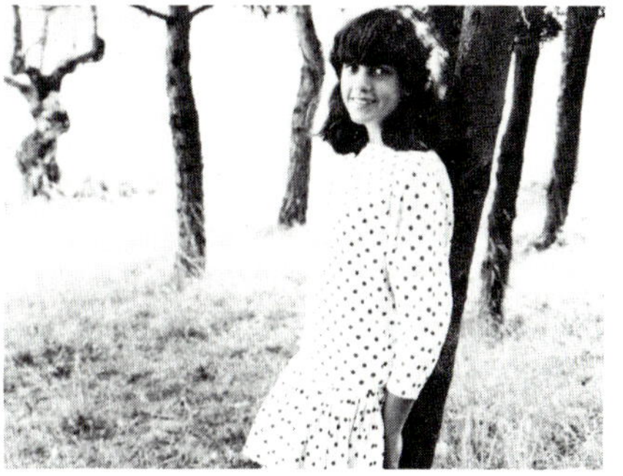

Special Lenses

There are a certain number of special lenses which can be of interest for the child photographer, although their use is limited.

Fish-eye lenses have an extremely short focus and produce a circular image. Their angle of view can be as great as 180° although 150° – 110° is more usual. As far as child photography is concerned, they could only be used as a gimmick as they produce very unattractive distortion at close range. Used occasionally, however, and in the right circumstances, they have an interesting and unusual effect. The macro lens is far more useful in this type of work as there will be occasions when very close face shots will be required. However, there are other methods of achieving the same result, at less expense; these are described on pages 140–1.

There are also lenses of extreme focal length, 500 mm or 1000 mm, which are manufactured using spherical mirrors in place of certain lens elements. This design is used to cut down the weight and bulk associated with lenses of such long focal length. They are useful for photographing at long distances, and the very compressed perspective produces a unique effect. Depth of field is almost negligible, and focusing on subjects moving at speed is almost impossible.

Accessory auto-focusing lenses are available to fit certain SLR camera bodies, though as a rule they are slower in use than those fitted to fixed-lens compact cameras. They are reassuring for achieving sharp focus under difficult conditions. Unfortunately, these lenses are very expensive and, as the reflex camera already has a most efficient focusing system, the extra cost might not be justified. Of course, it is possible to hire certain special lenses from camera dealers, and this is not too expensive for a day or two.

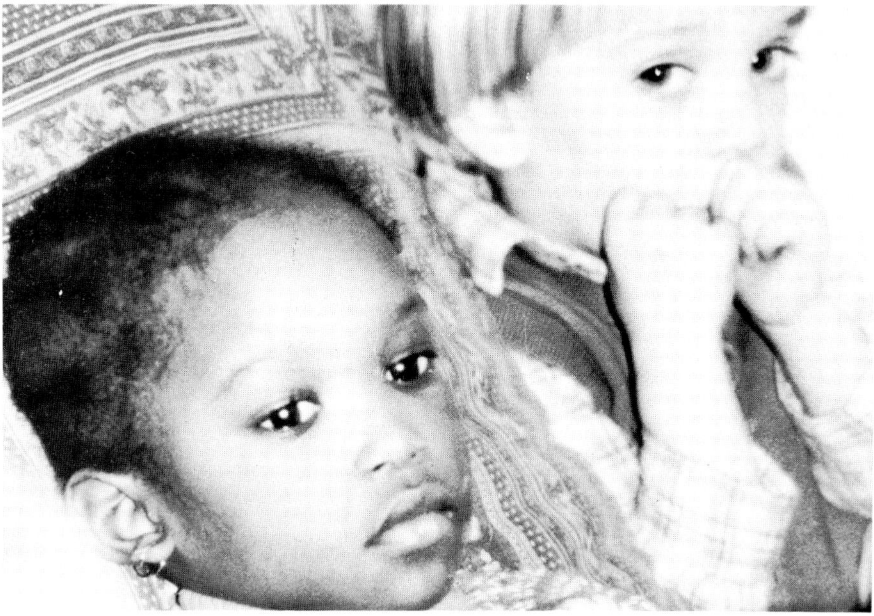

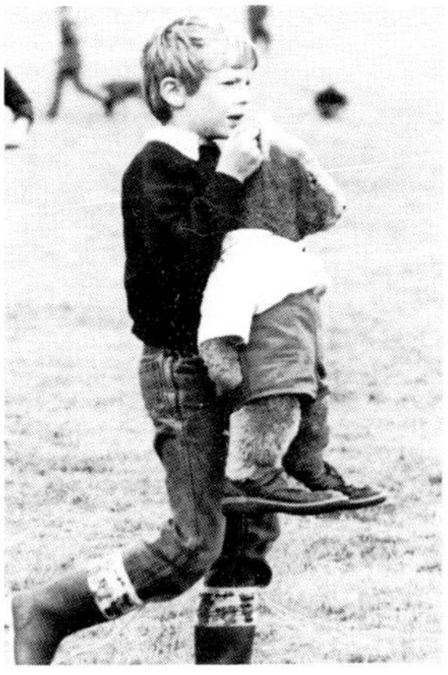

A candid subject photographed with a 500 mm lens (above). Such lenses are very difficult to focus on moving subjects of this type.

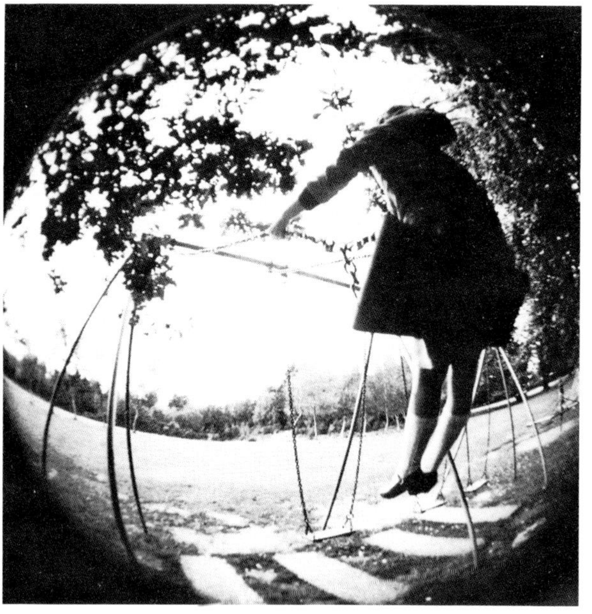

A fish-eye lens used in two ways to photograph a girl on a swing (right). The effect of such lenses is interesting for certain subjects, but they must not be used merely as a gimmick as the results soon become very boring.

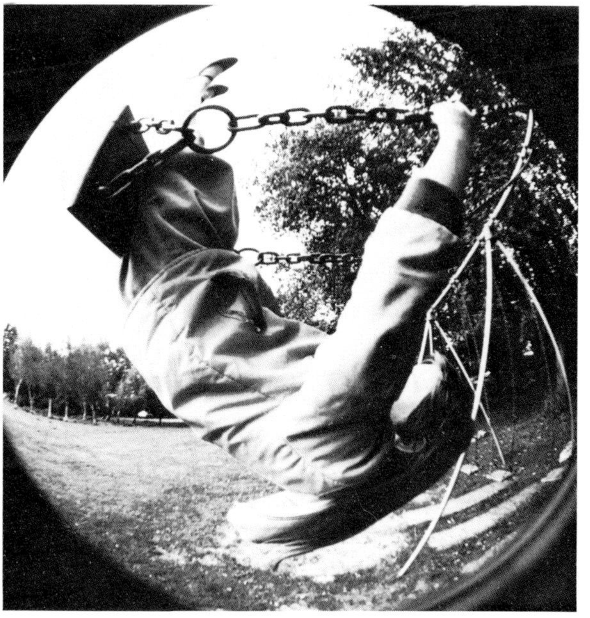

Very long-focus length lenses are ideal for close-ups of children. Because the lenses are bulky and heavy and best used with a tripod-mounted camera, they are most suited to photographing static subjects (left).

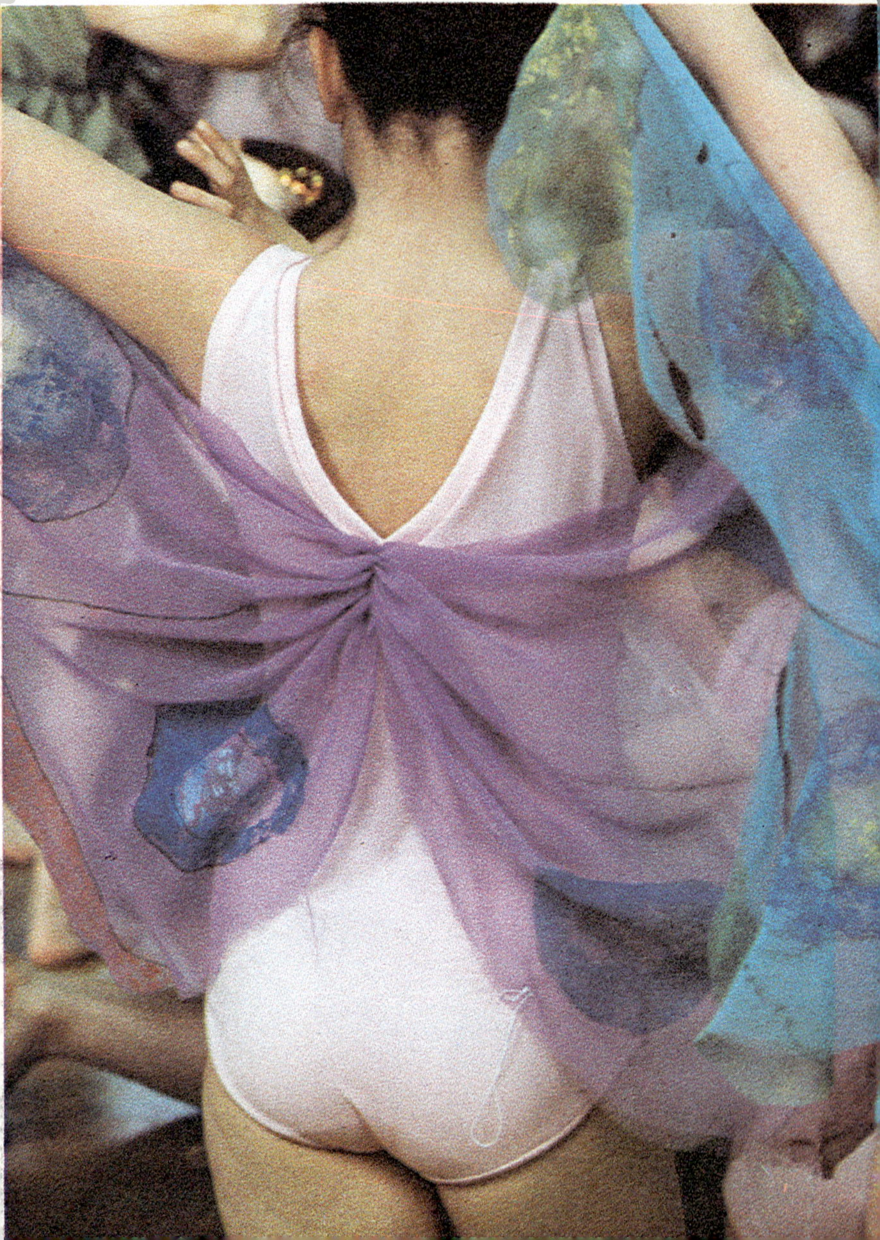

FILM AND PROCESSING

In the simplest terms, a photographic film consists of a transparent acetate base, which is coated with an emulsion of light-sensitive silver bromide crystals suspended in gelatine. When the film has been exposed to light in the camera it must be 'developed' to change the latent or unrevealed image into a visible one, composed of metallic silver. Those parts of the image receiving most light produce the heaviest deposits of silver, while those receiving less exposure produce lighter densities. When the film has been 'fixed' to make the silver permanent and no longer sensitive to light, the developed image can be viewed as a 'negative', an image of the subject with the tonal densities in reverse. This negative can be used for making a print, by projection on to light-sensitive paper and subsequent development.

This description is necessarily concise and simplistic, and takes no account of the varying types of film available and the differences in manufacture and processing. There are three main types of film in common use: colour negative film, colour reversal film and black-and-white film. Colour reversal film is made for the production of direct colour transparencies, while the other two types are used to make prints by enlargement.

As photographs are taken under a diverse range of lighting conditions, films of all types are manufactured to different levels of sensitivity or speed. Slow films produce results of the best photographic quality, and as the speed of films increases, so too does the level of grain in the negative or slide. Developed film is composed of silver crystals, which clump together to form the basis of the image. This clumping effect is the grain, and it becomes more noticeable as an image is enlarged, becoming more evident in proportion to the speed of the film used. Ultra-fast films are very grainy indeed, especially when they are push-processed for extra speed.

Because graininess effects the resolution – the ability to record fine detail in a photograph – it would be theoretically correct to use the slowest film appropriate in any given lighting situation. In practice, of course, many photographers will not know when they load their cameras what conditions are likely to be encountered, and compromise by using a medium-speed film, with a good balance of grain, resolution, contrast and exposure latitude, and only choose a faster film when they know that conditions will be unfavourable.

Film-loading systems have changed dramatically in the last two decades, with an emphasis on easy-loading methods such as cartridge and disc. However, the commonly used 35 mm system, pioneered by Leica in the 1920s, is still the most popular. Although the range and quality of film has improved enormously since that time, the loading system has remained virtually unchanged. To the beginner the range of films available can be confusing. However, it is only necessary to decide whether transparencies or prints are required, and whether they should be black-and-white or colour, and then select the appropriate film speed.

Black-and-white Film

Black-and-white materials are rapidly losing popularity among amateur photographers, mainly because manufacturers no longer advertise these products extensively, but also because of the simplicity and cheapness of modern colour print films and processing. It is a pity that black-and-white materials are not used more often, as in many ways this is a more sensitive medium than colour and particularly suitable for child photography. The tonal subtlety which can be achieved in a black-and-white print cannot be matched in a colour equivalent, and in many cases in fact a picture can be better suited to a monochromatic treatment.

Black-and-white film is now used almost exclusively by devotees who do their own developing and printing, and it is in the darkroom that the true potential of a 'mono' photograph can be realized by selection and control at the printing stage. Film is available in a wide range of speeds from 25 ASA to above 1000 ASA. It is best to use a medium-speed film of about 125 ASA, such as Ilford FP4, for outdoor work during the summer months, as a film of this type produces fine grain and a good tonal range. In the winter when the intensity of light is generally lower, a faster film of 400 ASA (Tri-X or HP5) would be better, giving a reserve of speed, with tolerable grain size. For very low lighting conditions, the ultra-fast films referred to on pages 124–5 will prove invaluable, making photography possible in conditions which were unthinkable only a few years ago.

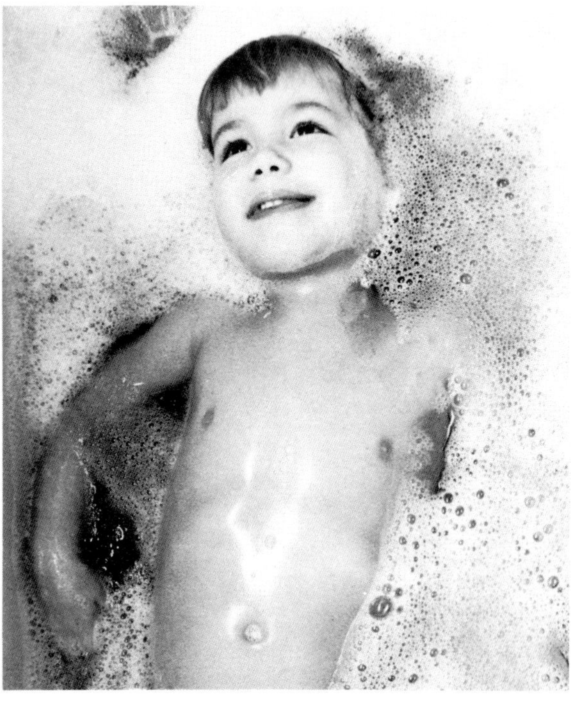

A medium-speed film of 125 ASA, such as Ilford FP4 which was used to take this shot, will have a good tonal range, wide exposure latitude and fine grain. This is especially important for subjects with fine detail, like the soap bubbles in this picture (left), which would not be resolved so clearly with a film of higher speed.

A fine-grain film gives the photographer the opportunity to blow up small parts of a negative without undue loss of quality. This picture (right) was enlarged from a very small section, and although the grain is quite evident it is not over-obtrusive or objectionable. Grain can even add a certain graphic quality to a picture which can be very pleasant when used appropriately.

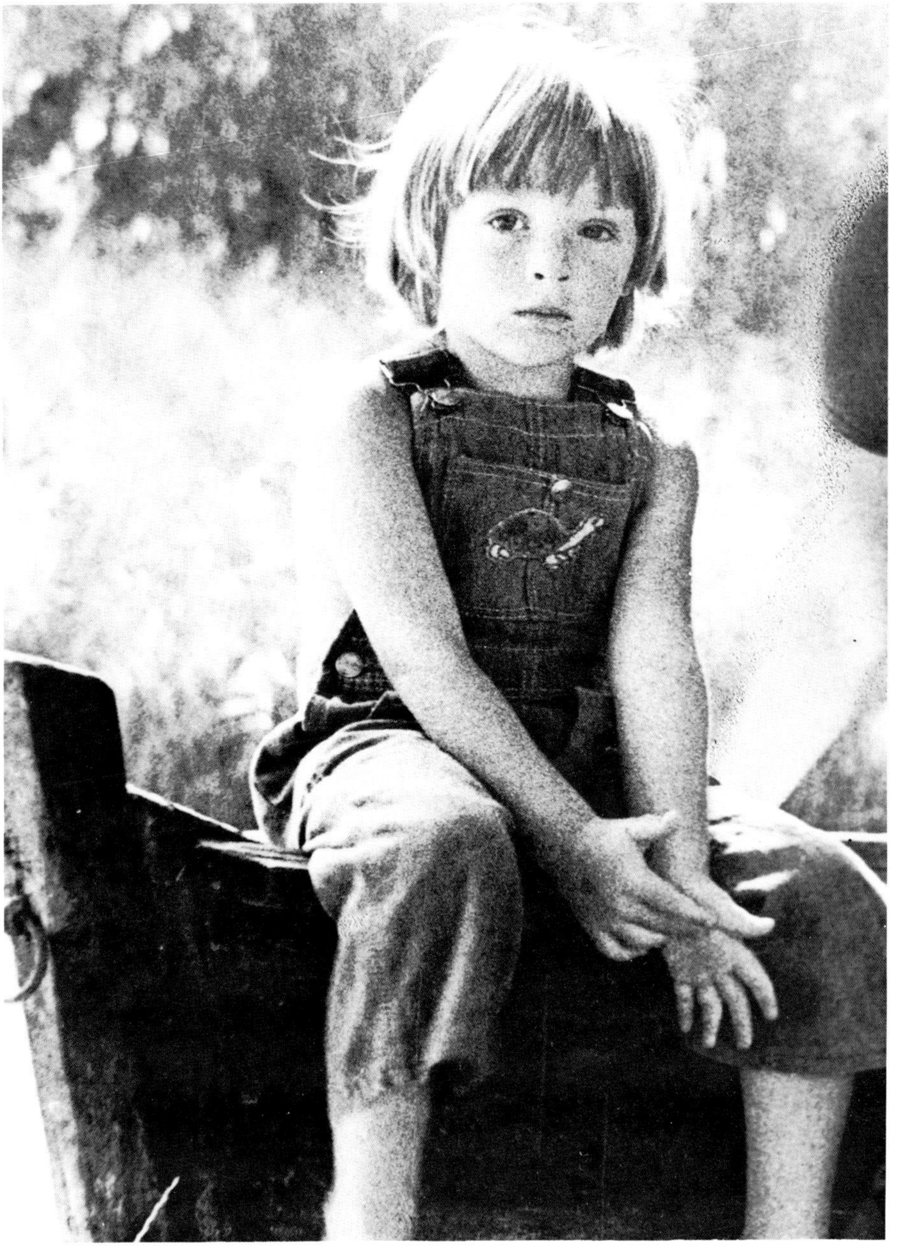

Colour Film

Colour film is often the immediate choice of the child photographer. It is an excellent medium with which to capture the gaiety of childhood, the colourful clothes, rosy complexions and bright toys which are so much a part of it.

The decision whether to shoot colour prints or transparencies is dictated by the final use which is to be made of the pictures. If the main aim is to put them in an album a print film would be best. On the other hand, if slides are required for projection, a reversal film is essential. If there is a dilemma, reversal film should be used, as it is possible to make colour prints from slides, though at greater cost.

Colour negative films are available in a speed range from 100 ASA to 1000 ASA. For general purposes, medium-speed films such as Kodacolor VR 100 or 200 are best as they have good latitude, very fine grain and record skin tones in a very pleasant manner. Faster, grainier films should be reserved for really bad lighting situations, when the results will be surprisingly good.

Colour slide films are available in a similar speed range, though for projection purposes it is best to use the slowest type that light conditions will allow. Graininess can be objectionable when a slide is enlarged on a screen and particularly when a grainy shot appears in a mixed bag of slides. For slide projection Kodachrome film is excellent as the grain is exceedingly fine and the colours well saturated. However, with a speed rating of 25 or 64 ASA the film is slow and only suitable for photography in strong light.

When photographing indoors by artificial light, a slide film balanced for tungsten light must be used. It is possible to convert daylight-type film for use in artificial light with special filters, but the loss of film speed is so great that this is not practical.

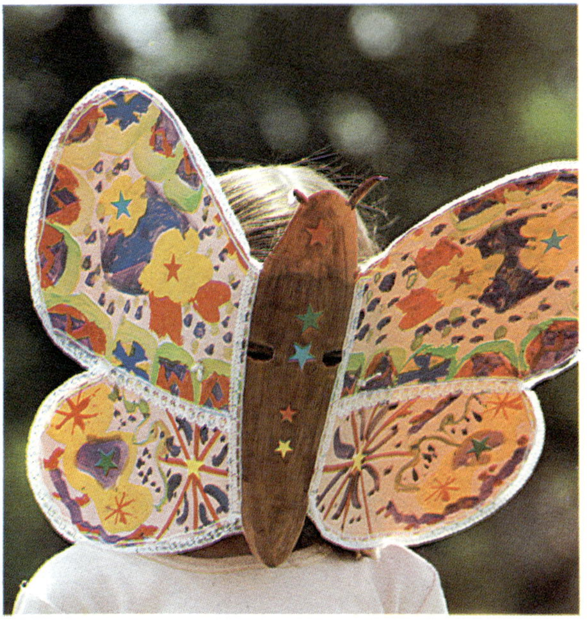

Outdoor events in the summer, such as fêtes and children's competitions, are ideal for photographing in colour. The light will often be strong and clothes and costumes are usually vibrant and colourful wherever children congregate (left).

A medium-speed colour film, Fujichrome 100, was used for these photographs of a competition of children's masks (right). A film of this type will have relatively little grain and will be capable of rendering a wide range of tones and colours accurately.

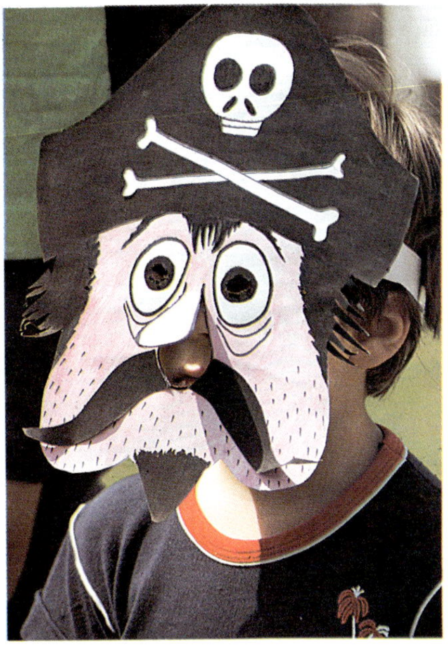

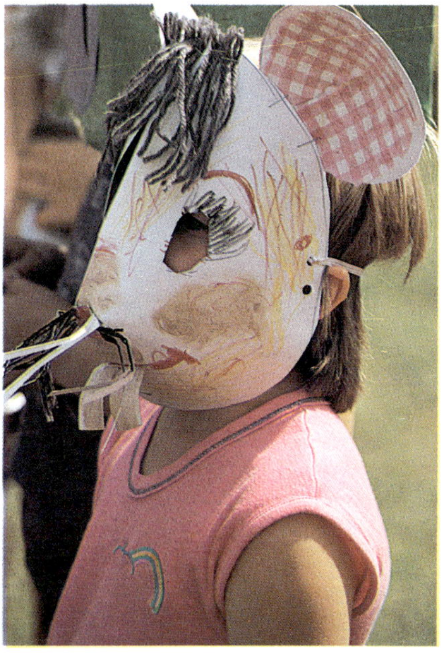

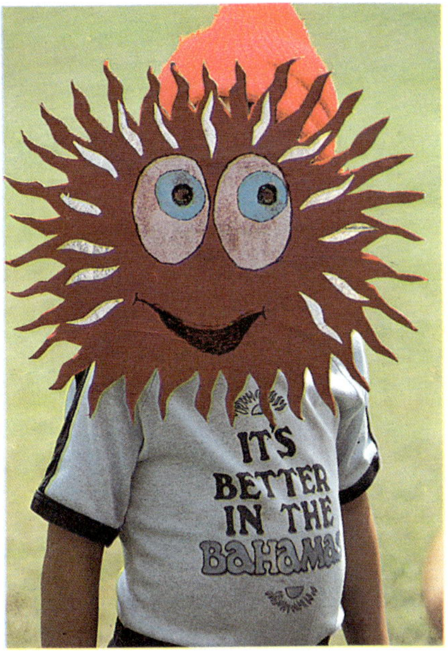
IT'S
BETTER
IN THE
BAHAMAS

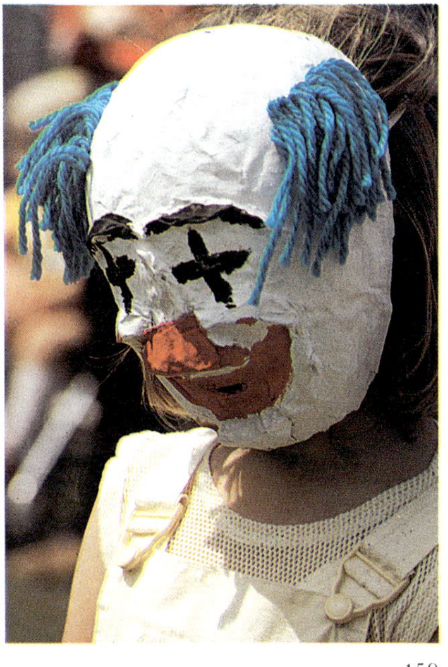

Choosing a Film

Film materials are produced by a number of manufacturers, and when their similar products are compared there is very little difference between them in terms of price, quality and specification. Sometimes one manufacturer will make a break-through in terms of technology, but it usually takes only a very short time for rival companies to produce a film of comparable quality.

It is a good idea to test a variety of differ-

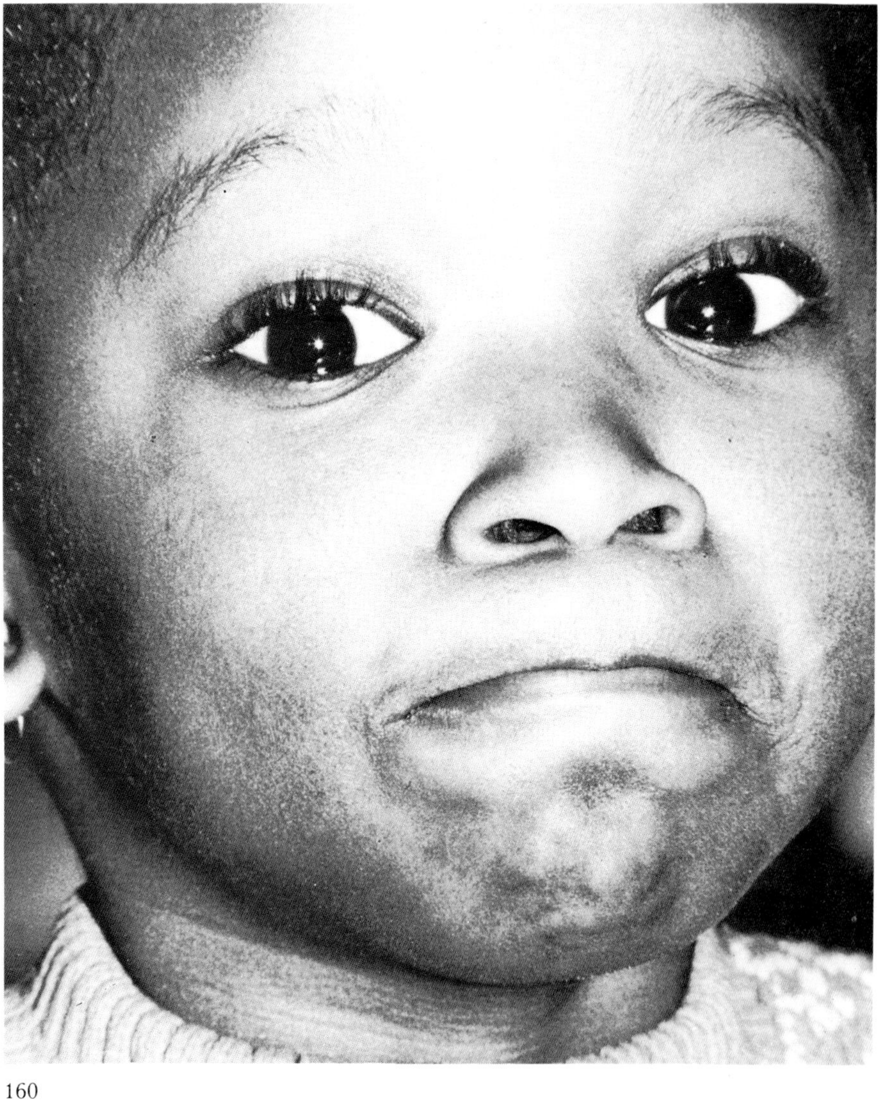

ent films to find one or two that have the qualities suited to your style of child photography. When you have discovered which films are the most suitable, use them exclusively so that you really get to know them, their strengths and weaknesses, and how they behave under varying conditions. This will enable you to predict the nature of your results more readily and a consistency will show in your work.

For flash photography it is rarely necessary to use a very fast film. A medium-speed film will give a far better rendering of skin tones, because the tonal range of the film is wider (left). A fast film is only required for flash work when using a unit of low output or when working at a great distance from the subject.

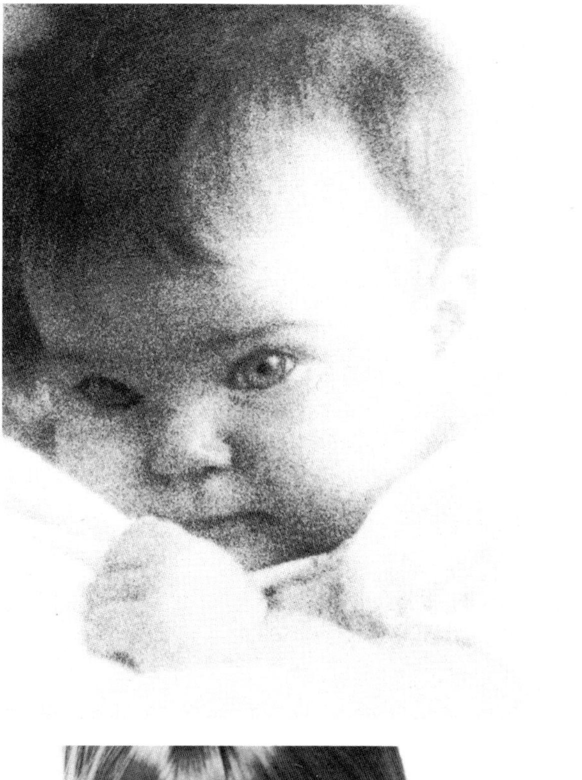

This picture (right) is an enlargement from a small section of a high-speed film negative. The effect of grains of silver clumping together will be readily seen in this example, although it will be slightly reduced in reproduction.

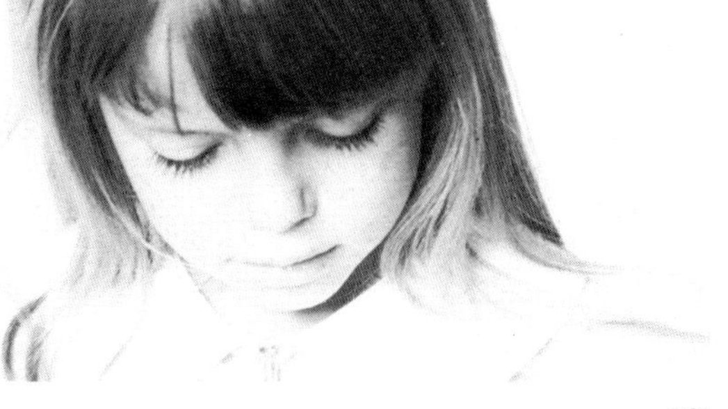

Choice of film is usually dictated by the amount of ambient light. In indoor situations, a fast film will enable a smaller aperture to be used to give greater depth of focus (right).

Processing and Printing

It is not within the scope of this book to deal at length with the subject of developing and printing photographs at home, and in any case, many readers will be content to send their films to a laboratory and will be entirely satisfied. However, the dedicated photographer will not always be happy with the standard treatment at a laboratory and will wish to process his own photographs.

Developing and printing your own films means that you have far greater control on the end-result, the print. Different sections of a negative can be selected for printing, and a photograph can be virtually re-composed at the enlarging stage. Varying depths of printing can be tried, and individual areas of a picture can be lightened or darkened. The art of photographic printing is in many respects more creative than the act of taking a picture, as the final print can be manipulated and controlled in many different ways. It can be immensely satisfying, and the photographer has complete control at every stage.

Processing black-and-white film is extremely simple and the only requirements are a thermometer, a light-tight developing tank and a small quantity of pre-packed chemicals. Colour films are rather more difficult and require more care. As this is a strictly mechanical process, and no creative possibilities present themselves at this stage, it is better to have colour films processed by a laboratory under controlled conditions. This is particularly relevant to colour transparency film which can easily be spoilt.

If you want to make prints, you will have to have an enlarger, and a model equipped to make colour prints from negatives will cost in excess of £100. Other necessary apparatus will include dishes, safelight and a print dryer. The same equipment can be used for black-and-white work, and for making colour pints from transparencies, using the Cibachrome or Agfaspeed reversal processes.

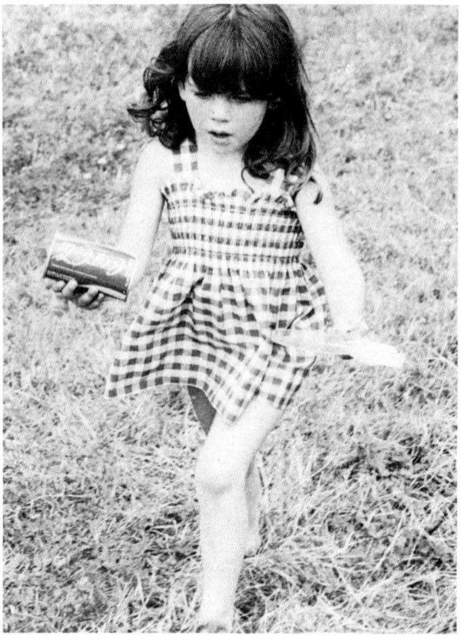

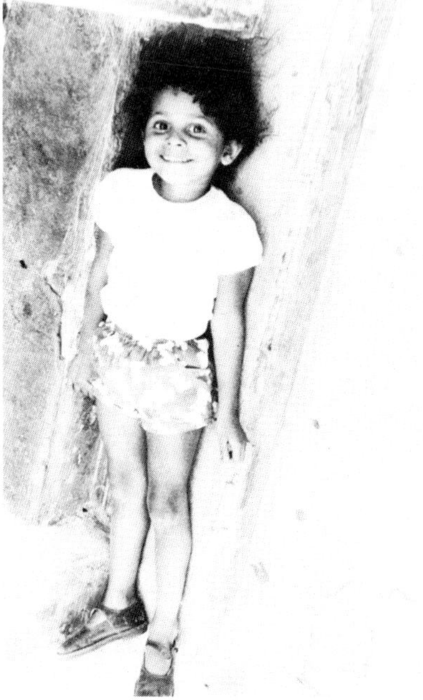

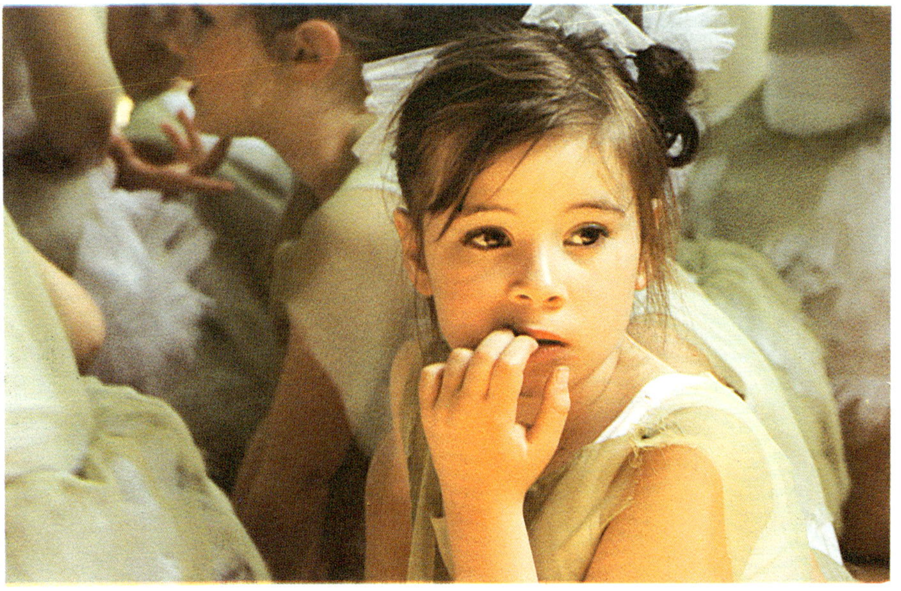

Colour printing is a little more difficult than black-and-white, but incredibly satisfying to the family photographer (above).

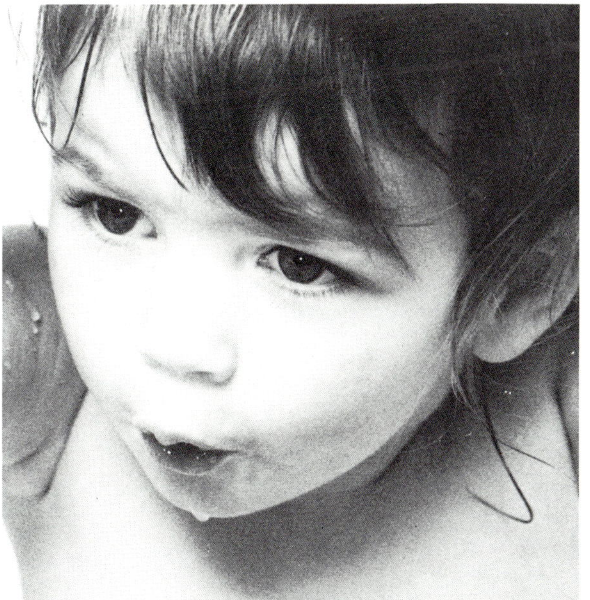

By printing your own photographs you will have complete control over the picture-making process. In both these examples (left), the photograph was re-composed at the enlarging stage to form a more satisfying image, and selected parts of the print lightened or darkened.

By selective printing, a close-up portrait of a child can be made, even in situations where it was not possible to shoot a full-head image on the negative (right).

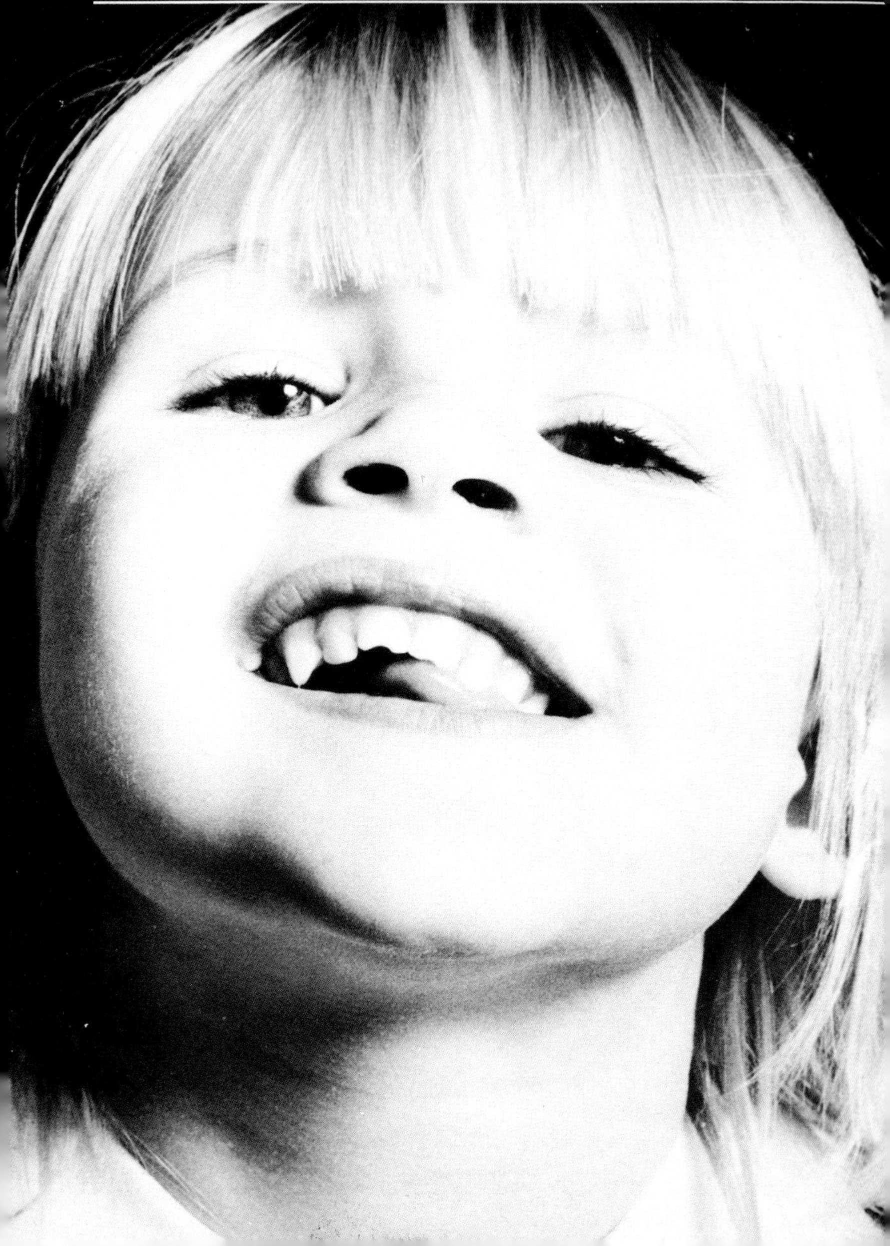

USEFUL ACCESSORIES

Most readers will be familiar with the cartoon characterization of an amateur photographer, with numerous cameras strung around his neck and lenses and accessories bristling from every pocket. To some photographers the acquisition of cameras and accessories reaches such a pitch that interest is lost in actually taking photographs, so overcome are they by the mania of collecting apparatus. While a certain amount of ancillary equipment is desirable for child photography, it is by no means essential, and very successful pictures can be taken with a minimum of equipment. Using accessories will not necessarily make your photography any better, but it can broaden the scope of subject-matter and make certain operations simpler.

When going on a photographic expedition, there is a temptation to take all your equipment, just in case, but this often leads to general confusion and boredom on the part of the model. It is usually preferable to take only certain items, say one lens and one filter, and to exploit that particular combination to the full. While it would be quite wrong to say that accessories are totally unnecessary, having too much to think about at any one time can be counter-productive.

The first accessory that a serious child photographer will buy will probably be a flash-gun. Photography depends upon light, and there are occasions when there is just not enough of it. A flash unit provides instant illumination in a neat and handy form, and if used intelligently can be an attractive and flexible light source. Because of its simplicity, however, there is a tendency to use flash at times when low-level ambient light would produce a better, more natural-looking picture of a child.

Other accessories can either make the photographer's job easier – such as motor drives and tripods – or more creative – such as filters and lens attachments. Whatever the accessory, there will often be a choice between that made by the camera manufacturers and an almost identical product made by an independent company; this applies equally to accessory lenses. In most cases, the independent product will be just as good as, and often cheaper than, that made by the camera manufacturer.

Choosing a Flash-gun

Flash-guns differ in two major respects, by the amount of light or power they produce, and by the way they ensure correct exposure. There are three main types of flash-gun – manual, computer and 'dedicated' – all available in a range of power outputs.

The manual gun is the cheapest and least sophisticated type. Exposure assessment is made by reference to a chart or by using a guide number to calculate the correct lens aperture. Whichever method is used, the exposure will only be approximate, as no allowance is made for the reflectance of the subject or the surroundings. Manual guns are no longer to be recommended as it is possible to purchase far better computer types for very little extra cost.

The computer flash contains a light sensor which measures the illumination reflected from the subject as the gun fires, and cuts off the flash instantaneously when the correct exposure level has been achieved. All the photographer has to do is to enter the film speed on a dial on the unit, which will then offer a range of lens apertures. Once the most suitable f-number has been set on the camera and on the flash, the exposure will be automatic and accurate. Most computer flash units have a swivelling head which means that the flash can be bounced off a ceiling or wall for a softer effect, and some types have two heads, one fixed and the other swivelling, to give a combination of bounced and direct light. Some computer flashes are 'dedicated' to certain camera types, allowing information from the flash to be read in the viewfinder.

TTL 'dedicated' flash units are a fairly recent development and are usually manufactured to fit specific makes and models of camera. The advantage of the TTL 'dedi-

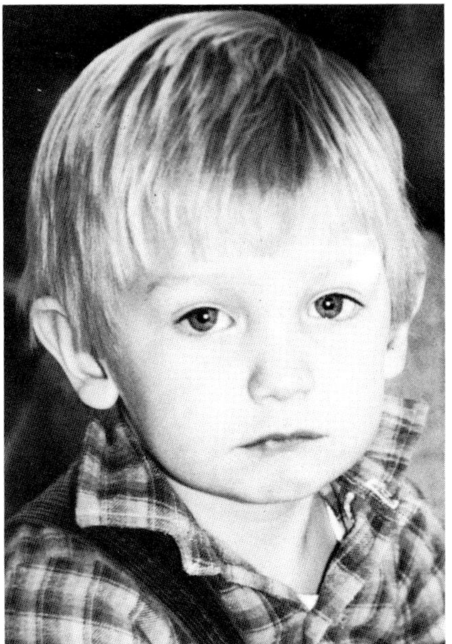

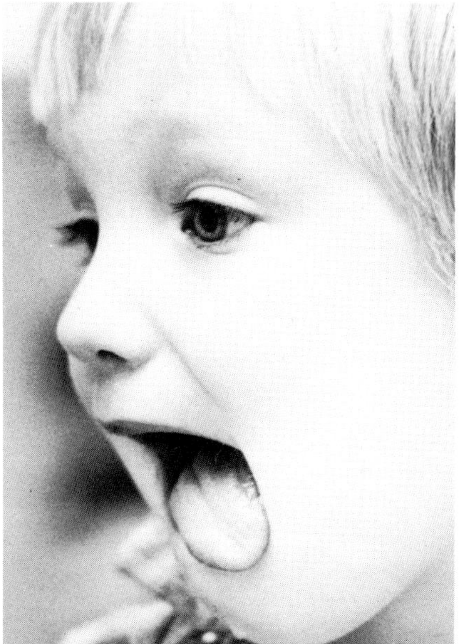

cated' unit is that the flash exposure is actually computed within the camera body, in the same manner as ambient light is measured within a TTL metering camera. All factors relating to the exposure, film speed, subject distance and reflectance, lens aperture and any filter factors are automatically taken into account when the flash is fired, and only a suitable intensity of light given to provide correct exposure. A further advantage is that the level of ambient light is evaluated at the same time, and when this is sufficient, it is used to contribute to the final exposure, giving a more realistic combination of flash and natural illumination. Most manufacturers of SLR cameras, including Pentax and Nikon, produce cameras with TTL 'dedicated' flash facilities, and the guns to go with them.

When choosing a flash it is a false economy to buy a model with a low power output. The only advantage of such a unit is its very small size, useful for carrying around as an emergency standby, but it will not provide enough light for working at any distance, particularly for bounce flash. It is far better to choose a slightly bulkier unit with a high output and know that in most circumstances you will have enough power to hand.

As regards the difference between computer and TTL 'dedicated' types, it is important to remember that although the latter are very much simpler and more flexible in operation, they can only be used on certain models of camera. If you own one of these models it is well worth paying a higher price to buy the appropriate flash, which will then work as an extension of the 'brain' of your camera. Computer models are still a good, and accurate, alternative, with the advantage that they can be used on any make or model of camera

An electronic flash unit is not only a handy and portable form of illumination, it also has the unique property of providing a very rapid burst of light, sometimes as brief as 1/1000 sec. This means that very fleeting facial expressions can be captured (far left), even the boy's extended tongue (left).

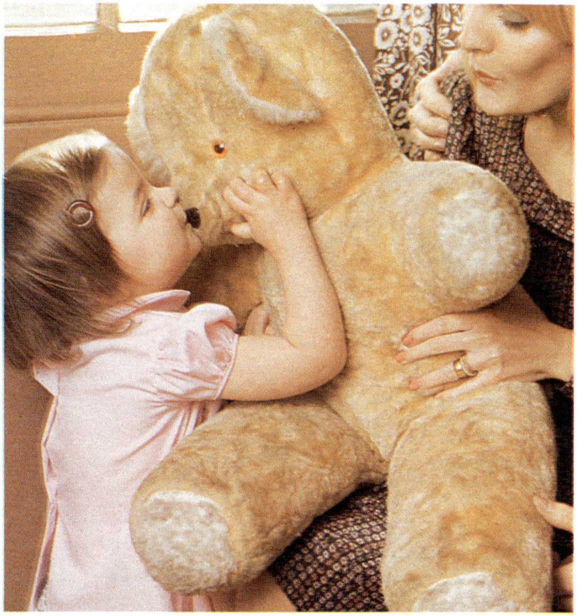

When there is insufficient daylight to use available light, a flash can be used as a substitute. For the best results, direct flash should not be used with the unit attached to the camera, but instead held above and to one side. This method was used in this picture (right) to provide more natural modelling.

Flash Techniques

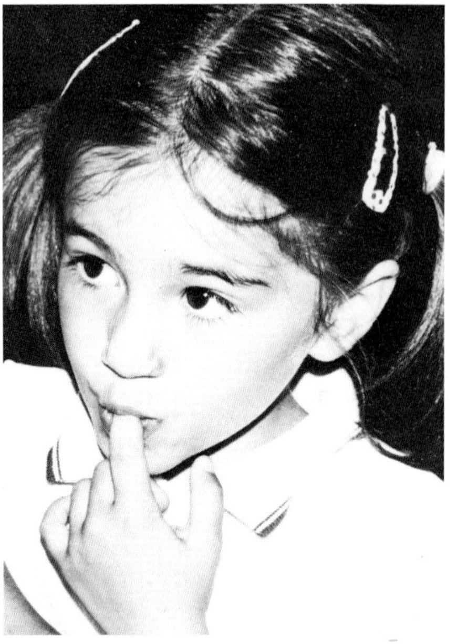

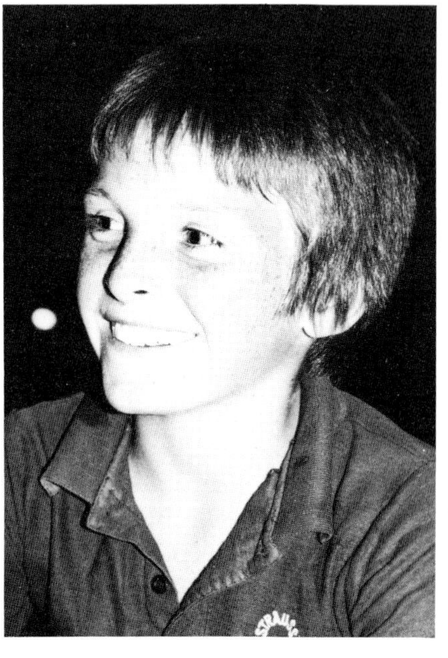

Many flash photographs are spoilt by the harsh and uncompromising nature of the light source, and the use of a flash-gun without some forethought will often result in a very unattractive picture. Children, especially, with their subtle skin tones and rounded features deserve better treatment, and there are ways of producing more natural results using flash. Whenever possible, when photographing children, it is best to bounce the flash from a suitable reflecting surface to soften the light, but in some circumstances, such as outdoors or in a large room, this is not possible and direct flashlight must be used.

Because most cameras are fitted with 'hot shoe' flash contacts, there is a natural tendency to fit the unit straight on to the camera body and to shoot using the direct flash method. Although this is convenient, the position of the flash unit, directly over the axis of the lens, is the least suitable place, giving flat, undirectional light with harsh shadows beneath the facial features. Direct flashlight can be improved in two ways, by softening and by removing the light source from the camera. The first can be achieved by taping two or three layers of white tissue paper over the flash tube, taking care not to obscure the sensor of a computer unit. This will have an immediate softening effect on the light source, though the flash output will be slightly reduced. Then, by moving the flash away from the camera, preferably above and to one side, a far more pleasant lighting effect will be produced, with fuller, but less dense shadows and better modelling and texture of skin tones.

Whenever circumstances allow, reflected or bounce flash should be used, as the effect will be softer and more flattering to the subject and will look more natural. Providing the flash unit has sufficient power, the technique is easy and always successful. Aim the flash head at the ceiling towards a point mid-way between the

The portrait of the girl (left above) was taken by direct flash with the flash mounted on the camera. The effect is very harsh with hard shadows beneath the model's nose and chin. By moving the flash above and to one side of the camera, far better modelling is achieved with softer and less pronounced shadows (left below).

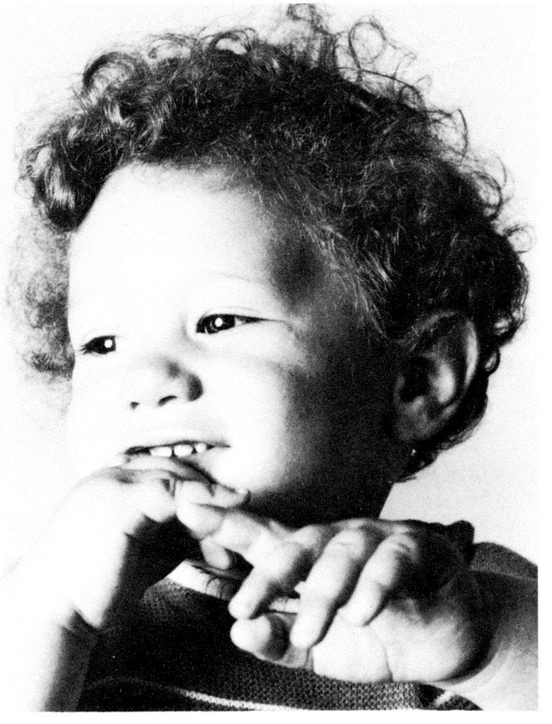

This picture, taken with one flash reflected in an umbrella at about 45° to the subject, shows the softer style of lighting that can be achieved using this method (right). By using another umbrella flash of lesser power, the darker area of the face can be filled in, if a more even effect is required.

camera and the subject. The light will bounce and spread when it reaches the reflecting surface, with the result that the subject and surrounding area will be illuminated by a sweep of soft, natural light. When shooting in colour, take care to ensure that the reflecting ceiling has a fairly neutral hue, otherwise the light will take on the colour of the surface. Obviously, white or light grey is ideal, but a cream or light pink ceiling would not upset the colour balance unduly. When the colour of a ceiling is unsuitable or if it is too high, a vertical wall can be used to equally good effect.

When using the bounce technique with a computer flash, the light sensor must remain aimed at the subject. Most models have a swivelling flash head, so that the main unit can remain fixed on the camera with the sensor pointing in the right direction, while the head is aimed independently at the reflecting surface. Some flash-guns, such as the Vivitar 283, have a detachable sensor which can be fixed at the camera position and attached by cable to the flash head positioned well away from the shooting position.

An alternative to the bounce technique is the use of umbrella reflectors, which provide excellent, soft, yet directional lighting (see pages 102–3). Owing to the lack of mobility of the units they are best used in a set-up situation, when the cameraman and model are working in fixed positions.

Synchro Sunlight

Although the flash-gun is usually considered to be an accessory which is used only indoors or after dark, there are times when it is invaluable in the strongest lighting conditions. When shooting in broad daylight, there are occasions when the strength and angle of the sunlight cause harsh shadows on the subject's face which might be objectionable and spoil the photograph. In other circumstances, with the sun behind the subject, the child's head and hair might be fully illuminated from behind, leaving the face totally shadowed. In both cases, a flash can be used to fill in the shadow areas and restore the effect of even lighting to the subject's face. This technique is known as 'synchro sunlight' or 'fill-in flash' and is widely used by professional photographers.

As a flat light is required, the flash can be mounted on the camera and the fastest shutter speed suitable for electronic flash selected. On some reflex cameras this can be as slow as 1/60 or 1/125 sec. Using this shutter speed the exposure should be set in the normal way, making no allowances for

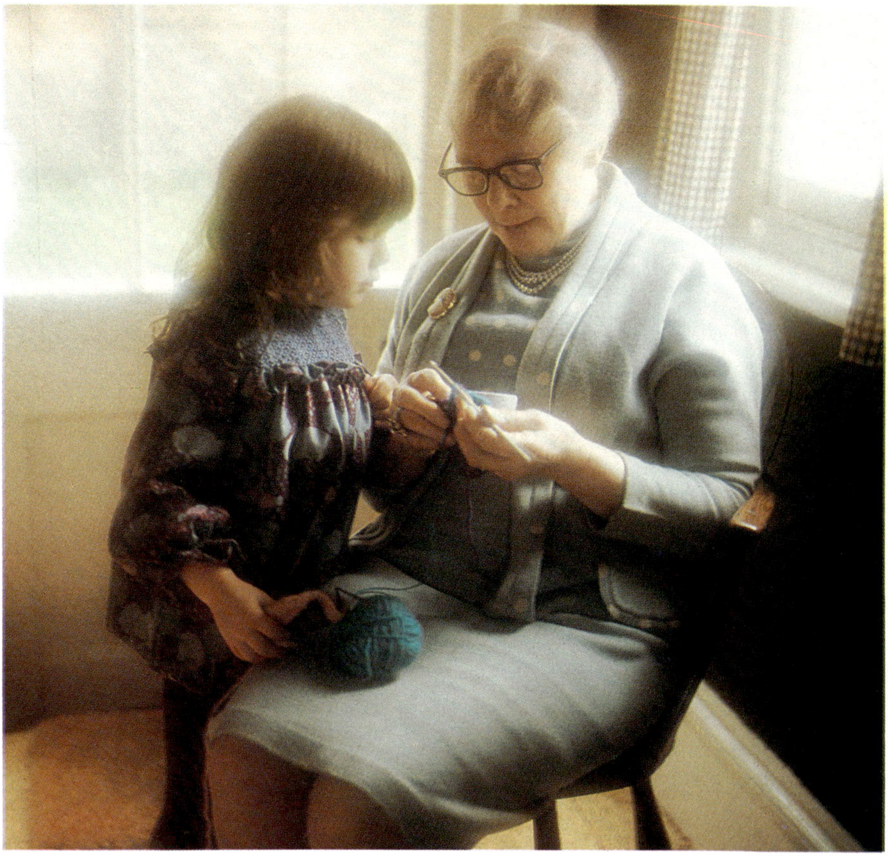

The sunlight for this outdoor shot (right) was coming from immediately behind the model, so a low-intensity flash was used to lighten the model's face just enough to give a natural, balanced effect.

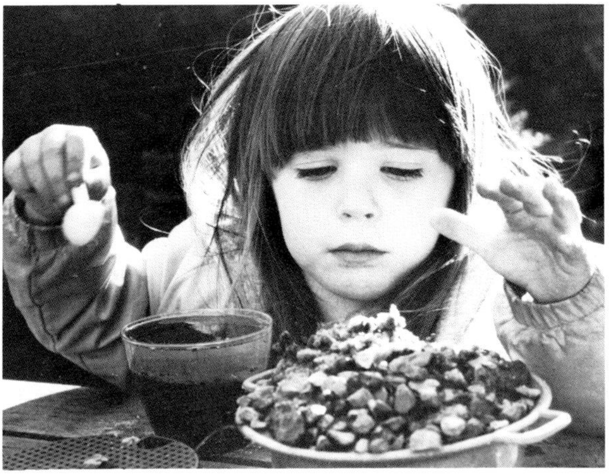

The main light source for this photograph (left) was daylight from the windows. This light alone was too contrasty, so a fill-in flash was used to lighten the shadowed areas of the grandmother's face and body, producing a more even effect, but not enough to destroy the natural effect of the picture.

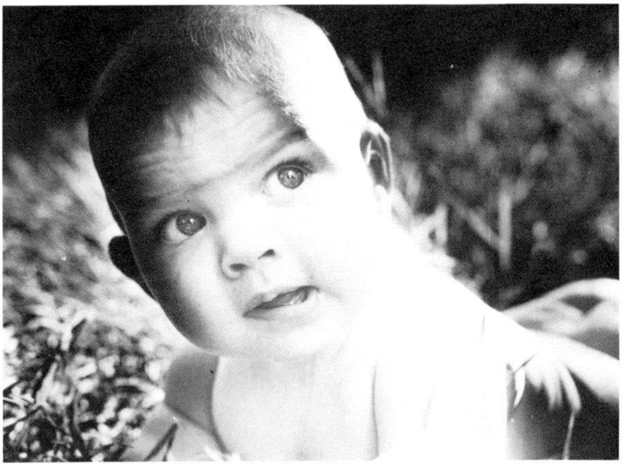

This photograph (right) was taken under very harsh sunny conditions. The only way to even out the shadows was to use a flash exposure, with the unit held above and to the right of the camera.

the secondary flash illumination. To ensure that the flash does not kill the ambient lighting it should be set to provide an exposure of a half or a quarter that needed to expose correctly by flash alone. If you are working with a computer unit you merely have to adjust the ASA setting to twice or three times the speed of the film in use. You can then make the exposure, confident that the flash will only provide enough light to fill in the under-exposed shadow areas without affecting the rest of the image. If you have any doubt about the correct ratio of flash to daylight, you can make a few exposures at different settings, in order to ensure one correct result. If your camera has a TTL 'dedicated' flash unit, the camera will in most circumstances make up its own mind about what is the correct ratio of daylight to flash, and will usually produce a reasonably balanced photograph.

Motor Drives and Tripods

It may seem strange to link together such apparently different items as motor drives and tripods, but their uses are in many ways complementary. They are both devices that in one way or another enable the photographer to ignore the camera and to concentrate his attention on the subject. This is particularly useful when taking child portraits as having a camera equipped with motor drive or winder and mounted on a tripod allows the photographer complete freedom to move away from the equipment to devote himself fully to the child. Motor drives are also useful for action shots, when many a good opportunity can be missed while you are winding the film.

Motor drives and winders are available for most SLR cameras, and are usually attached to the base plate at the bottom of the camera. They often incorporate a hand-grip, with a trigger for easy handling. The main difference between a motor drive and a winder is the speed at which they operate. A motor drive, in the continuous mode, can usually shoot at a variable rate of between 2 and 8 frames per second. Winders have a slower, fixed continuous shooting speed of 1½ or 2 frames per second, but are considerably cheaper to buy. Both devices, whether used for continuous or single exposures, relieve the operator of the need to wind the camera manually, which is much to his advantage when photographing children, whose behaviour can be unpredictable.

Tripods have two basic functions: they are used to locate a camera in a fixed position, framed and focused on the subject, while at the same time keeping the apparatus completely still and steady to avoid camera movement at the time of the exposure. This second function is particularly important for exposures of fairly long duration such as when photographing a child indoors by subdued light. The best tripod is undoubtedly the heaviest one, but for practical purposes a compromise must be made between weight, size and portability. The most sensible way to choose a tripod is to take your camera along to the photographic shop and test the various types for rigidity. A tripod which is light and fully collapsible is easy to transport, but is no use at all if the camera wobbles in the slightest breeze. Tripods should also have a substantial pan and tilt head, enabling the camera to be manoeuvred easily and positively.

There is a great temptation to buy a cheap tripod, as it is a less than glamorous accessory, but this is really a false economy. It is worth buying a more expensive one as it will be stronger and more rigid and will stay that way for many years of use.

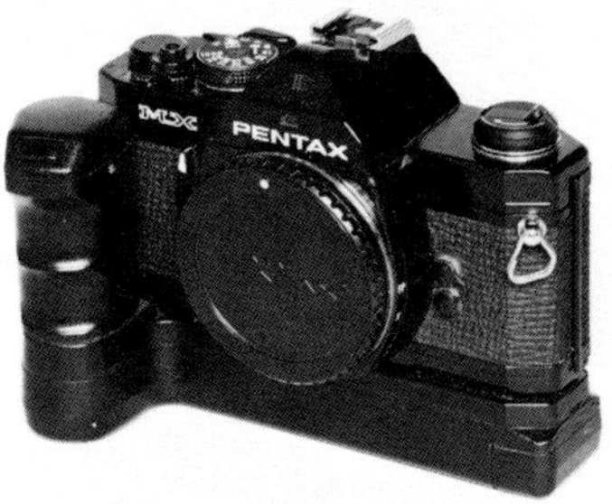

Pentax camera with motor winder attached ready for shooting.

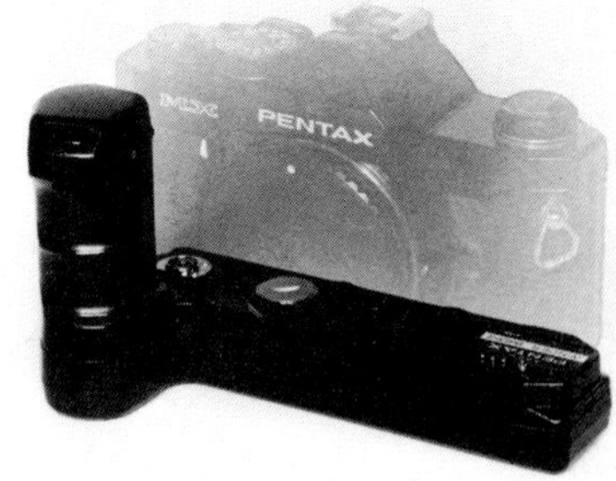

Winder unit showing electrical contacts and base plate fitting to camera.

Motor drives and winders are most useful for sequence photography, when there is insufficient time for the film to be wound manually between individual shots. This sequence (right) showing a girl taking breath, doing a handstand under water and resurfacing could only have been taken with great difficulty without the use of a motor drive, which allows the photographer to concentrate completely on the positions of the subject.

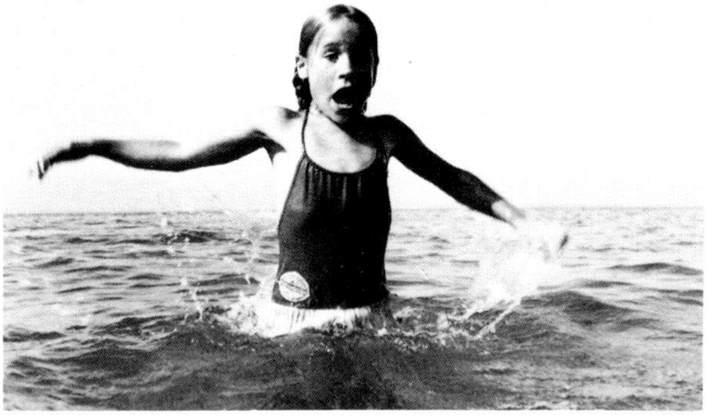

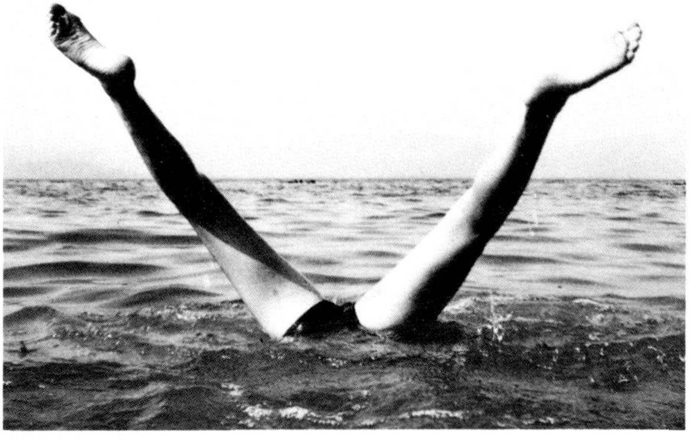

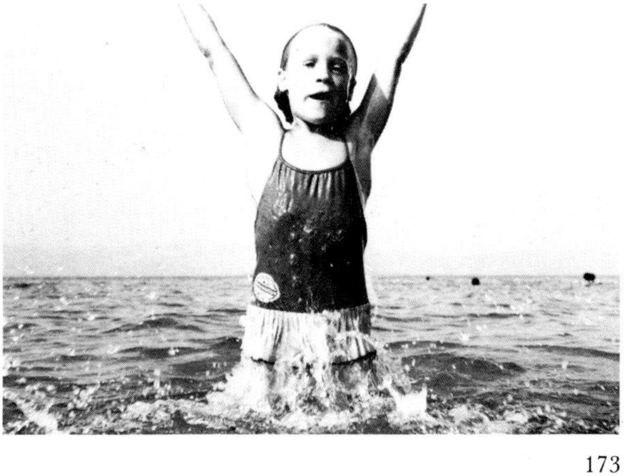

Filters and Lens Attachments

Filters and optical attachments are used in front of the lens to modify the photographic image. As a rule, filters influence the colour of a photograph while other attachments alter its character. There is a great vogue for accessories of this type and there are so many varieties available that the photographer sometimes feels duty bound to use one on every occasion. However, there are very few types that can be utilized in child photography without the result becoming artificial and pretentious. The important thing about all filters and attachments is that they should only be used when the photograph specifically warrants it and will be improved as a result.

The accessories are mounted in one of two ways. They are either circular in shape, with a threaded mount attaching directly to the camera lens, or they are square, slotting into a special plastic holder fixed to the lens mount. The square filters are made from optical resin, and are cheaper than the circular glass type which are individually mounted. Many different types are available in each range: graduated filters for darkening and colouring

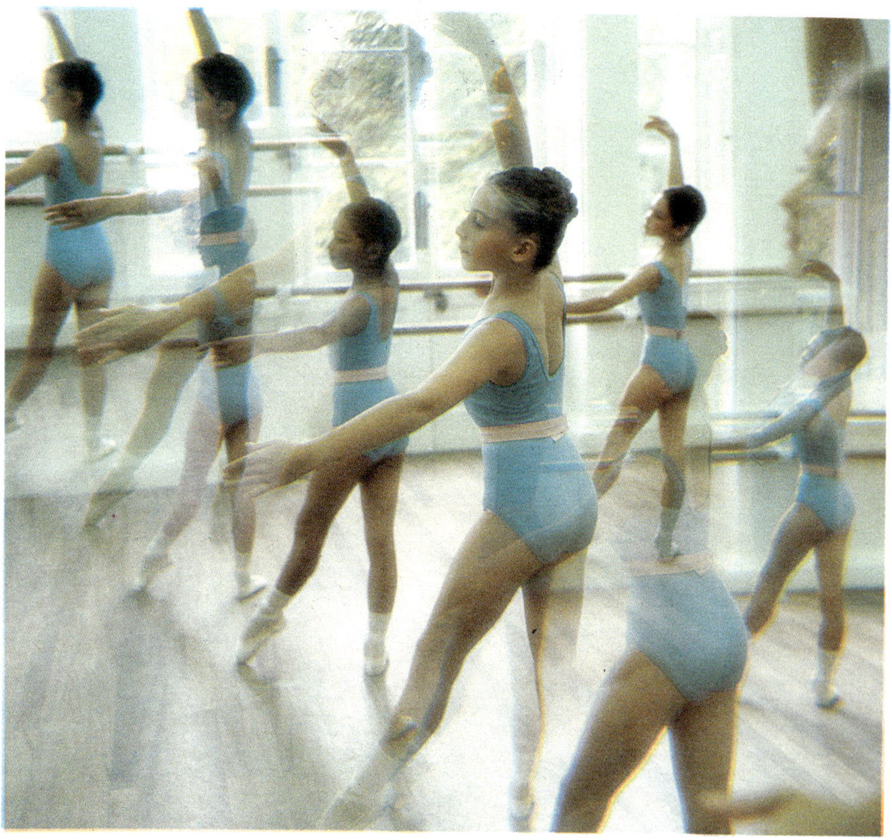

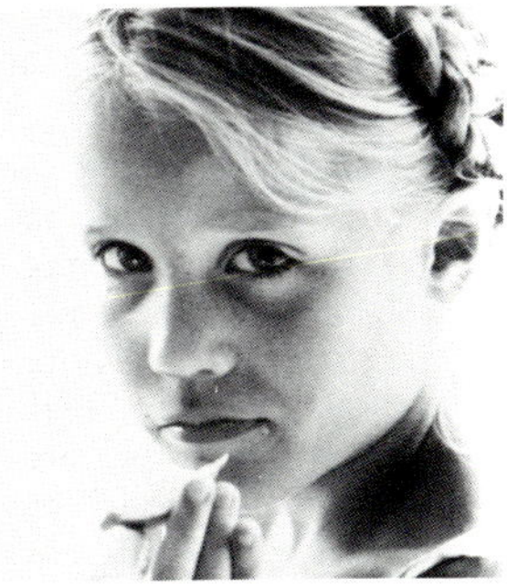

A soft-focus attachment was used to produce a gentle effect in this portrait (above).

A diffuser and a warm-tone filter were used for this mother and child study (right) to produce a warm, romantic picture.

Compare this shot taken using a multiprism (left) with the similar picture on page 115, taken without a lens attachment.

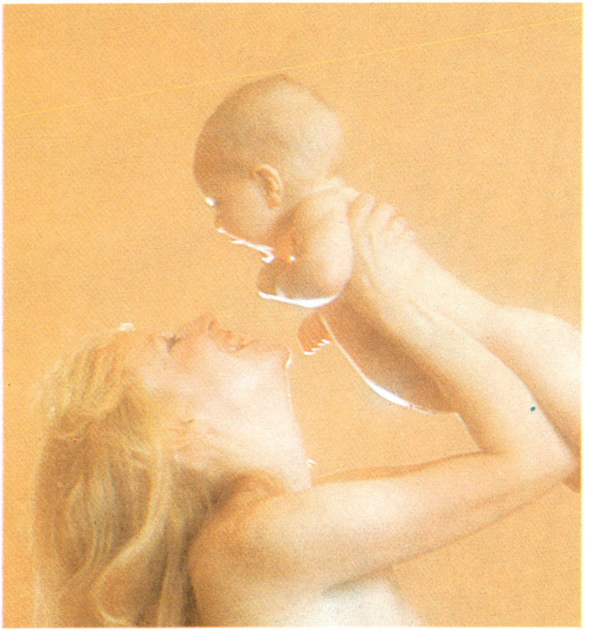

skies; stars and rainbow effects; colour filters for tinting; soft-focus and diffusing lenses; polarizing filters and multi-prism devices. Some of these attachments will be of use in child photography, so it is worth collecting a limited selection.

Of the many colour-effect filters, the only one which will be regularly applicable to child photography is the light amber filter used to warm up skin tones. This is particularly useful in winter and will give pale-faced children an apparently healthy sun-tan. These filters are marketed under different names according to the manufacturer, but if you ask your dealer for a 'warm-tone filter' he will probably know what you mean.

Diffusers and soft-focus lenses are frequently confused, as their appearance and function are quite similar. The surface of a diffuser is etched with little dimples which have the effect of diffusing light from the highlight areas into the adjacent tones, giving a romantic feeling to the picture, while the central core of the image remains relatively sharp. A soft-focus attachment reduces the lens definition throughout the photograph, producing a slightly out-of-focus effect, and is used when an impression of gentleness is required. It is also useful for hiding skin blemishes, when photographing children close-up.

Other types of optical attachment have more limited use. A star-burst filter, for instance, can sometimes be effective, especially at Christmas time to give a fairy-tale effect to the lights on the tree. Multi-prism devices, which produce multiple images of the subject in one exposure, can also be successful when used very occasionally, but if they are used too often they soon lose their originality.

Camera Cases and Other Accessories

The well-equipped photographer will probably possess an expensive camera, with a range of lenses, a flash-gun, tripod, a range of filters and possibly a motor drive or winder. An outfit of this size will have a considerable value and is best protected in some form of carrying case. A number of different types are available, each with its particular advantages and disadvantages. The choice will obviously depend on the working methods and priorities of the photographer.

The person requiring quick and easy access to his equipment will favour a fabric or leather case with a zippered opening, worn over the shoulder. Cases of this type have adjustable interior partitions, as well as a number of smaller compartments to take packs of film, filters and other small accessories. They are compact and light in weight and reasonably robust, giving a fair degree of protection to their contents, and good access when worn on the body. More substantial aluminium cases, built on the

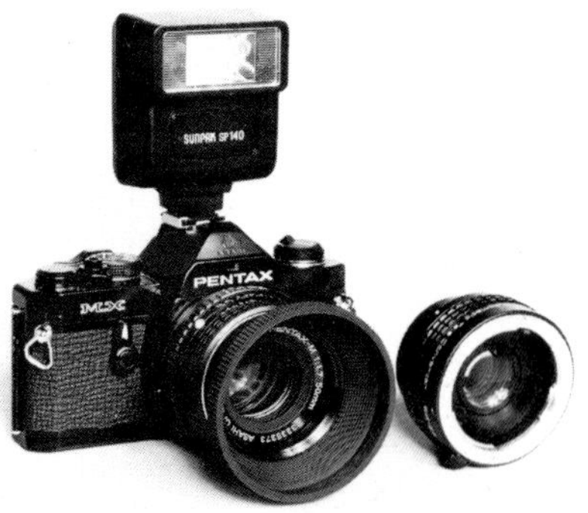

A basic camera outfit, comprising camera fitted with standard lens, lens hood, tele-converter and flash.

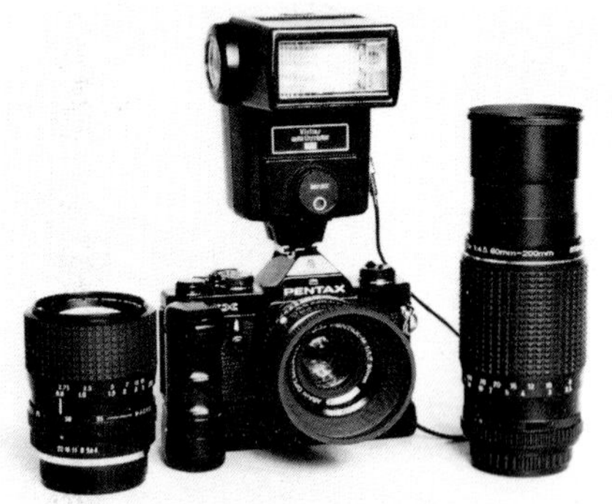

An advanced outfit comprising camera, standard and two zoom lenses, lens hoods, motor drive and swivel-head computer flash.

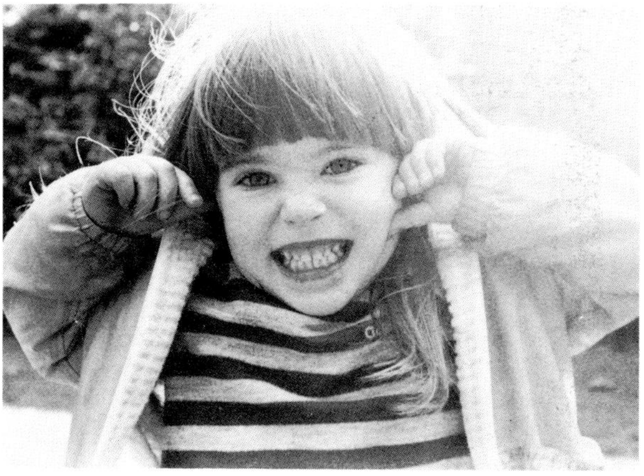

A lens hood is a most important accessory which is often overlooked. It prevents stray light from entering the lens and degrading the image in the form of flare. It is imperative to use a lens hood when shooting towards a light source, as otherwise lens flare is inevitable. The example shown here (left) was photographed towards the low winter sun without a lens hood, and consequently the right-hand part of the shot has been degraded.

suitcase principle with a sponge-rubber interior, offer a greater degree of protection and are good for travelling, but are considerably heavier and bulkier. Their major disadvantage is that they must be laid flat for opening and a piece of equipment cannot be removed in a hurry.

There are a large number of additional small accessories which will help to make the photographer's job easier in certain situations. Such items are not at all essential but are in some cases quite desirable. Just two examples among many are right-angle viewers which allow an SLR camera to be used at floor level, and infrared shutter releases for firing a camera by remote control. However, it is very easy to buy too many accessories, and to find that some are rarely or never used. The best policy is to study the brochures published by the manufacturer of your camera to find out what is available, and to purchase an extra accessory only when you are absolutely sure that you need it.

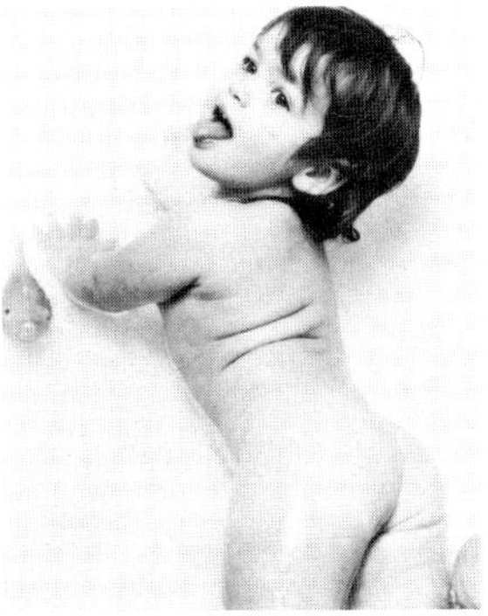

A camera case will protect your equipment from various hazards and is extremely useful for keeping water out of the works, be it rain, sea-spray or even bathroom splashes (above).

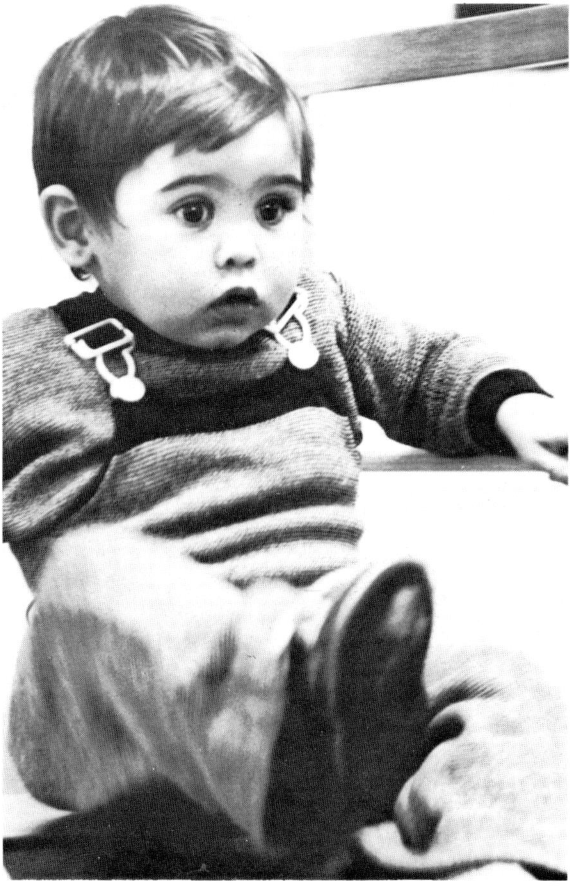

When photographing children it is often a good idea to shoot from floor level, in order to get a natural-looking perspective on the model (right). As this can be very difficult unless you lie full-length on the floor, a right-angle viewer can be attached to the eyepiece of the camera, enabling a low-angle shot to be taken from a more comfortable position.

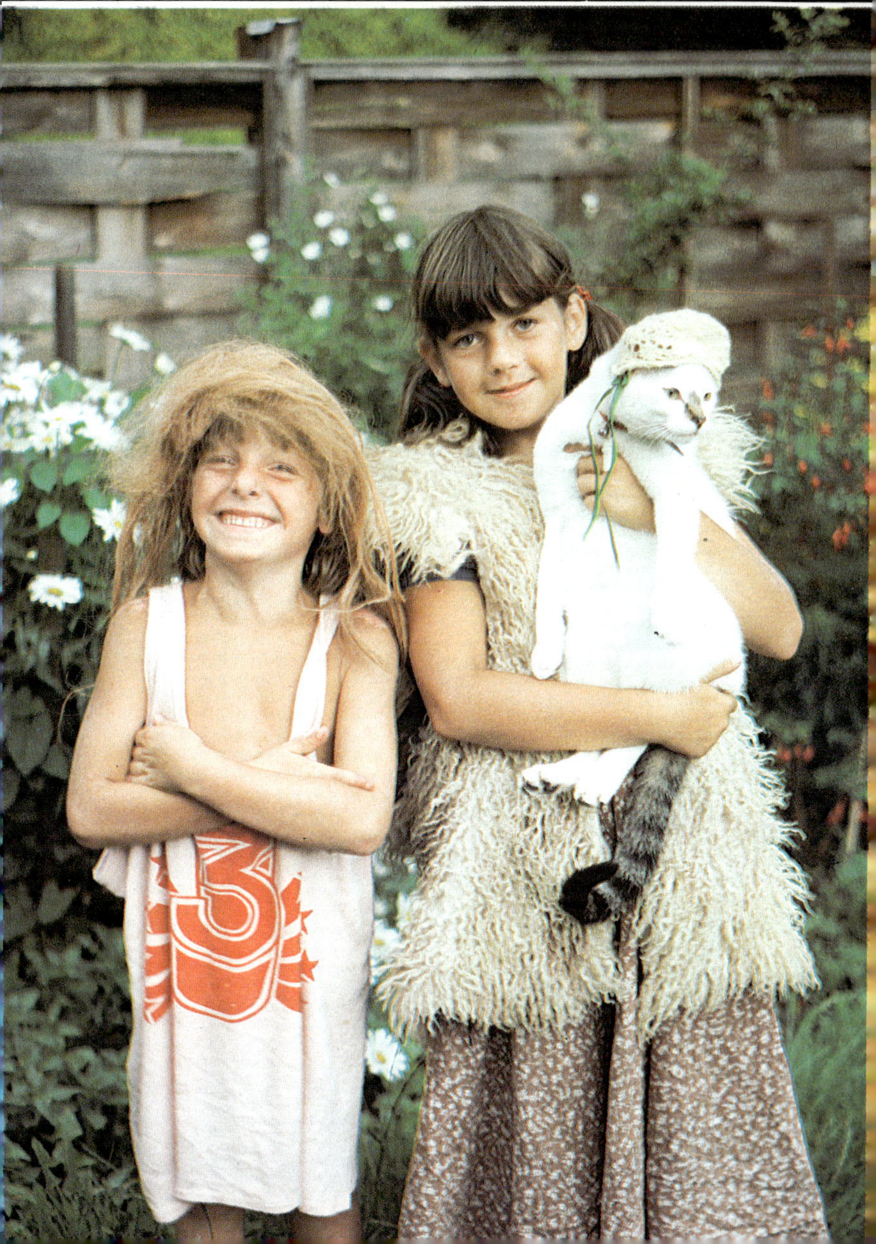

PRESENTATION

It is surprising how often a person will invest hundreds of pounds in camera and ancillary equipment yet make very little attempt to present his expensively gained photographs in an attractive and enjoyable way. Photographs often remain for ever in dog-eared wallets, provided by the photo-finisher, frequently without either dates or captions, so that in future years the circumstances are forgotten and the interest diluted.

Depending upon your personal preferences, there are two main methods of presenting family photographs, either as prints in an album or as a programme of projected colour slides. Whichever method is chosen, a complete family record can be compiled over the years, forming a chronicle of your children's lives from birth to teens. This record should not only include important landmarks such as birthdays, holidays and school events, but also pictures taken on a day-to-day basis charting the interests and development of the child. All the pictures, however they are to be presented, should be accompanied by notes or captions carrying relevant information.

It is quite difficult deciding whether to present your work in the form of prints or slides. The advantage of prints is that they are cheap to make, easy to duplicate if they get lost or damaged, and extra copies can be made to give to friends and relatives. In album form, they are easily viewed and handled, and take up comparatively little storage space compared to slide magazines. An album can be produced and shown at a moment's notice, whereas for a slide show you have to set up a projector and screen in a darkened room. On the other hand, there is nothing better than a well-exposed, well-projected colour slide, screened under perfect conditions; the image will often be larger than life, crisp and bright, and will have a realism which cannot be obtained in the small pages of an album.

Presentation is all too often overlooked because family photographers tend to see their work in terms of single pictures. Many amateurs are mean with film, even though it is just about the cheapest photographic commodity, and take only one shot when a set or series would be much better. It is not necessary to follow the example of the professional, who frequently takes several rolls of film to satisfy a client requiring one published picture, but the fact is that when more shots are taken, the success rate goes up. With many more successful pictures, the presentation can be varied and exciting, and events can be dealt with in a more comprehensive and detailed manner, which in years to come will be far more entertaining than a single shot.

Making an Album

The album will be the final product of the photographer's efforts and the final test of his expertise and aesthetic judgement. A thoughtfully planned album will show his work in a good light, and will hopefully be a record which is both informative and visually exciting. The essence of a well-designed album is its variety, in the choice of pictures and their shape and size as well as in the way they are distributed on the pages.

When you are selecting pictures, remember to study the complete film. Photographs with technical imperfections should be discarded, unless the subject-matter is so important that they must be included. Most rolls of film will contain repetitions, and it is important to choose only the best. Above all, select the greatest possible range of shots, including establishing shots, medium shots, close-ups and incidentals.

An album composed entirely of standard-sized prints can be extremely boring, so when you have made a selection from

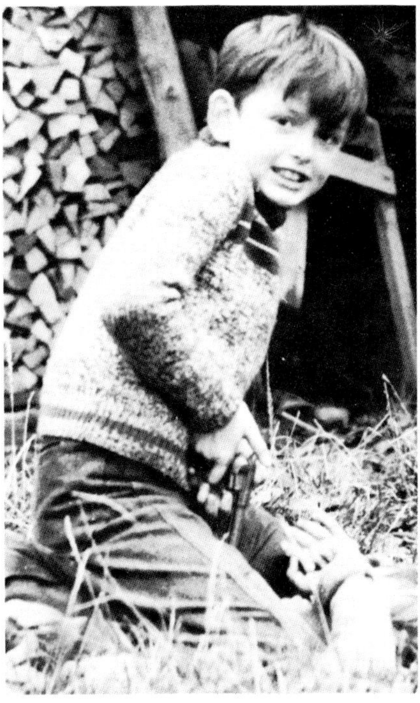

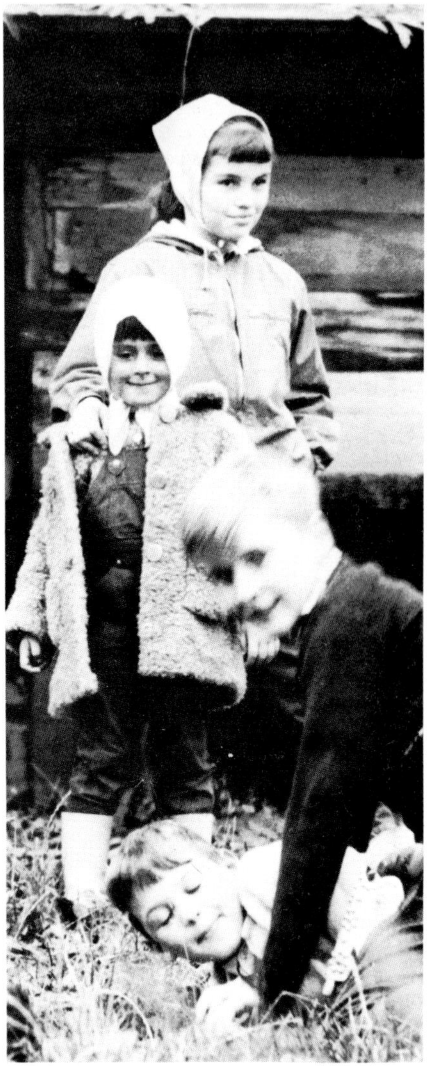

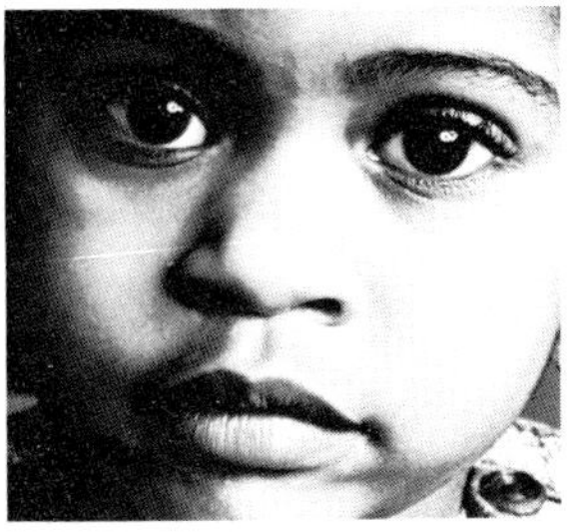

Although they look like different photographs, these two pictures were made from the same negative (above and right). Always look for different and unusual ways of cropping a shot.

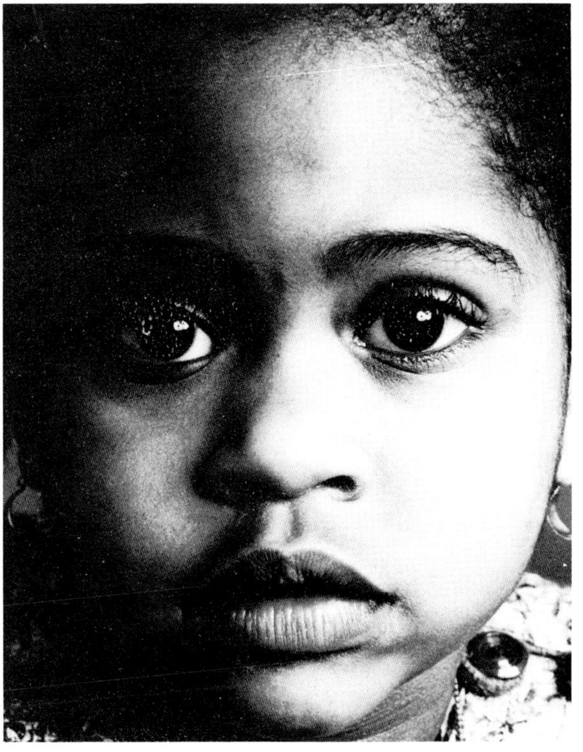

When you study a photograph, you will often realize that it can be made into two pictures (left and far left). Obviously, most pictures work best as a whole, but when trimming pictures for mounting, look for the possibility of splitting a photograph for layout purposes.

the en-prints decide which are worth printing to a larger size. Look again at the en-prints and see if any could be improved by cutting down; trim these carefully with a sharp blade and metal straight edge.

A range of enlarged, cut-down and standard-sized prints can be used as a basis for your layout. The design of pictures on a page is obviously a subjective matter. For initial inspiration, study a well-designed magazine or picture book, to see how pictures of different shapes and sizes can be juxtaposed to give a balanced look to the publication as a whole. You will notice, for instance, how the use of a large picture can be complemented by the use of smaller, yet similar, shots around it. Often it will be appropriate to fill a whole page of an album with a particularly good shot, which can be set off against smaller shots on the opposite page. Whichever way the photographs are finally laid out, there must be a consistency of style, with variations within that style to keep it visually alive.

The final touch to the album will be the addition of dates and captions. Captions should not be too long, but they should contain relevant information and, where appropriate, a touch of humour as well! They can be written directly on the page, in ink, but this leaves no margin for error, so it is advisable to use plain self-adhesive labels which can be discarded and rewritten if you make a mistake.

Albums, Frames and Mounts

Photographic albums come in a range of shapes and sizes, and in a diversity of materials. The simplest type is known as a 'flip-over' album. This consists of a number of transparent pockets, bound together, each large enough to accommodate one en-print or super en-print. They are designed to take one complete film load of 36 or 24 prints. Although only one or two shots can be viewed together with this system, and there is no scope for designing a properly laid-out page of pictures, this simple design is nevertheless useful as a pocketable means of showing and protecting prints, before they are transferred to a more permanent album.

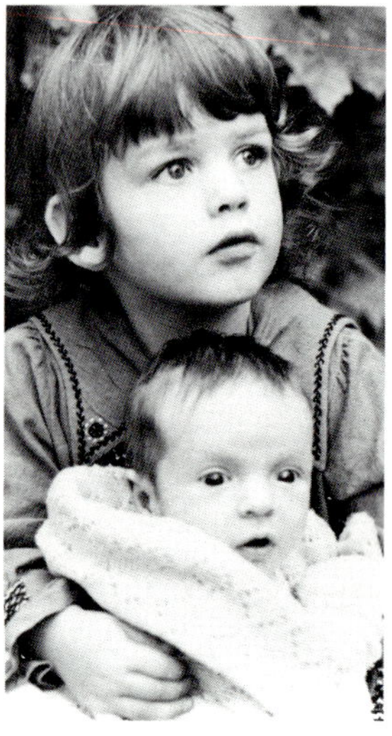

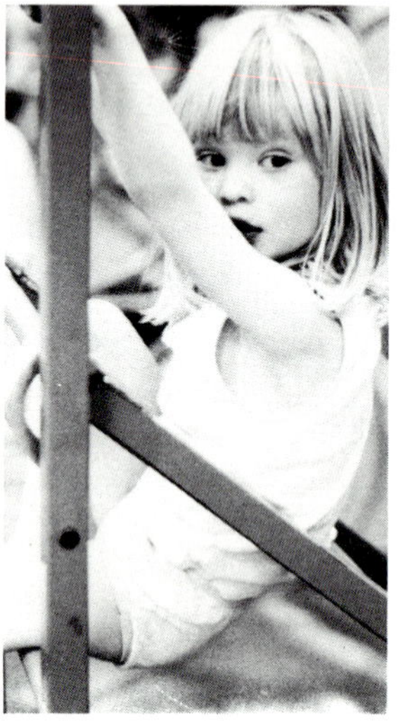

Unusually shaped pictures always make a photographic album look more interesting. Try long narrow upright or horizontal photographs like the examples on these pages.

Colour pictures work especially well as long, narrow, horizontal shots, like a Cinemascope screen in the cinema. Try if possible to let the action fill the whole of the print area (below and opposite).

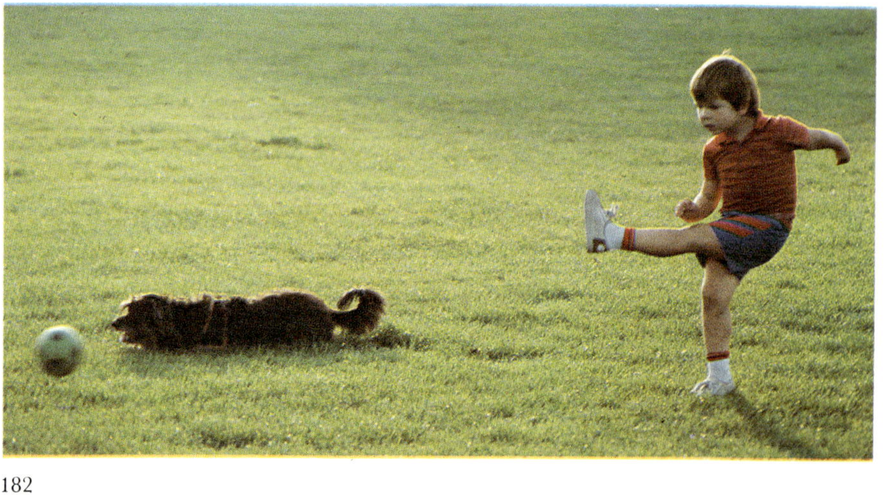

Some larger albums have pages with specially treated, clinging, transparent overlays which retain the prints in position. These are particularly convenient as they allow the prints to be removed and replaced at will, but they are not so suitable for larger prints as the adhesive effect is lost when there is insufficient contact between the overlay and the treated page underneath. Most albums of this type can be extended by enlarging the spine with metal bushes and adding further leaves.

The best albums for creative use have plain paper or card leaves of neutral tone, usually grey or black. A special aerosol adhesive must be used to mount the prints in the album, and the effect will, of course, be permanent. Using this method, there is no limit to the number of possible designs on every page, and different arrangements and proportions of prints can be used to gain visual interest.

Sometimes, individual prints will be required for decoration or to be presented as gifts, and there are a number of ways in which they can be mounted. To avoid the expense of going to a picture framer, you can purchase kits in standard sizes, or made to order, which means that you can frame your own prints. Made in wood, metal or plastic, these frames are attractive and relatively inexpensive. An even cheaper alternative is to block-mount prints on to an expanded plastic base. This material is available in various thicknesses and is supplied with a self-adhesive backing. The print is rubbed down on to the base and the sides trimmed flush with a craft knife or razor blade.

When a flush edge is not required for framing or presentation, the print must be mounted on to card of suitable tone and colour. The safest choice is to go for grey or black, but coloured mounts can be most effective. Browns and sludgy greens are particularly suitable, but the colour of the mount must be in sympathy with the colours of the picture. Selecting the correct mount will often be a case of trial and error, and the best way to decide is to take the print to an art shop and test it against card of different colours before making a purchase. Some colours will immediately kill the picture while others will complement and enhance it.

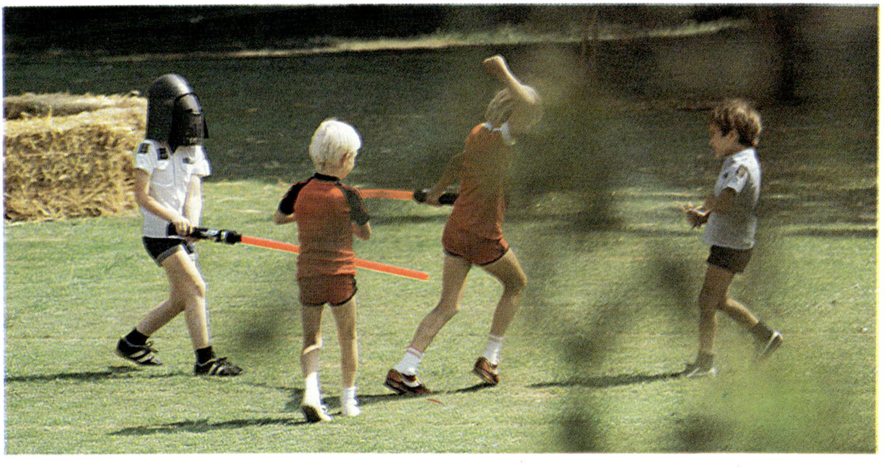

Slide Projection

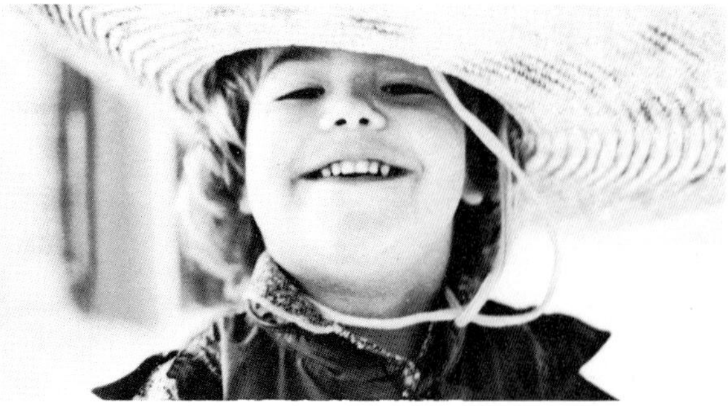

A shot of this kind will often capture the essence of an occasion very well and looks good in a varied slide show (left).

Close-ups are most impressive when projected and will often appear to be larger than life when enlarged on the screen (right).

Although many family photographers like to present their work in a readily accessible album, some prefer to show their pictures in the form of a colour slide programme. A slide presentation actually requires just as much attention to detail as an album, with a similar range and variety of shots. When selecting transparencies for projection a definite sequence should be attempted, in the same way that a ciné photographer edits and mixes lengths of film to produce a cohesive whole. To ensure the continuing interest of the audience, each slide should relate to the preceding and following ones whenever possible, and the presentation should follow a logical progression.

Take as an example a slide programme of a day spent with children at a zoo. To establish the setting it should start with a long shot, perhaps the children walking through the zoo entrance. This should be followed by mixed shots of the subjects riding animals, looking into cages and perhaps eating a picnic lunch, all interposed with close-ups of the animals and of the children reacting to them. The programme should finish with a closing shot, perhaps of the children walking back to the car. To keep the interest going, it is essential to have a good mix of subject-matter, and to vary the format between horizontal and vertical slides. The screen time for any particular slide should relate to the amount of information it gives, and the temptation resisted to show any slide for too long.

When you are showing a set of slides which are less closely related, perhaps a number of photographs taken of the same child over a period of years, try to ensure nevertheless that the sequence is cohesive and in good chronological order. Whenever possible, avoid mixing slides taken on different types of film stock, as the differences in colour rendition and graininess can often be very jarring on a big screen.

To ensure a smooth-running presentation, make all the necessary preparations before the audience gathers. Set up the projector and screen and then frame and focus a test slide, using the whole area of the screen. To ensure a smooth sequence, the slides should have been preselected and placed in order in a projector magazine, of either the straight or circular variety. Nothing disrupts a good slide show more than a shot being shown upside down. There is a simple way of avoiding this, by marking all slide mounts with a self-adhesive spot in the top right-hand corner when viewed inverted ready for projection. When the slides are assembled it is easy to check that all the spots appear in the correct position. Finally, most slide shows will benefit from the addition of soft music, even if it is used solely to mask the hum of the projector blower motor.

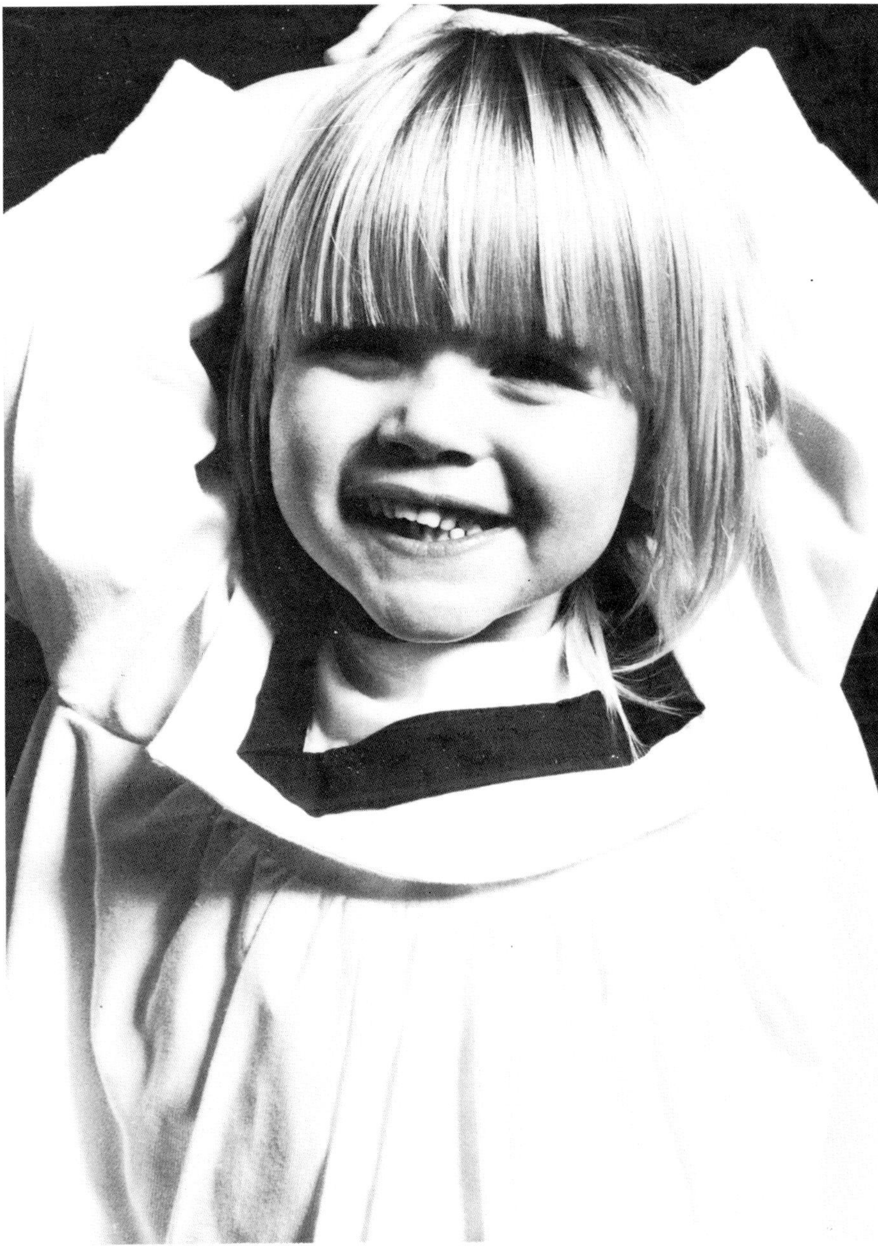

A Simple Audio-visual Show

Professional audio-visual shows involve the use of two or more projectors, with the ability to dissolve smoothly from one slide to another. A sound-track, on tape, is used to carry a voice-over, music and sound effects. This same tape emits electronic pulses instructing the projectors to change slides at the appropriate moments. Although such presentations use still photographs throughout, they can be just as visually exciting as a ciné production.

The amateur photographer equipped for simple slide projection can make up a basic audio-visual programme with very little additional equipment, merely a portable cassette recorder and a music deck with a tape-to-tape facility. When you are photographing with an audio-visual in mind, you should make a basic sound-track at the time of shooting. On the beach, for instance, you can record the sound of crashing waves, lapping water and children screaming with pleasure for use as a 'wild track'. At the same time, children can be 'interviewed', so that pertinent comments can be edited into the sound-track. Another example might be a visit to an exotic market on a foreign holiday. The 'wild track' would then carry sounds of general hubbub, street vendors' calls and strains of travelling musicians. When abroad, the purchase of a tape of locally recorded music can add extra authenticity to the presentation.

Back at home, the photographer will have at his disposal background sounds, children's speech recorded on the spot and probably a source of suitable music. When the required colour transparencies have been selected and edited, the sound-track can be made up using a tape-to-tape recorder to mix these three elements together. You may want to add a commentary as well, and this can also be done by using a mixer.

The only real difficulty is synchronizing the slide changes to the various parts of the sound-track without resorting to the use of expensive equipment. Pulsing apparatus is available for amateur use, but this is expensive, so instead some simple signal must be incorporated into the sound-track to alert the projectionist that a slide change is required. This could be a momentary sound fade, or an inconspicuous yet audible bleep on the track. An alternative is to use simple stop-watch methods, changing the slides at, say, ten-second intervals. You can get round the problem completely by using a more general sound-track which is not allied directly to individual pictures on the screen, and this could be faded out gently at the end of the showing.

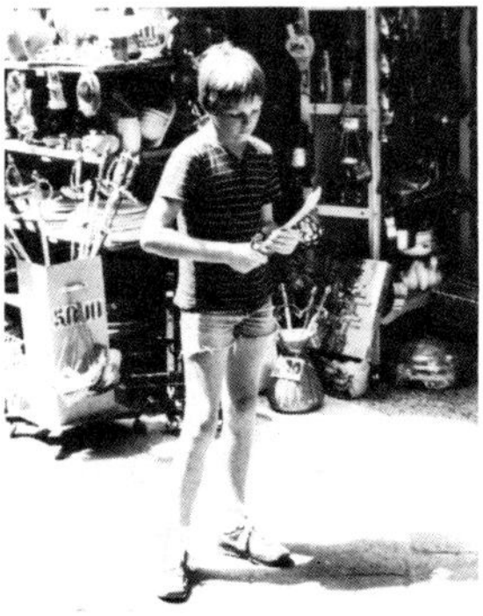

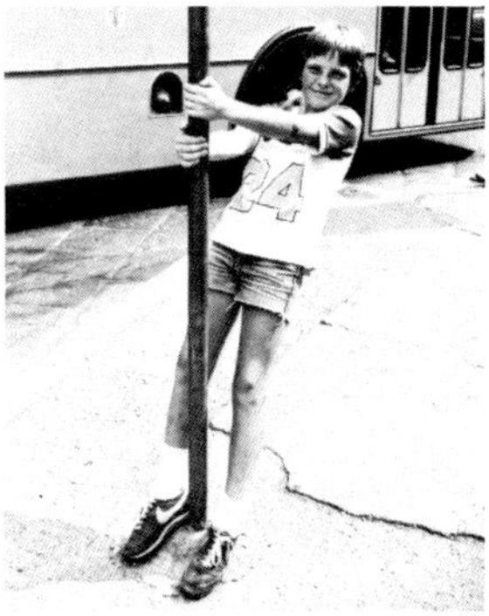

Street scenes are good for establishing locations in a slide show, especially when local artefacts can be included (far left).

Even when no locational clue is given, a street scene is useful for conveying the feeling of your child moving around a town or city (left).

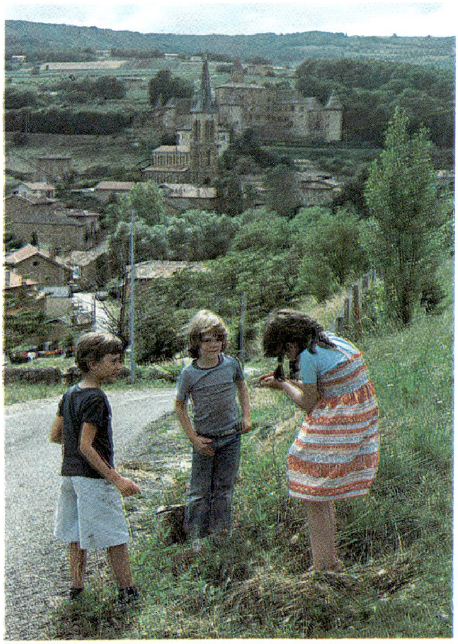

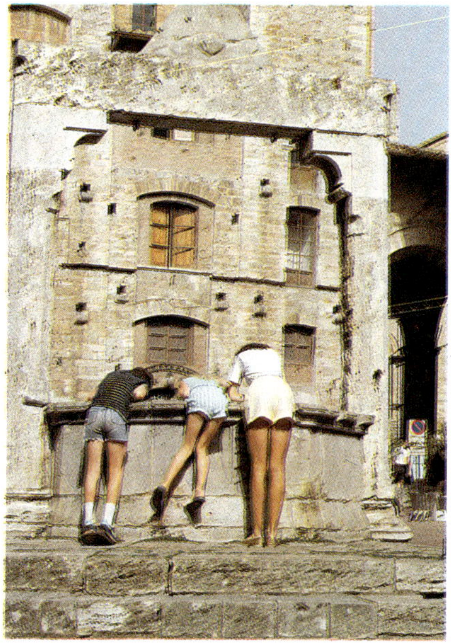

When shooting holiday views for a slide presentation, include your children at all times. They will add colour, scale and their own personalities to the shots and will add a continuity to the presentation as a whole (above).

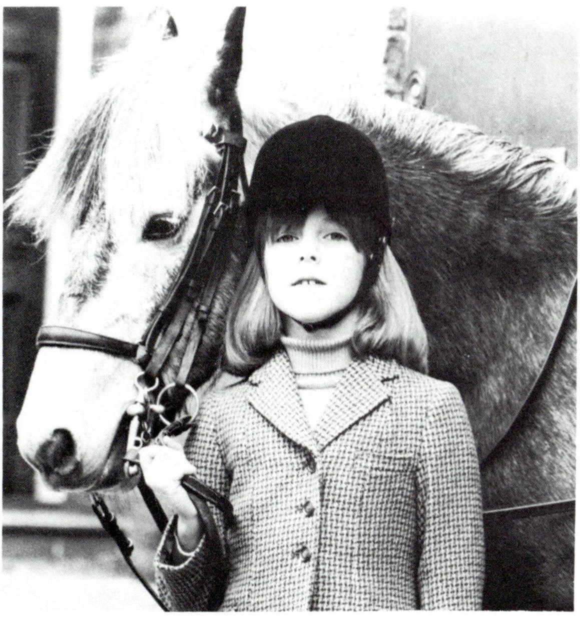

Special events like a first riding lesson will give added interest to a slide show, charting chronologically the life of your child. Such shots need only be simple close-ups, showing the essential ingredients of the event (right).

INDEX

Numbers in italics refer to illustrations

FURTHER READING

Bailey, David and George Hughes, *Begin with Bailey*. Dent.
Beaton, Cecil and Gail Buckland, *The Magic Image*. Little, Brown & Co.
Bernard, Bruce, *Photodiscovery*. Thames & Hudson.
Busselle, Michael, *Encyclopedia of Photography*. Octopus.
Campbell, Bryn, *World Photography*. Hamlyn.
Freeman, Michael, *Photographic Techniques and Materials*. Phaidon.
Gibbon, David, *Classic Colour Photography*. Colour Library Books.
Glanfield, Colin, *Photography by Available Light*. Colour Library Books.
Glanfield, Colin, *Techniques of Filters and Special Effects*. Colour Library Books.
Harker, M., *The Great Photographers: Julia Margaret Cameron*. Collins.
Hedgcoe, John, *What a Picture*. Mitchell Beazley.
Hicks, Roger, *Colour Photography, the Creative Art*. Colour Library Books.
Langford, Michael, *The Instant-Camera Handbook*. Ebury Press.
Langford, Michael, *The Pocket-Camera Handbook*. Ebury Press.
Mager, Alison, *Children of the Past in Photographic Portraits*. Dover.
Time–Life Books, *Photographing Children*.

ACKNOWLEDGEMENTS

The author would like to thank the following:
Merle Park C.B.E., Principal of the Royal Ballet School, for permission to photograph at the White Lodge School, Richmond Park.
The Michael Sobell Sports Centre and the Camden Staff Day Nursery, for permission to photograph on their premises.
Barry Austin of C.L.I. Ltd and John Munday of Transworld Publishing for permission to use certain pictures in this book.
Polaroid (UK) Ltd and Kodak Ltd for loan of cameras, and Pentax and Nikon for technical information.
Hilary Dickinson and David Fordham for their hard work in editing and designing the book.
Finally, all the children who modelled for the photographs and their parents.
All the photographs in this book were taken by the author with the exception of:

pp. 6–9: Hulton Picture Library
pp. 27 (left), 182 (right): Anne Moore
p. 50: Andrea Davies